Keeping the State Weak

Even if a state is democratic, it will fail its citizens if it cannot raise sufficient revenue or distribute public goods effectively. *Keeping the State Weak* points to widespread economic informality as a key feature that keeps poor democracies unstable. Jessica Gottlieb traces the colonial roots of this pernicious type of embedded informality and theorizes how it impacts both state citizens and state actors. Quantitative and qualitative evidence show how widespread informality prevents a would-be middle class from coordinating programmatic claims on the state and how informal intermediaries who benefit from their status resist attempts at formal state-building. The book concludes with a sobering perspective on the potential for formalization campaigns to initiate sociopolitical transitions and more optimistic suggestions for where a programmatic transition might originate.

Jessica Gottlieb is a Distinguished Associate Professor in the Hobby School of Public Affairs at the University of Houston. She is also codirector of the Democratic Erosion Consortium and a board member of the Evidence in Governance and Politics (EGAP) network. She has published articles in high-impact journals, two of which have won Best Article awards from the African Politics Conference Group (APCG).

Keeping the State Weak

Economic Informality and the Weak-State Trap in Sub-Saharan Africa

JESSICA GOTTLIEB
University of Houston

CAMBRIDGE
UNIVERSITY PRESS

CAMBRIDGE
UNIVERSITY PRESS

Shaftesbury Road, Cambridge CB2 8EA, United Kingdom

One Liberty Plaza, 20th Floor, New York, NY 10006, USA

477 Williamstown Road, Port Melbourne, VIC 3207, Australia

314–321, 3rd Floor, Plot 3, Splendor x Forum, Jasola District Centre,
New Delhi – 110025, India

Cambridge University Press is part of Cambridge University Press & Assessment,
a department of the University of Cambridge.

We share the University's mission to contribute to society through the pursuit of
education, learning and research at the highest international levels of excellence.

www.cambridge.org
Information on this title: www.cambridge.org/9781009846660

DOI: 10.1017/9781009846707

When citing this work, please include a reference to the DOI 10.1017/9781009846707

First published 2026

Cover image: Street block. Philippe Lissac / GODONG / The Image Bank Unreleased /
Getty Images

Intertwining stairs on the back of San Niccolò's fortified ancient city walls in Florence,
Italy; Busà Photography / Moment / Getty Images

A catalogue record for this publication is available from the British Library

A Cataloging-in-Publication data record for this book is available from the Library of Congress

ISBN 978-1-009-84666-0 Hardback
ISBN 978-1-009-84671-4 Paperback

Contents

Figures

Tables

Acknowledgments

This project grew out of a puzzle I stumbled onto while moving around Dakar, talking to store owners. I am grateful to those busy businesspeople for taking time out of their workday to indulge my curiosity. I am indebted to Fodé Sarr, a longtime research partner without whom my data collection in Dakar would not have been possible. I first met Abdoulaye Ndiaye while doing scoping work for the project in 2017 and was humbled by his openness and intellectual generosity. He remained a sounding board throughout the life of the project, and his interest in the work encouraged me to continue with it.

Because I wrote this first book at a later stage in my career, the work has been informed by innumerable research partnerships that have contributed to shaping the ideas found in these pages. Some of the research I report on has been coauthored, which I indicate in the text. I am grateful to these collaborators for their permission to weave our joint work throughout the book to enhance the evidence base for the theory. To Abhit Bhandari: I am grateful for our shared interest in firms in Dakar and the way in which we were able to join our study samples to answer questions around the 2022 elections. To Adrienne LeBas: I am grateful that you brought me onto your Lagos tax project in 2018 and shared your wealth of knowledge about the case which ended up serving as a key point of comparison to my primary case in this book. To Jaimie Bleck and Katrina Kosec: thank you for our continuing partnership in Mali, which turned out to provide a helpful example of when and how intermediaries obstruct programmatic transitions. To Jonathan Weigel, Pablo Balan, and Nikhar Gaikwad: thank you for sharing your qualitative insights from your Metaketa projects that help me illustrate backlash to formalization campaigns by political intermediaries that would otherwise be very difficult to observe.

I am eternally grateful for the generosity of my book workshop participants: Beatriz Magaloni, Noah Nathan, Emily Sellars, Pavithra Suryanarayan, Leo Villalón, and Nic van de Walle, whom it was so special to meet and learn from just months before his passing. The workshop conversations helped me figure out what the book was actually about and reflect that in a much-revised introduction and theory. I am thankful to Cathy Boone, whose early writing on the political economy of Senegal made my work on understanding the case so much easier and who helped refocus my book on what I really cared about in the last stages of writing and framing. I am also grateful to three book reviewers for engaging deeply with the material and providing constructive feedback to help me improve the manuscript.

To Amanda Robinson and all the women at Le Professoresse Scrivono, thank you for making the process of book revisions as enjoyable as I could possibly imagine. I am grateful to Kelly Clancy for helping me early on to think more like a book author. And I am grateful to my writing partner in Houston, Sandra Zalman, for our mostly productive writing days at Pondicheri.

Last but not least, I am grateful for the support of my family. Book writing is the headiest thing I have ever done as an academic, and I know there were dinners and kid pickups where my mind was still churning rather than fully present. When I submitted my manuscript, my husband told me I was like a different person. So thank you to JB, Claire, and Remy for putting up with me while I birthed this thing, and for giving me the best excuses to put it down and take a break. Thank you to my parents, Mark and Diane, for always encouraging curiosity and facilitating my search for answers – even when that meant traveling to Mali alone as an undergraduate.

1

Introduction

Can democracy be an engine for state-building? Today, over 85 percent of the world's poor live in the Global South,[1] most in sub-Saharan Africa and South Asia. Over the last several decades, a majority of them have come to live in states that are at least nominally democratic. Many scholars of development have thus been focused on how democratic institutions can reduce poverty and improve welfare in such contexts. But even if elected leaders are disciplined by elections to act as good stewards of public resources, that may only make a marginal difference in the lives of citizens *when the state is weak*. That is because government programs and public goods that contribute to economic growth and development require important state capacities. To administer social programs, enforce property rights, and ensure physical security, states need informational capacity, capable bureaucrats, and fiscal capacity.

If competitive elections can sometimes induce politicians to be better stewards of existing government funds (Stasavage 2005; Besley and Kudamatsu 2006), can they also motivate politicians to invest in building state capacity? I argue in this book that, at least in initially weak states, elections fail to motivate politicians to invest in the state, and may even motivate them to keep the state weak – setting up the conditions for

[1] I use this term in the book because of its common usage to describe low- and middle-income countries outside the "West." But as recently articulated by Mampilly (2025), the term is a euphemism to divide the White and non-White world. In Chapter 3, I describe how colonial projects that created a global order of White colonizers and colonized nonwhite peoples contribute to the scope conditions of the book: The creation of weak postcolonial states with high levels of informality inherited from dual legal systems born out of colonial rule.

a *weak-state trap*. I then argue that economic informality poses a key constraint to escaping the trap. The breadth of the informal economy in weak states means that most citizens, even some relatively well-off ones, have largely informal or irregular contact with the state. For reasons I will soon explain, this forecloses the possibility of an economic majority or interest group that will self-interestedly push for state investments. In addition, the intermediaries who are empowered to connect citizens to the state in the informal economy form a constituency that is actively opposed to growing state strength.

Why the focus on informality? State-building has been argued to occur when leaders are motivated by external forces like the threat of interstate war (Tilly 1990; Scheve and Stasavage 2016) or internal forces like a long time horizon that allows them to reap the benefits of greater economic productivity in the far future (Olson 1993; Besley and Persson 2009). But in today's weak-state democracies, neither of these motives are likely avenues for state-building. First, credible external military threats have become relatively rare (Herbst 1990; Bates 2001) and global capital markets and loans have become a plausible alternative to taxation in financing wars (Queralt 2019). Second, elected leaders concerned with winning reelection are more likely to attract votes with feasible, short-term promises such as gifts, cash, or selective access to the state (Kitschelt and Wilkinson 2007; Stokes et al. 2013) rather than with less credible promises of programmatic goods that require longer-term investments (Keefer and Vlaicu 2008; Hicken and Nathan 2020). This raises the question of whether there are constituencies in weak-state democracies that will demand investments in the state from political leaders – constituencies that will be willing to support costly investments today for the promise of greater economic payoffs in the longer term.

There are some historical examples of this happening, but they come from states that were not initially so weak. Across early industrializing countries, intra-elite competition led to increases in taxation of and spending on the capitalist elites who were gaining political power relative to the agricultural elite (Beramendi, Dincecco and Rogers 2019). As private businesses developed new forms of corporate management in the United Kingdom and the United States, corporations and the national business organizations that represented them became instrumental in pushing parties to adopt programmatic reforms, including investments in state capacity (Skowronek et al. 1982; Kuo 2018). In more recent decades, coalitions of exporters in Latin America increased demands for public goods due to a commodity boom, and governments responded with large investments in infrastructural and financial capacity (Saylor 2014).

In each case, there was a substantial economic constituency for state-building – what I will call a *constituency for programmatism* (following Shefter's (1977) idea of the role of a constituency for bureaucratic autonomy in historical programmatic transitions). I argue that, in initially weak states of the Global South, such a constituency is less likely to emerge because the vast majority of economic actors operate largely in the informal sector. In other words, this important push factor to incentivize democratic leaders to invest in state-building is less likely under conditions of high economic informality. I attribute this to two distinct mechanisms: (1) Members of the informal economy are less likely to have shared economic preferences for investments in state capacity and the ability to coordinate political action around them; and (2) informal interactions between these citizens and the state are often intermediated, creating a constituency that benefits from the status quo and may actively oppose increases in state capacity that could undermine its lucrative position.

Imagine the median voter in an industrialized democracy. She is probably working for a mid-sized firm, making a low but living wage and spending most of her monthly paycheck on necessities – rent, food, and clothes. Now imagine the median voter in a weak-state democracy. She is probably working for herself or in a small family enterprise, making just enough to scrape by. These women likely share a lot of similarities: They have little disposable income, but are still able to feed, clothe, and house their families. But there is a key difference between them: The first is working in the formal sector; the second, in the informal sector. This book uses a broad definition of informality because it is ultimately interested in the effects of *informal or irregular relationships* between the state and citizens, which can manifest among people who have no formal economic activity, just as they can among those who split their time between formal and informal economic activities or those who have informal positions in formal companies.

When a primary economic activity is unregulated, key interactions with the state are necessarily irregular. You might imagine how infrequent, unsystematic, and discretionary encounters with the state will lead the woman operating in the informal sector to have lower expectations of the state's capacity to tax and provide services relative to her formal-sector counterpart whose state interactions are prescribed by some public policy or administrative code and independent of her particular identity or connections to the state. The woman in the informal sector may not even prefer that the state invests in large-scale public goods provision, such as public education, if economic success in her sector does not depend on it. Further, the sheer variability and uncertainty of the experiences of others in her sector make it difficult for her to coordinate with others and to jointly make claims on the state. And finally, she might liaise with a well-connected community member or low-level bureaucrat to negotiate payments owed to the state or plead for individual access to goods or services rather than making direct payments or claims based on her responsibilities or entitlements as a taxpaying citizen.

These features of informal relationships between citizens and the state will, I argue, make a constituency for programmatism less likely to emerge. And when this key demand-side factor to invest in state-building is undermined, we should be less likely to see democratic leaders making costly investments in state capacity. Sometimes, however, democratic leaders are motivated by something other than electoral incentives. Rarely, there are technocratic visionaries who lead state-building campaigns (Dercon 2022); more often, external factors like credit crunches or the lack of aid availability can induce investments in the state (Albers, Jerven and Suesse 2023). Extensive informality also threatens these supply-side opportunities to state-build. When intermediaries necessarily facilitate personal and discretionary connections between citizens and the state under the status quo, they form a constituency actively opposed to programmatism because they would lose access to rents and special privileges.

These consequences of informality help explain why democratic gains in the Global South have not translated into greater state-building projects in initially weak democratic states. Figure 1.1 illustrates the dramatic upward shift in democratic institutions across the Global South and Eastern Europe in the 1990s (b) compared with the very slow and stable increases in state capacity over the same period (a).

It is only by understanding the particularities of these constraints on state-building that we might begin to generate recommendations for domestic and international actors seeking to invest in state capacity. Many of the practical implications of the book are about what not to do. Advocates of programs to formalize the relationship between citizens and the state through, for example, massive state registration or formalization campaigns, should be aware of the potential backlash from actors who stand to lose from such an innovation. Even if these resistors were somehow compensated or otherwise deterred, simply changing the legal status of informal economic actors would be unlikely to induce a

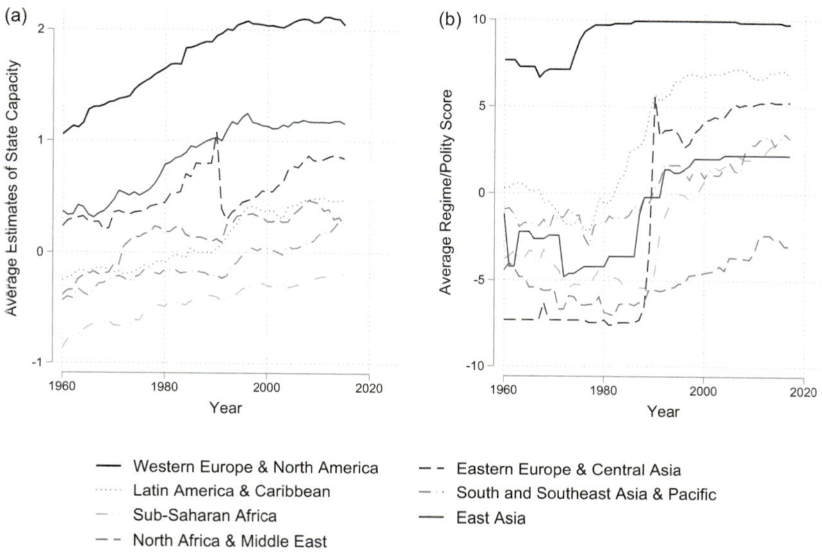

FIGURE 1.1 Trends in state capacity and democracy over time.
Note: State capacity is measured by a multidimensional indicator of state capacity from Hanson and Sigman (2021), and regime type is measured using the Polity IV regime data (Marshall, Gurr and Jaggers 2018). Panel (a) illustrates mostly slow secular upward trends in capacity across regions (with steeper gains in Western Europe, North America, and East Asia); the gap in state capacity between regions of the Global North and South has remained relatively constant. Panel (b) illustrates rapid growth in democratization in sub-Saharan Africa, Latin America, and South and Southeast Asia that has substantially closed the gap in regime scores between regions of the Global North and South.

change in the way they make claims on elected leaders if not accompanied by a much more regularized, impersonal relationship with the state.[2] Such a change necessitates major investments in the informational, administrative, and bureaucratic capacities of the state, which do not often accompany one-off formalization or registration campaigns.

On a more optimistic note, the theory implies that a programmatic constituency will be born of actors who have economic interests in a stronger state and can better coordinate shared policy demands. This suggests

[2] This warning echoes Gallien and Boogaard's (2023) "evolutionary fallacy" that from the creation of one type of linkage with formal state structures, other positive externalities will necessarily follow.

experimenting with interventions that help small businesses coordinate, for example, by disseminating information about shared grievances, such as abuses by government or challenges they face to expansion. This could help a fractionalized set of small businesses see commonalities as the basis for future organization and mobilization. It also suggests experimenting with identifying and connecting businesses that are typically on the losing end of discretionary politics or who do not have access to well-connected intermediaries, such as political minorities or outgroups.

1.1 CONTRIBUTIONS

Part of the motivation for writing this book was understanding why a more programmatic form of politics, with its attendant benefits for state-building, has not yet taken hold in young democracies of the Global South. Limited academic scholarship in this area may simply be a consequence of the fact that we see relatively few programmatic transitions in the Global South – and it is harder to study something's absence than its presence. This challenge is what led me to the importance of the informal economic sector in answering the question. In cases where democratic states have transitioned away from patronage politics and toward more programmatic forms of electoral competition, economic constituencies that advocate for programmatism are often partly responsible. In these cases in the Global North, the bourgeoisie or the formal corporate class has been key in disciplining the state to invest in nondiscretionary policies and programs. In contexts where the formal sector is very small – too small to play this role effectively, then more "middle-class" economic actors in the informal sector may be the next best hope. Whether they begin to make these demands from within the informal sector or only after formalizing is an open empirical question. But entrepreneurs who have managed to accumulate capital in the informal sector deserve our attention.

One advantage of introducing a focus on the informal economy in discussions of state-building is that the economic actors in the informal sector are both a key constraint on state-building and potentially the best hope for exiting the weak-state trap. By shining a light on informality and by highlighting its implications for state-building, one of the book's main contributions is to draw our collective attention to the informal sector, the people in it, and their role in constraining or stimulating economic development through electoral pressures. Because of their very nature – an absence of legibility to the state and economic and political marginalization, members of the informal sector are paid insufficient attention in theories of mass politics.

In line with a growing literature on endogenous state capacity which focuses on the incentives of political and economic actors to build (or destroy) state strength (Suryanarayan 2024), this book asks when individuals and groups of voters in weak-state democracies will make demands that are consistent with state-building. It comes to a novel conclusion, in part, by considering the reality of the majority of economic agents in most postcolonial countries who operate in the informal sector with irregular and idiosyncratic ties to the state. While democratic leaders should be motivated to invest in state capacity when the majority of voters has an "encompassing" interest in the market (Olson 1993), it is unclear what happens when that majority operates in a market outside state regulation.

I argue that the informal sector is unlikely to be a constituency for programmatism (even though they can and do organize politically). Instead, clientelism (or other non-programmatic forms of vote mobilization such as populism)[3] is more likely in cases of widespread informality, and such appeals do not promote the same incentives for state-building. This book thus proposes a new explanation for persistent informality alongside persistent state weakness. Informality is not only correlated with weak state capacity but also makes programmatism less credible and reinforces the utility of clientelistic electoral linkage mechanisms. This, in turn, undermines incentives to invest in state capacity. In other words, informality and state weakness are not only correlates but comprise a particularly stable equilibrium from which it is hard to escape. Below, I discuss several areas of literature to which the book contributes.

Explanations for the Programmatic Transition

Drawing insights from explanations of programmatic transitions in the Global North (and recognizing their limitations) (Shefter 1977; Skowronek et al. 1982; Boulay and DiGaetano 1985; Reid Jr. and Kurth 1992; Kuo 2018), the book adds to a smaller set of explanations for the programmatic transitions in the Global South (Geddes 1994; Asunka 2017; Nathan 2019). When democracy itself is born out of

[3] Because it is empirically the most common non-programmatic linkage mechanism (Kitschelt 2013), the book's theory and empirics focus on clientelism. However, I consider the implications of populist or charismatic linkage mechanisms for the theory in Chapter 7.

a class struggle, as was often the case in earlier historical periods, politics are more likely to cleave along programmatic lines from the start. Constituencies that are negotiating over the expansion of the franchise will naturally form the bases of political parties with differing preferences over economic policies of redistribution.[4]

But democracies in the Global South were not typically born out of pressure from a disgruntled bourgeoisie or working class. Poorer classes did not fight their way into representative institutions (Przeworski 2009), as universal suffrage was typically granted immediately in these cases, and former colonial powers as well as international financial institutions offered new external incentives for regime change (Aidt, Albornoz and Gassebner 2018).[5] Furthermore, scholars of the developing world have questioned the applicability of a class-based voting model in contexts where the relationship between the middle class, the private sector, and the state is more complicated (Roberts 2002; Handley 2015).[6] This is a key insight for postcolonial states, where what today might be referred to as the "middle class" often grew out of state employment or heavy reliance on state-run companies (Melber 2017).

Perhaps more relevant to the question of the rise of programmatism in the Global South is how democracies in the Global North transitioned from more clientelistic or patronage-based forms of politics to more programmatic ones. This transition is already more likely in modernized, industrialized societies because the rise in the incomes and homogeneity of voters makes patronage less efficient (Reid Jr. and Kurth 1992). But, more promising for contemporary low-income democracies, Shefter (1977) argues that a programmatic transition can also occur when externally mobilized parties, or ones that are not organized by members of the existing regime and thus do not have access to state resources for

[4] Two sets of logics have been advanced to explain the rise of parties with economic bases of support that ultimately offer distinct programmatic policies. First, the bourgeoisie advances democratic claims and forms a constituency for nondiscretionary politics and redistribution (Moore 1966; Easterly 2001; Acemoglu and Robinson 2006). Second, the working class advances democratic claims and forms the basis of socialist parties (Rueschemeyer et al. 1992; Collier 1999).

[5] Ansolabehere et al. (2022) describe how franchise expansion along economic lines in the US resulted in political and economic development.

[6] Lankina and Libman (2021) highlight the importance of the autonomy of a middle class from the state. In Russia, they distinguish between an older, more autonomous bourgeoisie and a newer, state-engineered middle class, finding that only the former is conducive to prodemocratic development. Rosenfeld (2021) similarly finds that state-sector careers diminish support for democracy.

patronage distribution, become sufficiently popular.[7] This, however, depends on having a large and well-resourced group that is independent of the dominant political class, again highlighting the importance of an economic constituency that is autonomous from the state.

On its face, there is no reason why economically autonomous members of the informal sector could not play this role in pushing politicians and parties to deliver programmatic policies. But I argue and show that they often do not do this in contemporary weak states, contributing to a small body of research on programmatic mobilization in the Global South. Some of this work has argued that institutional differences, such as electoral systems and decentralization, can contribute to the rise of programmatic parties.[8] Others argue that characteristics of the electorate matter: In Ghana, politicians are more likely to make nondiscretionary investments in resource allocation when voters have weaker party attachments and thus clientelistic targeting to loyal voters is relatively less effective (and abstention from targeting will not put off large swaths of loyal voters) (Asunka 2017). And finally, characteristics of the state matter: Also in Ghana, middle-class voters who might otherwise be attracted to programmatic promises do not see them as credible when the state is weak (Nathan 2019).[9]

While most of this research can help explain variation within and across developing democracies with respect to the attractiveness of programmatic parties, only Nathan's (2019) work helps explain why most of these countries' politics are still largely non-programmatic in nature.[10] Consistent with his explanation, my argument also invokes the

7 Grzymala-Busse (2002) argues that the loss of access to clientelistic mobilization when they were forced out of power post-transition is what set up the communist successor parties in the Czech Republic, Hungary, Poland, and Slovakia for potential programmatic success.

8 In Morocco, programmatic parties are more likely to garner votes in proportional relative to majoritarian systems (Pellicer, Wegner et al. 2013). And, comparing Paraguay and the Dominican Republic, Schuster (2016) finds that the likelihood is higher when the locus of control of patronage lies outside the executive. This is consistent with Fergusson, Molina, and Robinson's (2022) insight from Mexico that investing in patronage for vote mobilization is a comparative advantage for incumbent parties.

9 Habyarimana, Schipper et al.'s (2022) findings in Tanzania are consistent with this explanation. They show that the programmatic *promise* of the incumbent's secondary education expansion policy had immediate electoral benefits, but those benefits turned into electoral costs in the election following the policy's *implementation* which was disappointing to voters.

10 Nathan (2019) similarly recognized Ghana as being caught in a clientelistic electoral trap, but our diagnoses of what creates this trap differ in a key respect. Nathan's trap is

importance of state weakness. However, the book goes further in helping to explain the persistence of that state weakness. Not only is the informal sector a symptom of state weakness, but it also helps perpetuate it by limiting the likelihood of a programmatic transition.

Politics of Informality

Much of the literature on the informal sector is situated in the economics discipline. A Google Scholar search yielded five times as many economics articles with "informality" or "informal sector" in the title as political science articles. But this book makes a case for how one's status as an informal or formal sector economic agent, and the way in which informality manifests in society, should have implications for an individual or group's political behavior. In this way, it adds to a small but growing literature on the politics of informality.

The book weighs in on a first key question in this literature: whether or not the informal sector can successfully organize meaningful political action. Bringing disparate views into conversation,[11] it recognizes that informal sector workers can often successfully mobilize to make particularistic demands, but not programmatic ones.[12] This book also adds to the conversation about the state's political incentives to engage

robust to a changing environment in which the middle class, and with it programmatic demands expand, because of turnout inequality: middle-class voters are more likely to opt out of a political system that cannot meet their demands. The trap I describe is instead robust to such change because the middle class is largely growing in the informal sector, where demands are less likely to be programmatic to begin with and where people underestimate the capacity of the state to provide public goods. These forces are not mutually exclusive, although they may be likely to arise in different contexts. For instance, middle-class voters in the formal sector may be more likely to opt out of politics in more ethnically divided electoral systems like Ghana than in Senegal, where ethnicity is less of a determining factor in vote choice. In fact, voter turnout correlates positively with economic formality in my sample from Senegal which contrasts with Nathan's (2019) findings in Ghana.

11 Some scholars are quite pessimistic about the ability of the informal sector to exert political influence, either because the members of the sector are alienated from the formal state system (King and Rueda 2008) or because the sector is too fragmented to engage in successful collective action (Roberts 2002; Meagher 2014). Others are more optimistic, citing evidence of successful political mobilization among all types of informal workers from self-employed street vendors in Mexico (Cross 1998) to informally employed contract workers in India (Agarwala 2013).

12 Auerbach (2019) explains variation in the success of collective claim-making in another site of informality – urban slums – by the uneven distribution of party networks in slums, itself explained by social diversity and population.

with the informal sector (Holland 2016; Hummel 2017), introducing a new strategic incentive with respect to how states and politicians treat the informal sector.[13] Not only might the state shift policy to appease the informal sector, but it may also have preferences over the size or existence of the sector itself.

The implications of the book's theory suggest that in contexts of widespread informality, politicians may do better to keep the informal sector large. First, the informal sector is less likely to make programmatic demands and more likely to make particularistic ones, and incumbents generally have a comparative advantage in responding to the latter. Second, politicians and their networks of intermediaries may benefit from the rent-seeking that is more available to them under clientelistic exchange than under programmatic exchange.

Endogenous State Capacity

The book seeks to extend the literature on state-building by putting it in direct conversation with the literature on economic informality. My arguments are consistent with existing theories that recognize the mutually reinforcing dynamics between clientelism and state weakness. Others have argued that clientelism is more likely to arise in weak states because opposition politicians are less likely to be able to credibly commit to deliver on programmatic campaign promises (Nathan 2016*a*) and because new parties with weak reputations have a harder time making credible programmatic promises (Keefer 2007). Fergusson, Molina and Robinson (2022) even name the "weak-state trap" as one in which lower capacity leads to lower revenues, making public goods provision less possible and leading to a substitution of informal relationships of exchange for formal ones. I extend this analysis by introducing the role of economic informality in keeping states trapped in this equilibrium. This is important because it contributes to our understanding of why this status quo in

13 There is evidence from Latin America of incumbents ignoring informal economic activities or forbearing on enforcement to court electoral favor (Holland 2016), and even of competitive elections inducing parties to improve conditions in the informal sector (Feierherd 2022). Somewhat counterintuitively, Hummel (2017) finds that the state may sometimes be incentivized to create or reinforce informal sector organizations – not so they can make costly demands on the state but rather so that they can reduce the state's own costs by taking on the role of monitoring and enforcement.

many low-income democracies is so stable, and it points to a constituency that may have the potential to spur a transition to a stronger state.

With this book, I thus join a growing group of scholars who consider weak state capacity as endogenous,[14] arguing that the failure to invest in capacity can be a politically strategic decision. Some have pointed to the financial costs of increasing state and fiscal capacity to political elites which can increase the de facto tax burden on themselves and their cronies (Garfias 2018; Hollenbach and Silva 2019) or shrink future political rents (Martin 2023). Others have identified the immediate electoral costs of increasing capacity which can make incumbents less popular (Prichard 2018; Christensen and Garfias 2021) or clientelistic strategies relatively less effective (Fergusson, Larreguy and Riaño 2022). Finally, one set of studies points to another cost – reduced social status – that incumbent coalitions might seek to minimize by undermining state capacity when they fear a formerly marginalized coalition would benefit from that capacity, thus threatening the incumbent's status advantage (Suryanarayan 2021; Suryanarayan and White 2021).

I argue that there is an additional cost to state-building, especially in a democracy: Increasing state capacity can shift the dimension along which voters evaluate politicians from a clientelistic to a programmatic one. Programmatic spending can have the downside of raising expectations and inciting new political activity (Cohen 1973; Gottlieb 2016). And being made to compete along programmatic lines can also put incumbents at an electoral disadvantage if programmatic promises are less credible and if they have less of an edge against opposition candidates. Even if it does not directly affect reelection prospects for the incumbent, the transition creates a constituency of unhappy intermediaries who lose out from the move away from discretionary politics. To the extent that those intermediaries wield political and economic power, they can indirectly impose future costs on the leader.[15]

I also contribute to a long literature examining how features of economic actors in the polity can condition state-building choices, focusing here on largely informal urban actors. Existing works describe how the collective action capacity, the need for public goods, and the political clout of economic actors affect leaders' incentives to invest in the state. Boone

[14] This literature is helpfully summarized by Suryanarayan (2024).

[15] In a similar vein, Garfias and Sellars (2022) describe how state-building that reduces the bargaining power of local elites imposes costs on the central government by reducing intermediaries' willingness to suppress future attempts at rebellion.

(1998), for example, described how the more organized and hierarchical structure of rural cocoa producers in Ghana compared to the weak and fractionalized indigenous planter bourgeoisie in Côte d'Ivoire incentivized greater local state-building in the former than the latter. I argue that, as in the latter case, the lack of organized demands in the informal sector induces greater complacency in state-building efforts. Beramendi, Dincecco and Rogers (2019) explain how the stronger faction among economic elites across early and late industrializers led to increases in state-led taxing of and spending for the capitalist elites in the former but not the latter, where agricultural elites held more sway. And Saylor (2014) argues that when states had exporters as constituent members of the majority political coalition, they granted more public goods such as transportation infrastructure and access to credit to help them maximize economic opportunities. I similarly argue that different preferences across the formal and informal sectors and their differing sizes and political salience will affect leader choices to state-build.

Revisiting Lessons from Older Works

A final contribution of the book is to revisit lessons from older scholarship, particularly on the notion of dualism in society. The way I describe the economic and political lives of the informal and formal sectors is inspired by the often more anthropological depictions of dual sectors, many from the 1970s. Informed by his experience in Brazil, Santos (1979) wrote about a theory of two circuits that map onto contemporary conceptualizations of the formal and informal sectors. He describes an upper circuit as consisting of the modern urban industry, trade, and service sector alongside a lower circuit consisting mostly of the noncapital-intensive forms of production and non-modern forms of commerce (generally at a small to medium, retail level). Drawing on his experiences in Nigeria, Ekeh (1975) argues for two publics: a primordial public that is identified with "primordial groupings, sentiments, and activities" but at the same time impinges on public interest; and a civic public that is based on civil structures such as the military, civil service, and police. And with reference to India, Partha Chatterjee makes a distinction between the "civil" and "political" society that can be seen as a corollary to the formal/informal divide. The idea being that this civil society makes claims on the state as fully enfranchised citizens, whereas political society often mobilizes the claims of those who are de facto disenfranchised (Chatterjee 2004).

A first observation is that little has changed in the structure of and the relationship between these dual sectors, pointing to the stability of large-scale informality that I discuss in the book. But whereas these older works considered the dualism from the perspective of people in the sector, I also consider dualism from a strategic perspective – from the perspective of the state or politicians. In particular, I theorize about how the effects of electoral accountability differ when the median voter is ensconced in the primordial public or informal economic sector compared to the civic public or formal economic sector. And, these different expectations of electoral accountability have knock-on effects on strategic incentives to state-build.

The book's insights are also complementary to those of Boone's (1992) earlier work, inspired by the Senegalese case. Both attempt to explain contemporary political and economic outcomes by looking to the social origins and material bases of states and social strata. But our arguments highlight distinct consequences of the colonial experience. Boone (1992, p. 4) faults postcolonial states for pathologies that constrain development, including corruption and the inefficient use of state power, saying "regimes seem to use state prerogatives in ways that erode the bases of their own power." I find fault in a pathology rooted in the colonial project itself – one that created severely bifurcated postcolonial markets.

1.2 THEORY

The outcome the book is ultimately interested in understanding is when states decide to invest in building their capacities. As a result, it takes a multidimensional view of state capacity similar to the empirical measure plotted in Figure 1.1, which captures extractive, administrative, and coercive capacities (Hanson and Sigman 2021). Such an approach acknowledges that these types of capacities are highly codependent (Berwick and Christia 2018); for example, the ability of the state to administer programs requires resources from extraction, which can itself require coercion (or a credible threat of it).[16] These manifestations of state capacity cannot be divorced from a professionalized, Weberian bureaucracy, which itself facilitates economic development through its

[16] Coercive capacity can be supplanted by norms of compliance as a way to ensure revenue extraction, but compliance is conditioned on the expectation of taxpayers on a return for their investment in the form of public goods (Bates 1981; Levi 1989), which itself requires administrative and fiscal capacity to produce.

hierarchical structure, division of labor, written rules, and meritocratic recruitment (Weber 1946). Thus, in addition to understanding when states invest material resources in extractive, administrative, and coercive functions, it is also interested in when the state apparatus moves from one that is more traditional or patrimonial in nature – marked by arbitrariness and personal loyalty – to one that is rational-legal in nature – marked by formal rules (Weber 1978). A constituency for state-building is thus one that would benefit from (and can collectively organize around) a stronger state and one with more meritocratic tendencies.[17]

As articulated above, the rise of a constituency for state-building is one feasible way out of the weak-state trap in contemporary democracies. I argue, however, that large informal sectors frustrate the development of such a constituency. They do so by dampening programmatic demands and making non-programmatic linkages between voters and politicians more robust. The type of party competition that dominates electoral politics is thus the key mediating variable in the theory. Informality, through its effect on the distribution of programmatic and non-programmatic party–voter linkages within the polity, will reduce incentives to invest in state capacity. I turn next to defining the mediating and independent variables – programmatic linkage mechanisms and informality, respectively – before summarizing the main argument.

Programmatic Party Competition

Office-seeking parties want to signal to voters with limited attention spans the differences between multiple candidates (Aldrich 1995). To do this, parties can choose to differentiate themselves from competitors in a variety of ways. I focus here on the distinction between programmatic and non-programmatic appeals because each has unique implications for politician incentives to state-build. Like Mazzuca (2010), who writes about the quality of democracy in Latin America, this argument distinguishes between two sometimes conflated features of the polity – access to power (democratic vs. authoritarian) and exercise of power (rational-legal vs. discretionary or patrimonial). This reflects the empirical reality that many contemporary weak states have both relatively

[17] These might look like Progressive Era reformers in the US in the early 1900s pushing for civil service reform (Skowronek et al. 1982) or industrialists in post–World War II East Asia pushing for infrastructure, credit, and trade policy (Evans 1995) (although the latter are examples from authoritarian regimes).

competitive elections (scoring high on the access to power dimension) and relatively unprofessional bureaucracies (scoring low on the exercise of power dimension).

Democratically elected leaders are more likely to invest (or promise to invest) in state-building when they perceive electoral benefits to doing so (Olson 1993). But only certain types of citizen demands require high levels of state capacity to implement, for example, demands for public goods. These might be tangible goods and services like national roads and high-quality education, or intangible goods like property rights and contract enforcement. Public goods delivered at scale require intensive resource extraction to fund and can necessitate a large bureaucratic effort to deliver effectively. And, when goods are allocated on the basis of need or merit, the state requires informational and statistical capacity to identify legally eligible recipients for, for example, a welfare program or a property title.

Other types of citizen demands and political appeals – such as short-term transfers of cash, goods, or access to the state – require relatively lower levels of state capacity to effectuate. Not only are they smaller in scale and scope and less expensive, but they are more often distributed to individuals or groups based on discretion rather than rules and often in exchange for political support. Such exchange does not require the elected leader to deliver universal, large-scale programs that come with equivalently large fiscal and bureaucratic burdens. Instead, it requires them to credibly target available resources to political supporters, and perhaps organize extraction in a discretionary way as well. This type of claim-making and provision of goods benefits from investments in non-state institutions such as social networks and identity groups, because they can facilitate the personalized connections, group trust, and loyalty that make such exchange more efficient.

I call the former type of demand for nondiscretionary public goods *programmatic* demands. Voter demands and consequent party appeals are programmatic when they seek to address social problems through policy packages and where any targeting is based on legal or economic rationale rather than discretion, for example, raising taxes to fund a means-tested poverty reduction program (Kitschelt 2000). When electoral competition is primarily programmatic, preferences tend to diverge according to class or sectoral cleavages. Relative to poorer citizens, richer ones prefer lower tax rates and lower public goods provision because taxes are more costly to them, and they have better access to privately provided goods. Relative to agricultural elites, industrial elites tend to prefer higher levels of public goods and taxation (Beramendi, Dincecco and Rogers 2019). Political cleavages thus constitute dimensions that are durable and allow voters to select among distinct parties (Lipset and Rokkan 1967).

Contrast this with discretionary allocation of goods in which targeting tends to occur *de facto* through personal, often intermediated connections rather than *de jure* on the basis of universal principles or prescribed formulas. Instead of organizing along class or sectoral lines, we see constituencies congeal along ethnicity, caste, kin group, or religious lines. These identity-based groups and networks often demand goods exclusive to their group, and parties differentiate themselves by making promises to distinct groups based on shared identity or personal connections.

Notably, parties that appeal to voters primarily on the basis of programmatic policies or economic issues are rare in polities in the Global South, according to the most comprehensive expert survey of party-level linkages with voters (see Figure 1.2). More capable states, largely concentrated in Europe and North America, have the most programmatic party competition.[18] Instead, party–voter linkages in Global South countries are predominantly clientelistic, that is, the distribution of targeted goods to groups or individuals in exchange for electoral support; charismatic appeals, for example, populist or anti-elite rhetoric based on thin ideology, are relatively more common in these countries as well.[19]

Types of Informality

The International Labour Organization (ILO), which collects data globally on types of employment, defines the "informal economy" as referring to all economic activities by workers and economic units that are – in law or in practice – not covered or insufficiently covered by formal arrangements (International Labour Organization 2015). However, applying this definition in a binary way to people, businesses, or sectors becomes challenging and has been the subject of considerable scholarly debate (Gallien and Boogaard 2023). An individual may have

18 South Africa and South Korea are two notable exceptions.

19 Consistent with Hicken and Nathan (2020), I define clientelism in this book more flexibly than the standard definition that insists on a quid pro quo exchange (Hicken 2011) and implies monitoring, which has been found to be rare empirically. My broader definition includes unenforced but targeted, particularistic distribution to likely supporters. While such an approach has been considered wasteful, it is a viable strategy when more efficient than alternatives such as programmatic distribution (a strategy that can result in even more scarce resources being delivered to opposition supporters). Especially when unmonitored, it is easy to see how shared identity, such as ethnicity, can improve the efficiency of clientelism: It can serve as a heuristic to parties for expected vote choice (Nathan 2016*b*) or can work through local leaders who are good at mobilizing coethnics (Koter 2013).

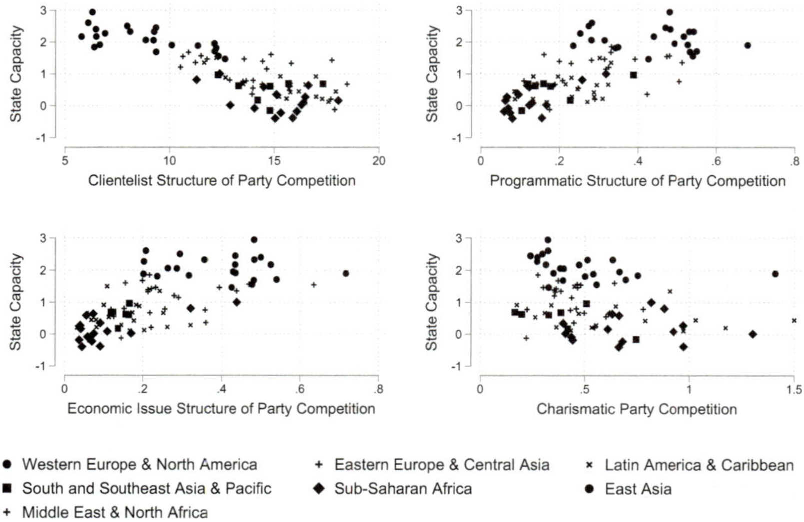

FIGURE 1.2 Cross-national comparison of modes of party competition and state capacity.

Note: Measures of party competition are from the Democratic Accountability and Linkages Project (DALP) dataset compiled in 2009 (Kitschelt 2013); party-level measures are weighted by party size and aggregated to the country level. The clientelistic structure of party competition is measured by an index of questions about the extent to which parties use exchange mechanisms in which promises of material goods, preferential access, or influence are used as inducements to secure votes. The programmatic structure of party competition is an index of questions asked about the parties' positions with respect to social spending on the disadvantaged, the state's role in governing the economy, public spending, tolerance of minority groups, and freedom from state interference into privacy. The indicator itself measures the cohesion of parties' appeals on an issue position, the salience of the issue position, and the degree of spatial distinctiveness or polarization of parties on issue positions. The economic issue structure measure is a subset of the larger programmatic measure focusing only on economic issues. State capacity is measured by a multidimensional indicator from Hanson and Sigman (2021); the 2009 value is used to coincide with the DALP data.

one formal job alongside an informal occupation or move fluidly between job types (Baker and Velasco-Guachalla 2018). A business may be formally registered but pay taxes through informal channels (Williams, Shahid and Martínez 2016; Ulyssea 2020). The informal sector's viability or profitability may be largely influenced by that of a related formal sector (Potts 2008), or there may be interconnected formal and informal firms within the same narrowly defined industry (Ulyssea 2018). This complexity suggests real variation in the types of actors and firms that comprise the informal sector – variation that is analyzed and described in the empirical chapters.

The argument in this book centers on the way informal economic *interactions* with the state condition political attitudes and behaviors. The logic should thus be relevant to any actor or business that has some foot in the informal sector if we make the straightforward assumption that economic actors with some level of informality have more irregular interactions with the state than actors squarely in the formal sector. This focus on the lived experience of informality rather than one's status as formal or informal also suggests that informality manifests on a spectrum. The way informality is measured empirically in Chapter 4 reflects this. Distinguishing between one's formal-legal status and the quality of one's actual experience with the state is also consistent with recent literature that has advocated for shifting focus away from firm registration as an end in itself that will necessarily bring about associated benefits such as tax payment, access to public and financial services, and compliance with regulations (Gallien and Boogaard 2023; Moore 2023). It also allows us to study the reality that even when informal firms pay formally defined taxes, they often do so in irregular ways, including through discretionary targeting, coercion, negotiation with state intermediaries, and limited to no formal recourse or return on their investment (Moore 2008; Haavik and Cissé 2024).

While the book's argument should apply to a range of actors with varying levels and types of informal interactions with the state, a key scope condition has to do instead with the extent and durability of informality within the polity (rather than within an individual or business). In other words, what proportion of economic actors experience frequent informal interactions with the state? Most countries exhibit some level of economic informality: Between 6 and 72 percent of GDP per capita is produced in the informal sector, and between 1 and 99 percent of employment is in the informal sector. The argument in this book is relevant primarily for countries at the higher end of this spectrum that exhibit features of what I will call "embedded informality."

As one might expect, informality is strongly negatively correlated with state capacity as depicted in Figure 1.3(b). More capable states have a greater ability to regulate and tax economic actors, establishing formal or regularized relationships with them. But it is important not to conflate these two constructs. There can be more capable states that *choose* not to formalize relationships with citizens or less capable states that use extensive enforcement capacity to go after economic actors.

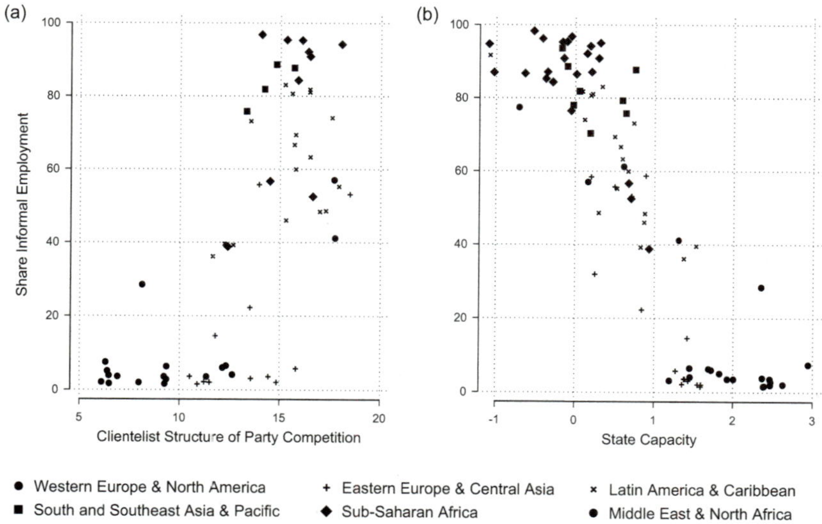

FIGURE 1.3 Cross-national comparison of economic informality, clientelism and state capacity.
Note: In (a), informality is positively correlated with the clientelistic nature of parties across countries. The latter is measured by an index of questions about the extent to which parties use exchange mechanisms in which promises of material goods, preferential access, or influence are used as inducements to secure votes from the DALP dataset compiled in 2009 (Kitschelt 2013). In (b), informality is negatively correlated with state capacity as measured by a multidimensional indicator of state capacity from Hanson and Sigman (2021). Informality is measured in both panels as the share of informal employment from the ILO. Because DALP data is only measured in 2009, and the ILO data is not measured every year in every country, all points reflect the mean value of available data for each indicator in a five-year range (2009–2014).

Observed variation in the size of the informal sector across contexts can thus be categorized along two dimensions: the *capacity* of the state to engage in enforcement, and the *motivation* of the state to enforce. In Chapter 2, I describe the four types of informality that manifest across these two dimensions. In contexts where the state has both high levels of capacity and motivation to enforce, we should expect very low levels of informality. Such contexts of *marginal informality* best describe countries in the lower right-hand quadrant of Figure 1.3b, primarily in Europe and North America. In contexts where the state has the capacity to enforce but relatively low motivation due to low incomes or profits in a substantial portion of the economy, we should see *extractive infor-*

mality.[20] In contexts with the opposite set of dynamics – where the state has the motivation to enforce but insufficient capacity – we should see *reactive informality*. In these cases, the state finds it lucrative to enforce taxation on certain sectors of the economy but cannot prevent high levels of evasion.[21]

The final type of informality is the one of interest in this book: when the state has neither the capacity nor the motivation to enforce taxation on much of the economy. Because neither economic actors nor the state is actively attempting to change their informal status, I call this *embedded informality*. This stable status endures over time and becomes embedded in not only the economic relationships between citizens and the state but also in the sociopolitical relationships citizens have with the state and each other. We should expect the largest informal sectors in contexts of embedded informality, which best describe the countries in the upper-left quadrant of Figure 1.3(b), located largely in sub-Saharan Africa and South and Southeast Asia.

A notable characteristic of embedded informality is that citizens and states still interact with each other – just in less prescribed and more idiosyncratic ways. Because informal sector members are not trying to hide from the state, as in cases of reactive informality, their economic activities will be more visible to the state and others in society. And because the state is not actively using forbearance to induce vote mobilization, as in cases of extractive informality, there are fewer constraints on the state enforcing upon citizens in a more informal way. Particularly in democracies where incumbents are motivated to mobilize political support from among the populous informal sector, citizens can still hope to gain something (if small) from the state, and the state can hope to extract political support, if not also some small amount of revenue, from citizens. These political dynamics encourage contact between citizens in the informal sector and the state, in spite of relatively weak state capacity.

This kind of informal exchange – by its very nature of being unregulated – is especially conducive to discretion. When politicians and bureau-

20 These most resemble cases in Latin America described by Holland (2016) and Tendler (2002) as examples of forbearance: Relatively capable states credibly offer to forbear on enforcement in exchange for something it wants more, such as political support.

21 Such is the case in parts of Europe and Central Asia, Latin America and the Caribbean, and the Middle East and North Africa with too-heavy regulatory and tax burdens (Vorisek et al. 2022). Indeed, the countries in the very middle of Figure 1.3(b) with middling levels of informality and state capacity are found largely in the regions of Latin America, the Middle East, and Eastern Europe/Central Asia.

crats find themselves in a position to offer some benefits or to impose some costs, they can target them to particular groups or individuals.[22] In a democracy, leaders can derive electoral benefits by engaging in targeted distribution and extraction based on a political logic, that is, offering discretionary benefits or withholding costs in exchange for political support. This type of clientelistic exchange is common in contexts of embedded informality. Figure 1.3(a) illustrates a strong positive relationship between informal employment and the clientelist structure of parties.

The Weak-State Trap

In Figure 1.2, we see a tight clustering of Global South countries, particularly those in sub-Saharan Africa and Southeast Asia, at low levels of state capacity and low levels of programmatic party competition. Of course, this cluster of polities has other things in common, such as relatively low levels of GDP and human development indicators. But I argue that these two phenomena – weak state capacity and the absence of programmatism – are not only strongly correlated, they are also mutually causal. They comprise an equilibrium that is unlikely to shift, barring some exogenous shock.

The logic is this: When the state is sufficiently weak and citizens condition their vote on the basis of programmatic performance, even well-meaning politicians will get kicked out of office. Honest politicians want to govern responsibly but simply do not have the capacity to meet voter demands. Knowing that they cannot satiate programmatic demands with a limited budget, they are more likely to shirk their duties (you might call this a damned if you do, damned if you don't mentality). In this case, voters are more likely to get nothing. By contrast, if voters in a weak state instead condition their vote choice on the basis of the receipt (or promise) of smaller, targeted transfers, then they at least have a chance of receiving some benefits in exchange for political support.

So the best voters can do in a democratic weak state is demand smaller, targeted transfers from politicians, which the state is more capable of providing. This explains why, even though voters on the whole tend to do better under programmatic politics (because they benefit from economies

22 Nathan (2023) points out that state weakness itself gives rise to the politically valuable tool of discretionary targeting because the increasing scarcity of state resources makes the little that is available increasingly valuable to the few who can access it.

of scale and investments in capacity that allow for larger and more substantial public outlays), they instead vote according to a clientelistic logic.

This stable equilibrium forms a trap because it has self-reinforcing dynamics. When voters prefer to condition their vote on the receipt of particularistic transfers, it undermines incentives for the incumbent to ever invest in building up the state to better deliver on programmatic policies. Politicians can gain an edge in the provision of targeted transfers by investing in the networks and machines that make transfers more electorally efficient through information gathering (who is susceptible to such exchange) and relationship building (to make promises of exchange more credible). These investments are made almost exclusively outside the formal channels of the state.[23]

This discussion gives rise to two stable states of the world depicted in Figure 1.4. The first is a weak-state trap where particularistic or clientelistic politics and state weakness are mutually reinforcing. The second is a public goods equilibrium where programmatic politics incentivizes the state to invest in the kinds of fiscal, bureaucratic, and infrastructural capacity that make programmatic promises credible, attractive, and efficient.[24]

Informality Blocks Pathways Out of the Weak-State Trap

Equilibria are inherently stable, but they are not fixed. Any system is subject to idiosyncratic or exogenous shocks that might lead to durable change. There are two main pathways through which polities might exit the weak-state trap. First, there could be a rare programmatic candidate or party that wins office and starts investing in the state, or a programmatic constituency that suddenly congeals and starts making programmatic demands on the state. Second, there could be a rare shock to state capacity that, in turn, changes the calculus of voters at the ballot box.

23 In fact, incumbent parties have a comparative advantage when they engage in clientelistic politics but not programmatic politics because they can use state resources as either clientelistic transfers or investments in sustaining the machine. So incumbents face an electoral *dis*incentive to invest in state capacity because reducing the cost of providing programmatic goods gives opponents a competitive edge (Fergusson, Larreguy and Riaño 2022).

24 While others have written about the weak-state trap (Fergusson, Molina, and Robinson 2022), the voter accountability model I introduce in Chapter 2 helps explain the conditions under which we should expect each state of the world to emerge and why they are stable.

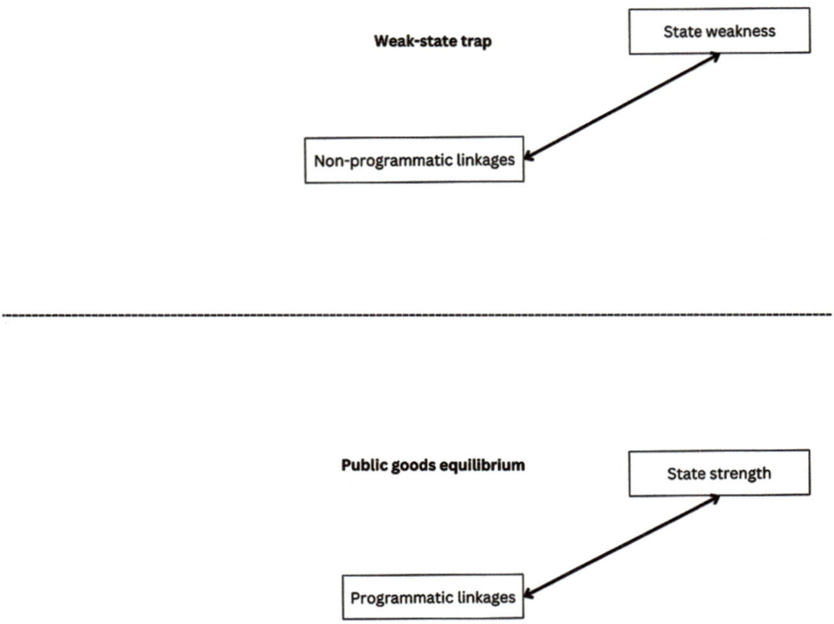

FIGURE 1.4 Two equilibria of accountability and state capacity.

I argue that embedded informality reduces the likelihood of either of these (already rare) occurrences.

We saw that embedded informality is co-occurring with both clientelistic linkages and weak state capacity in Figure 1.3. This is not surprising. Informal economic relationships are conducive to more particularistic and discretionary forms of politics because both rely on personal relationships and networks. And, intermediaries that facilitate informal economic relationships between citizens and the state or serve as sources of social insurance can be usefully leveraged as clientelistic brokers to facilitate bloc voting. By contrast, large formal economic sectors are conducive to more programmatic forms of politics, that is, organized corporate sectors are particularly good at advocating for programmatic demands (Kuo 2018). These different types of economic constituencies are represented in Figure 1.5 alongside their respective equilibria, for example, the weak-state trap or the public goods equilibrium. The pathways out of the weak-state trap described above are represented by the numbers (2), a shift in linkage mechanisms, and (3), a shock to state capacity.

Let's start by considering how embedded informality constrains pathway (2), or an increase in programmatic demands among voters, setting

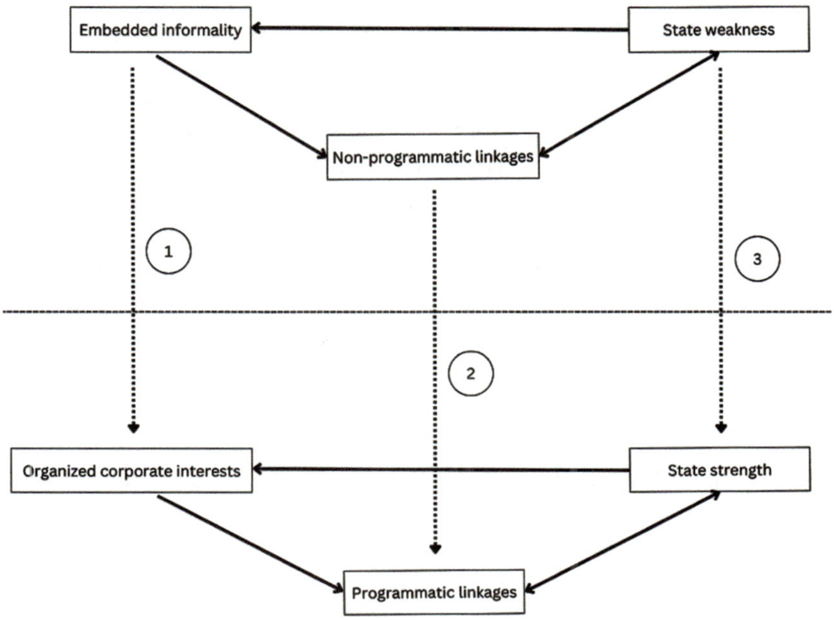

FIGURE 1.5 Potential pathways out of the weak-state trap.

off a virtuous cycle where accountability pressures now stimulate investments in capacities that facilitate public goods provision. Embedded informality stymies this pathway out of the trap by reducing preferences for programmatic goods and undermining the ability to coordinate collective claims on the state. First, members of the informal sector have especially low expectations of state capacity. Because of the irregular nature of their relationship to the state, they will underestimate the capacity of the state, which does form regularized economic relationships at times, but with a minority of citizens. Second, members of the informal sector have idiosyncratic relationships with the state and thus have a hard time developing accurate beliefs about what other members of their sector experience. These diffuse beliefs about their peers make it harder for members of the informal sector to perceive shared grievances and coordinate joint claims on the state.

Now, let's turn to pathway (3), whereby a sufficiently large increase in state capacity could increase the state's ability to implement programs and policies uniformly and with less discretion, making programmatic linkages the more attractive and efficient electoral mobilization strategy. Embedded informality additionally limits this pathway out of the weak-state trap by creating a constituency that will resist reforms to make the state more capable. Others, mainly writing about Africa, have made similar arguments (see, e.g., Bayart (1993)) with respect to different domains of intermediation. Writing about juridical sovereignty, Englebert (2009, p. 6) argues that weak central states share territorial authority with peripheral clients who, in exerting their command arbitrarily, create opportunities for intermediation between citizens and state agents – and intermediaries who "have an interest in maintaining the dysfunctional state." In the realm of property rights, others have argued that actors who gain from participating in informal or customary land governance institutions will resist land titling and formalization (Onoma 2009; Honig 2022).

I argue that, in the realm of economic transactions with the state, embedded informality also creates a need for intermediaries who can help connect states and citizens. When politicians and bureaucrats engage in discretionary tactics of provision and extraction, they do better to work through local knowledge brokers who have information about which citizens need what services and which economic agents have surpluses to extract. These knowledge brokers are often leveraged by political parties as vote brokers to increase the efficiency of clientelistic exchange. Intermediaries benefit from their role in bureaucratic and political exchange as they can demand material payment or privileged access for their services. But these services would no longer be necessary were the state to move to a less discretionary mode of provision and extraction and were parties to move to a more programmatic form of politics. As such, economic intermediaries prefer the status quo under the weak-state trap and resist moves to programmatic politics or stronger states.

Since embedded informality indirectly constrains exit from the weak-state trap (through the above two pathways), a final way out could be undermining economic informality itself – pathway (1). But I argue that this too is unlikely because embedded informality is particularly stable. Notably, the divide between economic sectors often overlaps with social characteristics like language, culture, and identity that create barriers to individuals seeking to exit the informal sector. Furthermore, success in the informal and formal sectors requires very different types of long-term investments in education and in insurance against risk, creating intergenerational path dependence. Once someone has begun investing for success in one sector for themselves and their family, it makes it difficult to switch pathways later, losing those sunk costs and starting again. This is not to say that formalizing members of the informal sector should necessarily have a direct effect on exiting the weak-state trap. Formalization will only accelerate a transition out of the weak-state trap when it contributes to creating organized interests that demand nondiscretionary policies and public goods.

1.3 EMPIRICAL APPROACH

To interrogate these theoretical ideas, I set much of the book in urban Senegal. This is arguably among the most-likely contexts for the emergence of a programmatic constituency on the continent. It is thus an interesting site in which to study why such a place has not transitioned to a more programmatic form of politics (at least as of this writing).

On the one hand, Senegal is a fairly average African country along relevant measures. As shown in Figure 1.6, Senegal scores about average for the continent in terms of its parties' linkage mechanisms (more clientelistic than programmatic) and in terms of state capacity. At 91 percent, Senegal's mean level of informal employment over the last decade is higher than that in sub-Saharan Africa on the whole (77 percent) but equivalent to the average in the subregion of West Africa, where informal employment is highest on the continent.

In other ways, though, Senegal is a most-likely case for making a transition to programmatic politics. It has been described as the oldest democracy on the continent because of its experience with real electoral representation under the French colonial regime and because it has been a presidential republic since independence. While elections have not always been competitive, it has never experienced military rule or civil war like many of its neighbors. Additionally, ethnicity is not a main driver of politics as it is elsewhere on the continent. In terms of its economy, Senegal has seen steady economic growth in recent decades, and there is a burgeoning entrepreneurial sector in its capital city, Dakar.

Existing explanations suggest that such stable economic development (Kitschelt and Wilkinson 2007) and urbanization (Reid Jr. and Kurth 1992) in a stable democracy contribute to the likelihood of a programmatic transition. But Senegal's politics have largely not cleaved along programmatic lines. In this way, we can think of Senegal as a deviant case to help us uncover new reasons that a programmatic transition has not been forthcoming (Seawright and Gerring 2008). Another way to observe Senegal's high potential for a programmatic transition is to look at its placement in Figure 1.6. In this plot of just sub-Saharan African polities, we again observe the two equilibria described in the previous section: Most countries cluster around lower values of programmatism and state

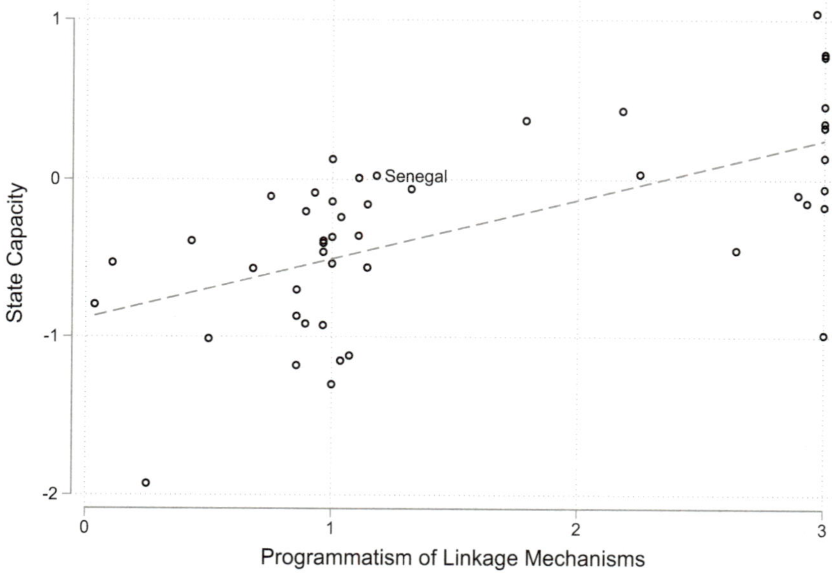

FIGURE 1.6 Cross-national comparison of programmatism and state capacity within sub-Saharan Africa.

Note: Each point indicates the average value for each African country for the years since 1990, when many countries transitioned to multiparty democracy. Programmatism is measured by an indicator of party system linkage mechanisms from the Varieties of Democracy dataset (Coppedge et al. 2023) instead of DALP since the former is available annually, whereas the latter is only collected in 2009. A 0 indicates entirely clientelistic linkage mechanisms, whereas a 4 indicates entirely programmatic linkage mechanisms. As before, state capacity is measured using Hanson and Sigman's (2021) indicator.

capacity, and a relative few form a cluster with higher values on both dimensions. Some in this latter cluster are not even nominally democratic, such as Rwanda and Tanzania, whereas others are island or microstates, such as Cape Verde, Mauritius, and Eswatini. Just considering the countries in the lower-left cluster, Senegal has among the highest levels of state capacity, but its politics remain firmly non-programmatic. (A value of 1 on this scale indicates some individual and collective clientelism.)

To introduce the case and explore the origins of embedded informality, Chapter 3 charts the history of indigenous capital development in Senegal. We see the ways in which the colonial regime depressed opportunities for formal capital development and contributed to the segregation of indigenous capital in the informal sector. We also observe some of the factors that make embedded informality so durable: Language serves as a key barrier to exit, and investments in social networks increase the comparative advantage of remaining informal. To interrogate the scope conditions of the book, I use cross-national data to show how patterns of colonial settlement map onto contemporary patterns of embedded informality.

In Chapter 4, I bring us to contemporary urban Senegal to empirically evaluate the argument that informality constrains the second pathway out of the weak-state trap. Specifically, I exploit variation in the irregularity of actors' fiscal relationship to the state to understand how that shapes demand for programmatic politics. Importantly, I sample economic agents who would be most-likely candidates for mobilizing around programmatic demands. The focus on urban Senegal is substantiated by evidence in Chapter 7 that shows that clientelism has been declining as an attractive electoral mobilization tool in urban but not rural Senegal.

In a face-to-face survey from 2017, I studied the political attitudes and behaviors of about 2000 members of the formal and informal sectors in Dakar who were self-described middle-class residents. I recruited people who had decent, stable employment or owned brick-and-mortar businesses. The extent of informality varies within and across both groups, specifically with respect to the regularity of how each firm owner or worker pays income tax.[25] I show how this variation in the regularity (or formality) of one's fiscal relationship to the state has consequences for political attitudes and behaviors. Greater informality is associated with lower expectations of the state, lower likelihood of coordination with other members of one's economic group, and lower likelihood of voting for a programmatic candidate. To show that this is not a novel moment in Senegal's history, I also trace the rise and fall of an informal sector union. While the union was able to organize targeted tax protests in the 1990s, the organization has since splintered, failing to coordinate successful lobbying efforts among its heterogeneous members with fractionalized interests. The empirical exercise in Chapter 4 thus helps to answer why programmatic demands have failed to emerge even in this most-likely context.

If a mobilized constituency for programmatism is one pathway out of a weak-state trap, then the state or external actors pushing for increased state capacity is another. I argue that intermediaries who informally link

25 Some informal sector businesses pay taxes only when tax collectors come to their stores, negotiate how much tax to pay, and do not get the benefit of a receipt. Others have more formal accounting records and demand receipts in exchange for tax payment. Even in the formal sector, some workers are paid in cash and only sometimes pay income tax, while others are paid by direct deposit and have taxes regularly withheld.

the state to citizens comprise a constituency *against* such a change, and can thus serve to block this pathway out of the weak-state trap. The empirical exercise in Chapter 5 travels outside Senegal to generate evidence for this claim. This is because observing resistance from intermediaries requires a real or perceived shock to state capacity. I leverage my involvement in other research collaborations where such a shock occurred or was imminent.

First, we travel to Mali, one of Senegal's neighbors, where a forthcoming performance-based funding initiative by the Government of Mali and the World Bank threatened to upset clientelistic linkages between local intermediaries and the elected mayor. Specifically, future transfers from the state to the municipality would be based, in part, on the mayor's performance in the prior year, and civil society would have a say in judging that performance. So civil society leaders face a choice: Call out mayoral corruption (where it occurs) and risk future informal transfers, or stay silent and implicitly consent to the misuse of funds. With Jaimie Bleck and Katrina Kosec, we conducted a survey of a large sample of these civil society leaders to ask them what they would do. We find that the most embedded leaders (who have operated the longest in the village and have the most ties to villagers) both benefit more from clientelistic transfers under the status quo and are the least likely to sanction a corrupt mayor.

While this evidence is suggestive of the idea that informal intermediaries are loath to support changes to the status quo, the chapter concludes with more concrete examples of intermediary resistance. These examples come from my participation in a coordinated multicountry study, called a *Metaketa*, in which teams of researchers and implementing agencies across six countries evaluated the effect of policies to formalize the relationship between states and citizens.[26] Not only do these cases represent relatively rare examples of a concerted top-down effort to strengthen the state in ways that decrease discretion and increase programmatic linkages, but they also have the benefit of being accompanied by research teams. While the field experimental evaluations tested the effect of formalization policies on citizen behavior, my participation in the Nigeria study with coauthor Adrienne LeBas motivated me to consider the potential for

26 See https://egap.org/our-work/the-metaketa-initiative/roundtwo-taxation/.

backlash from intermediaries who had something to lose from increasing formalization in each case. Conversations with the other research teams suggested this took place in at least two other cases – India and the Democratic Republic of Congo (D.R. Congo). Using evidence largely from outside the Senegalese context, I thus show how embedded informality stymies a second pathway out of the weak-state trap because of its reliance on individuals who mediate irregular relationships of extraction and provision between the state and citizens and are motivated to resist changes to the status quo.

After these two main empirical chapters provide evidence for how informality constrains two pathways out of the weak-state trap, the latter part of the book interrogates when we might instead expect to see a transition to programmatism in democratic, weak states. I first ask whether increasing electoral competitiveness in weak states might be a way to induce pressure for state-building and the provision of public goods. Chapter 6 provides evidence to the contrary: especially when politics do not cleave along programmatic lines, electoral competition is unlikely to have these salutary effects. The chapter opens with a case comparison of two public bureaucracies charged with tax collection in Senegal and Lagos State, Nigeria – both contexts of widespread economic informality and clientelistic electoral politics. However, as evidenced by interviews with current and former members of the Internal Revenue Service in Dakar and Lagos, investments in building the informational, bureaucratic, and technical capacity of the state have been far greater in Lagos than in Senegal. One explanation that emerges from these interviews is that greater electoral competition in Senegal might weaken incentives to regulate and tax the informal sector. The longer time horizon of the ruling party in Lagos state – unchanged since the onset of multiparty elections in 1999 – increases the perceived future benefits of making costly investments in fiscal capacity. I follow the case comparison with a cross-country analysis, generating additional evidence in support of this claim. Using a panel dataset of 31 countries from 1870 to 2010 (most from outside Africa), I show that increases in electoral competition *reduce* subsequent tax revenue collection, but only in polities where elections are largely contested along non-programmatic lines.

If clientelistic politics are standing in the way of the potential for electoral competition to induce investment in state-building, might the decline of clientelism be a way out of the weak-state trap? Chapter 7 considers the case of urban Senegal, where the efficiency of clientelism has waned in recent decades. There, the role of informal intermediaries as political brokers has been on the decline – at least in Dakar, which is home to most informal businesses. The chapter traces the decline of urban political brokers and clientelistic voting using historical, geographic, and electoral data. Instead, many of these voters seem to be attracted to populist promises of party leaders.

The final chapter considers nascent constituencies that might serve as advocates for a stronger, more programmatic state. In particular, it tells the story of Senegal's wealthiest businessman, who built an incredibly successful corporation and whose political interests are now at odds with those of the traditional economic elite. It then traces the rise of a new, externally mobilized political party (a recipe for success suggested by Shefter (1977)), that has a more credible claim to making programmatic promises than its predecessors, which have all been born out of elites from the *ancien régime*. Finally, it introduces two possibilities for exiting the weak-state trap suggested by cases outside Africa: mixing strategies (clientelistic and programmatic) and compensating intermediaries.

1.4 PLAN OF THE BOOK

Chapter 2 introduces the concepts of *embedded informality* and the weak-state trap before turning the main argument that the existence of the former makes it especially hard to exit the trap. To move from a clientelistic, weak state to a stronger state requires a transition to programmatic politics or substantial investments in state capacity. Embedded informality obstructs both pathways out (and is itself incredibly stable). First, economic informality depresses citizen expectations of the state and weakens coordination around programmatic demands. Second, informal intermediaries strongly prefer the status quo and thus resist transitions away from it. Chapters 4 and 5, respectively, provide evidence for each of these claims. Before these main empirical chapters, Chapter 3 introduces the country context of Senegal and illustrates how and why embedded informality can be particularly resilient. It thus explains how one pathway out of the trap, a slow shrinking of the informal sector, is unlikely in cases of embedded informality.

The question thus arises: Are initially weak democracies with large informal sectors doomed to stay weak forever? Chapter 6 examines whether increasing electoral competition can serve as one way out of the weak-state trap by looking at the more and less competitive cases of Senegal and Lagos, Nigeria, alongside a quantitative cross-country analysis. It finds that, if anything, electoral competition impedes investments in state-building under conditions of highly clientelistic politics. Chapter 7 then considers whether a decline in clientelism facilitates a transition to the strong-state, programmatic equilibrium. It does this by tracing the decline of the political influence of clientelistic intermediaries in urban Senegal but finds that populism rather than programmatism is the main mode of attracting urban voters.

Chapter 8 concludes with two more speculative discussions. First, it offers some optimism around the congealing of a constituency for programmatism by exploring the rise of a potentially programmatic candidate and of a more independent bourgeoisie in Senegal. It also considers what we might learn from other cases that have made strides toward a transition to more programmatic politics. Second, it reflects on how we might translate the theory and findings from the book outside of the African continent, with specific consideration of Latin America. It concludes with a discussion of the book's practical and policy implications.

2

A Theory of Informality and the Weak-State Trap

Political economists agree that weak states can limit a nation's economic development: States that cannot raise revenue or provide public goods will be unable to secure the institutional conditions that facilitate growth, for example, protect property rights (Besley and Persson 2010; Acemoglu, Moscona and Robinson 2016; Dincecco and Katz 2016). But economists are divided over the impact of informality on economic growth (La Porta and Shleifer 2014). At the microlevel, studies have found that formalizing firms has little to no immediate economic benefit (De Mel, McKenzie and Woodruff 2013; Benhassine et al. 2018). However, more aggregate shifts in levels of informality could induce growth by reallocating resources from low-productivity to high-productivity firms, inducing greater investments in human capital, and increasing high-skill wages (although these benefits can come at the cost of increasing unemployment) (Ulyssea 2020).

My theory posits an indirect negative consequence of informality on economic development. Large, embedded informal sectors can slow the development of state capacity by reducing the likelihood of a constituency for programmatism. Almost by definition, we would expect larger informal sectors to arise in places with weak states, so it is not surprising that we observe this empirically; Figure 1.3, for example, illustrates a strong negative correlation between informal employment and state capacity. But studies that consider ways to reduce the size of the informal sector – see Ulyssea (2020) for a good review – seldom consider the political calculus of the incumbent government to invest in the necessary capacity to increase enforcement or compliance. And studies that consider ways to increase state capacity have not considered how demand (or lack thereof) from a large informal-sector constituency affects the state's motivations to sustain increases in capacity (Suryanarayan 2024).

I argue that economic informality and state weakness are not only correlated but also mutually reinforcing. I posit two main ways through which informality keeps the state weak; both are mediated through politics. For leaders to make costly investments in state-building, they require motivation. In the absence of exogenous forces like war, that motivation can come from endogenous forces like constituent pressure. First, a constituency *for* state-building – which forms through programmatic linkages – is less likely to emerge in a context where informal economic agents make up an electoral majority. Second, a constituency *opposed* to state-building is more likely to form where contact with the state is frequently facilitated by intermediaries.

One puzzle that arises from this logic is why, in a competitive democracy, would citizens operating in the informal sector vote against their interests? Programmatic demands such as social insurance or other need-based state programs would likely benefit informal actors more than formal ones, and the tax burden of such programs would be less costly to them. I address this puzzle in the second section of the chapter, with a theoretical model. The counterintuitive result is explained by the fact that voters in a weak state expect the government to be too unlikely to deliver on programmatic promises, so they turn instead to particularistic promises, which are more certain. Specifically, voters in a weak state cannot distinguish between a bad incumbent who shirks and a good one who is just too constrained to deliver. To exact some modicum of accountability, voters instead demand particularistic benefits that are feasible to distribute under weak-state conditions. This result is consistent with other arguments linking the lack of programmatism (or clientelism) to state weakness that focus on, for example, the lack of credibility of programmatic demands under a weak state (Nathan 2019), the proclivity of clients to expect lenient state enforcement (Sy-Sahande 2017), and "that clients are relatively uninformed, do not act collectively towards the state, and are willing to break rules" (Fergusson, Molina, and Robinson 2022).[1]

This logic produces two distinct accountability-capacity equilibria: a non-programmatic, weak state and a programmatic, strong state

[1] There is a more substantial literature on the related relationship between clientelism and preferences for public goods (see, e.g., Stokes et al. 2013; Khemani 2015; Diaz-Cayeros, Estévez and Magaloni 2016).

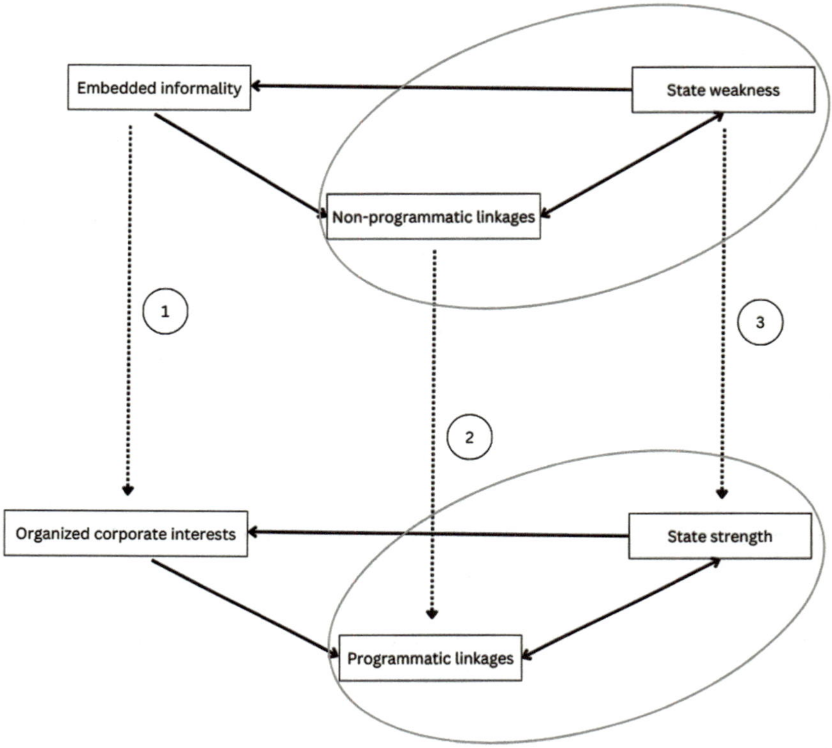

FIGURE 2.1 Informality and the weak-state trap.

(these relationships are depicted in the gray ovals in Figure 2.1). Each equilibrium is self-reinforcing because of the consequences of each linkage mechanism for investments in state-building. In the former, the non-programmatic electoral mobilization strategy reduces incentives to invest in the state; in the latter, the programmatic electoral mobilization strategy increases incentives to invest in the state. It is for this reason that I call the former equilibrium a weak-state trap; not only is it stable, but there are forces produced by equilibrium behavior that reinforce the parametric conditions. In simpler terms, equilibrium selection depends on the initial level of state strength. In a non-programmatic electoral system, there are incentives *not* to invest in the state or even to quash such investments, keeping the state weak.

Illustrating the durability of a non-programmatic, weak-state equilibrium and contrasting it with a programmatic, strong-state equilibrium begs the question of how polities transition from the first to the second. I argue that a key gap in our understanding of when and how this transition will occur in contemporary weak states concerns the role of informality. In particular, I show how three potential pathways out of the weak-state trap are constrained by a manifestation of the informal sector that I call *embedded informality*. The first part of this chapter is thus dedicated to explaining embedded informality, and where we should see it emerge. Next, the chapter describes how embedded informality is associated with clientelism and the weak-state equilibrium while a large formal economy is associated with a programmatic, strong state (see how the economic dimensions on the left side of Figure 2.1 correspond to each of the equilibria in the gray ovals). Finally, the chapter concludes by positing how embedded informality constrains three plausible pathways out of the weak-state trap (depicted by the three dashed lines in Figure 2.1).

2.1 DEFINING EMBEDDED INFORMALITY

The term informal sector can conjure up a number of quite different images. It can evoke the ambulatory peddler of wares, living on the edge of poverty. Or it might instead make you think of a slippery importer who bribes customs officials and profits from markups on illicit goods. What we likely don't think about are the more "middle-class" firm owners with brick-and-mortar stores but without any formal fiscal status. This type of informal sector member is conceptually puzzling. The state would likely see little benefit to taxing the peddler, and may be simply unable to tax the evasive importer. But with some basic informational and bureaucratic capacity, the state could more efficiently tax these legible store owners.

And yet, the state sometimes chooses not to. In Senegal, 97 percent of all economic units exist in the informal sector. Here, I use the definition of informal sector employed by the Senegalese state: economic units that fall into the category of entrepreneur or very small enterprise and thus qualify for a simplified tax regime (ANSD 2016). While some of these informal actors indeed look more like the poor peddler, many are also entrepreneurs or family-owned enterprises earning annual revenue of up to about 200,000 USD. During interviews with some such informal firms in Senegal's capital, I provided information about their tax obligations were they to register with the state, and the process for doing so. Almost all firm owners I spoke with were unaware of this regulatory status and the consequent (reasonable) tax obligations for small firms. About half even thought they would pay less under the formal status than they pay informally under the status quo.

This highlights two surprising features of the informal sector in some contexts. First, there are members of the informal sector who are not hiding from the state – and may even have some latent willingness to comply with the state. Second, informal firms still often pay tax to the state, in some form. Informal actors often pay formal taxes to the state such as presumptive tax, business licenses and user fees that do not require formal accounting or registration (Dube and Casale 2016; Anyidoho et al. 2025). This is on top of any social extraction (Lust and Rakner 2018) or informal taxes (Olken and Singhal 2011) they may pay to non-state actors to secure social insurance or communal goods. But as my interviews with informal firms reflect (Chapter 4), even formal taxes are often paid through informal means: Amounts and deadlines are irregular and often negotiated during ad hoc visits by a variety of state agents or intermediaries; and records of payment are not systematically kept nor receipts systematically offered.[2]

This manifestation of the informal sector appears less puzzling once we interrogate the state's competing motivations. In places like Senegal – democratic, weak states – incumbent governments have limited budgets to invest not only in maximizing economic growth but also in maximizing their chances of reelection. In the next section, I show why the electoral linkage mechanism most common in these contexts is clientelistic: Incumbents do better to mobilize voters with promises of small targeted transfers that they can safely deliver rather than with riskier promises of large-scale programmatic policies that take time and more initial investment of resources (they don't yet have) to effectively implement. Here, I describe when and where we are likely to see a particular type of informality: where the informal sector is not necessarily hiding from the state and the state is not necessarily seeking to increase enforcement.

Manifestations of Informality

I follow the ILO definition of the "informal economy": all economic activities by workers and economic units that are – in law or in practice – not covered or insufficiently covered by formal arrangements (International Labour Organization 2015). At an individual level, economic actors in

[2] See also Haavik and Cissé's (2024) interviews with informal firms in Mali whose experiences with taxation reflect similar (often disadvantageous) phenomena including bargaining with local authorities, targeting of marginalized groups and a lack of recourse.

the informal sector will necessarily have a more irregular relationship with the state than actors in the formal sector. This could mean that their economic activities completely elude the state, or it could mean that the state attempts to tax or regulate them in relatively more idiosyncratic ways than they do actors in the formal sector.

But on a collective level, the informal economy manifests differently across contexts. The size and durability of the sector differs dramatically across economies as does the type of social or political strata with which it tends to overlap. These variations in the size and composition of the informal sector have political implications. In this section, I develop a framework to categorize four types of macro-level economic informality in order to distinguish the category of interest in this book: embedded informality. I then describe the contexts in which we should expect this type of informality to arise.

Informality manifests differently in society depending on two key aspects of the state: the *capacity* of the state to enforce and the *motivation* of the state to enforce. In general, the state will be more motivated to enforce formal regulations and formal taxation when the benefits to doing so exceed the costs. Greater capital accumulation among economic actors is a key motivation for states to engage in enforcement and taxation. When capital accumulation is higher, the state will have a greater incentive to regulate and extract – pushing people and firms trying to escape the state into informal status. But when capital accumulation is lower, the state is not as interested in regulating and extracting. And members of the informal sector are not necessarily trying to evade the state; some may even see benefits to formalizing.

I describe four types of informality that manifest across different combinations of these two dimensions – capacity and motivation to enforce – in Table 2.1. First, in contexts where the state has both high levels of capacity and motivation to enforce, we should expect very limited levels of informality. In these contexts of *marginal informality*, we would expect to see the informal sector exist only on the margins of the economy where incomes or profits are so marginal that the cost of enforcement exceeds the benefits. Second, in contexts where the state has the capacity to enforce but relatively low motivation due to low incomes or profits in a substantial portion of the economy, we should see *extractive informality*. In these cases, the state has greater bargaining power relative to the informal sector; it can credibly offer to forbear on enforcement in exchange for something it wants more such as political support. Third, in contexts with the opposite set of dynamics – where the state has the

TABLE 2.1 *Types of informality by state capacity and motivation to enforce*

		Motivation to enforce	
		High	Low
Capacity to enforce	High	Marginal informality	Extractive informality
	Low	Reactive informality	Embedded informality

motivation to enforce but insufficient capacity, we should see *reactive informality*. In these cases, the state finds it lucrative to enforce on certain sectors of the economy but cannot prevent high levels of evasion, resulting in larger-scale informal firms that, here, have the upper hand and escape enforcement without giving the state anything in return. Finally, we observe the type of informality that I alluded to at the beginning of the chapter: when the state has neither the capacity nor the motivation to enforce on much of the economy. Because neither economic actors nor the state are actively attempting to change their informal status, I call this *embedded informality*. This stable status endures over time and becomes embedded in not only the economic relationship between citizens and the state but also in the sociopolitical relationships citizens have with the state and each other.

Multiple types of informality may emerge within a single context, especially as the state may have more or less motivation to enforce across different sectors. There are some generalizations we can make about where we might expect these different types of informality to emerge and why. A World Bank report on how informality manifests differently across regions helps illustrate regional trends (Vorisek et al. 2022). In South Asia and sub-Saharan Africa, pervasive informality has been associated with low human capital and large agricultural sectors. This is consistent with embedded informality in weak states, where there is relatively low motivation to enforce. In Europe and Central Asia, Latin America and the Caribbean, and the Middle East and North Africa, heavy regulatory and tax burdens and weak institutions have contributed to informality.[3] This

[3] Loayza (1996) similarly argues that Latin America is an example of this. The "informal economy arises when excessive taxes and regulations are imposed by governments that lack the capability to enforce compliance."

is consistent with reactive informality where weak institutions place too high regulatory burdens that they cannot enforce.

Examples of extractive informality have most often come from Latin America. Inspired by her work in Brazil, Tendler (2002) describes "the devil's deal" as one in which government officials strike implicit understandings with members of the informal sector where the government forbears on tax collection and the enforcement of other burdensome regulations in exchange for electoral support. Holland (2016) further exposes the ways in which relatively more capable states may exchange forbearance for political support, citing other cases in urban Latin America. She makes a clear distinction between institutions that meet some minimum capacity standard and so *can* enforce but choose not to, and those that fall below that capacity standard and so cannot credibly use forbearance as a distributional politics tool, differentiating between our categories of extractive and embedded informality.

We should expect the largest informal sectors in contexts of greatest embedded informality, where states have neither the capacity nor the motivation to enforce policies to regulate and extract from the formal sector. But even in these weak-state settings with relatively low capital accumulation, the state still exists and interacts with members of the informal sector, even if according to a more informal logic. We should expect to see more frequent (if unregulated) interaction between the state and the informal sector in these settings than in the other manifestations of informality. Because informal sector members are not trying to hide from the state as in the lower left quadrant of Table 2.1 (reactive informality), their economic activities will be more visible to the state and others in society. And because the state is not actively using forbearance to induce vote mobilization as in the upper right quadrant (extractive informality), there are fewer constraints to the state enforcing upon citizens in a more informal way. In other words, neither the citizens nor the state have incentives *not* to interact with each other. And in spite of relatively weak state capacity, there will still be members of the state's political or bureaucratic apparatus that have individual incentives or capabilities to extract from or provide to the informal sector.

A key feature of embedded informality is thus that citizens and states still interact with each other – just in more idiosyncratic and unregulated ways. This is partly because there are fewer disincentives for citizens to evade the state and for the state to avoid citizens – there is nothing pushing against citizen–state interactions. Citizens and states will also interact in contexts of embedded informality because there are mutually beneficial consequences of interaction. This is particularly true in democracies where incumbents are motivated to mobilize political support from among the informal sector. In these contexts, citizens can hope to gain something (if small) from the state, and the state can hope to extract at least political support, if not also some small amount of revenue. This type of informal exchange is different from extractive informality because the state is offering positive goods such as jobs, cash, or club goods in exchange for political support rather than negative goods or forbearance.

Just as there are political and economic benefits to a formal social contract (where economic actors give up some autonomy in exchange for public goods), there can be similar benefits to an informal social contract even outside of electoral clientelism. Representatives of the local and/or central state can hope to extract some revenue through informal taxation, and citizens can hope to extract some benefits from the state through informal claim-making (Kruks-Wisner 2022). In a democracy, the social contract is reinforced by competitive elections. Voters are more likely to comply with state regulation and extraction when they feel represented by their elected government officials. And government officials are held accountable for the distribution of public goods by electoral competition. The same can be said for informal exchange. Voters are more likely to accede to informal extraction when they can hope to exchange votes for particularistic transfers. And states are more likely to distribute particularistic transfers when their competitors can credibly promise to do the same.

2.2 DEFINING THE WEAK-STATE TRAP

I have just made the case that states with embedded informality will engage in some contact and exchange with citizens in the informal sector and that citizens and the state are not always motivated to avoid each other in these cases. Given that the majority of informal sector members are low- to middle-income, they would likely benefit from holding the state accountable for providing some nondiscretionary, programmatic goods. In a competitive electoral system, why then wouldn't a party or politician seeking to mobilize voters distinguish themselves from their competitors by offering a programmatic platform? I answer that question with a simple formal model, the details of which are in the chapter appendix. The model helps explain why voters in a democratic, weak state choose a non-programmatic, often clientelistic, mode of politics. And in doing so, they incentivize incumbent governments to invest in social identity networks and clientelistic machines at the expense of investing in the state – further entrenching the status quo.

While writing down a model requires that we abstract away from key nuances in context, it can also help to shed light on the main actors in a strategic situation and the forces driving their behavior. This clarity can lead to a greater understanding of seemingly intractable or puzzling phenomena as well as help inform where and when the theory can generalize. In short, the model shows that particularistic or non-programmatic party competition is stable (or rational for voters and parties) under certain conditions. Specifically, when the likelihood that the government will have a budget to provide programmatic goods is low, that is, in a weak state, an honest politician will be unable to provide public goods even if he wants to. So voters who are disciplining politicians on the basis of public goods provision will kick him out anyway. The voters thus do better to condition reelection decisions on the basis of the receipt of smaller, private goods. Under a weak state, the politician can better keep his job this way, too. By contrast, when the state's likelihood of having the capacity to provide public goods is high, voters and politicians do better under a programmatic linkage mechanism.

The weak-state equilibrium in the model does not require parties to use clientelistic linkages with voters. It only requires that politicians campaign on the transfer of smaller goods or promises that do not require high state capacity, instead of larger goods or policies that do. The weak-state equilibrium is thus consistent with politicians using charismatic or populist appeals as long as those appeals are similarly credible under a weak state. But because clientelism is the most common non-programmatic linkage mechanism (according to DALP data (Kitschelt 2013)), the book focuses its attention here. The argument that informality constrains programmatic claim-making should hold irrespective of which non-programmatic linkage mechanism is being used. However, the argument that intermediaries will resist transitions to programmatism is weaker in the context of populist or charismatic linkages relative to clientelistic linkages because intermediaries are less valuable for vote mobilization. Chapter 7 explores whether the decline of clientelism (in favor of more populist appeals) can advance a polity's exit from the weak-state trap.

I use the term clientelism in both the theory and the rest of the book to represent the distribution of smaller, particularistic transfers to political supporters. Note that this more flexible definition departs from some that insist on a quid pro quo exchange (Hicken 2011) and imply strict monitoring, which has been found to be rare empirically. Consistent with Hicken and Nathan (2020), this broader definition includes unenforced but *targeted, particularistic distribution* to likely supporters. Such a strategy is often assumed to be wasteful because some voters will get transfers and fail to reciprocate with a vote. However, it can be a highly viable strategy when it is more efficient than alternatives such as programmatic distribution (a strategy that can result in scarce resources being delivered to an even greater number of opposition supporters). Especially when unmonitored, it is easy to see how shared identity, such as ethnicity, can improve the efficiency of clientelism. It can serve as a heuristic to parties for expected vote choice (Nathan 2016*b*) or can work through local leaders who are good at mobilizing coethnics (Koter 2013).

Two Accountability-Capacity Equilibria

Standard models of voter control of politicians consider how voters solve the moral hazard problem when it comes to democratic accountability. Just as individuals have temptations to take risky actions once they have acquired insurance, self-interested incumbents have temptations to act against the public interest once they are elected. If we assume incumbent self-interest is not perfectly aligned with the public interest, then the only thing that keeps them from acting against the public interest is the fear of voters sanctioning them in the next election. These models generate insights into when we should expect incumbents to be more likely to act in the public interest.

I extend these models to consider the related question of *when politicians will be motivated to invest in the state*, or more concretely, when politicians will compete along a programmatic dimension versus a non-programmatic one.[4] Different types of electoral competition have different implications for state capacity. Simply, programmatic competition motivates larger investments in bureaucratic, fiscal, and administrative infrastructure than does non-programmatic competition. A key distinguishing feature of programmatic politics is that policies and programs are either universal or targeted based on some rational-legal

[4] This setup, modeling the choice between programmatic and non-programmatic appeals, is similar to that of Robinson and Verdier (2013), who find that clientelism is more likely when voter monitoring is weak or income inequality is high, and to that of Lizzeri and Persico (2001), who find that clientelism is more likely when politicians face concentrated constituencies or majoritarian incentives.

criteria rather than on an individual's identity or personal connections. Informational and statistical capacity is required to deliver broad-based or formulaic policies and programs such as these. Larger programs and larger bureaucracies are also more expensive and imply a larger fiscal burden than do non-programmatic policies.

Programmatic performance is what models of democratic accountability often have in mind, whether the model has voters selecting their favorite candidate or sanctioning the incumbent based on some performance threshold (Fearon 1999). Specifically, voters prospectively evaluating politicians could compare party platforms with distinct ideologies with respect to redistribution, that is, how much tax is extracted from which citizens and who it is spent on, or they might retrospectively evaluate a candidate on the basis of a valence measure of performance, that is, how much of the budget was spent in the public interest relative to spent with corruption. In either case, it is incentive-compatible for politicians to invest or promise to invest, in state infrastructure that will make them more competitive, either by making their prospective promises more credible or by making their retrospective performance more efficient.

But empirically, not all democratic polities cleave along programmatic lines. In fact, in the weak-state democracies that are the focus of this book, the vast majority of parties are not programmatic. Kitschelt (2000) defines two alternative linkage mechanisms to programmatism: charismatic and clientelistic. The former is "symbolic or personalistic, based on citizens' likes and dislikes of grand gestures and personal styles," while the latter has to do with directly exchanging targeted material benefits for electoral support. According to a cross-national expert survey conducted in 2009 (Kitschelt 2013), parties with charismatic linkages are the rarest.[5]

In the model, I focus on the voter's choice to discipline the politician on the basis of their programmatic performance or on the basis of their non-programmatic performance. For the latter, I focus on the more common manifestation of non-programmatic politics – clientelism. Under clientelistic accountability, rather than observing changes in policy

[5] While parties can choose multiple linkage mechanisms and polities can have parties that vary in their primary linkage mechanism, party systems tend to be structured primarily around clientelistic appeals or programmatic appeals. Indeed, the variance in linkage mechanisms between countries is more than five times greater than the variance within countries (Kitschelt 2013).

or programs, the voter instead observes whether the politician directed goods or cash directly to them or their group in exchange for past political support. Among non-programmatic linkage mechanisms, clientelism is actually a best-case scenario in that voters can still extract goods from politicians, compared to charismatic or personalistic candidates who can inspire support without distributing much of anything except perhaps rhetoric and empty promises.[6]

Chapter 7 helps illustrate that clientelism is not the only non-programmatic linkage mechanism that will fail to incentivize state-building. In it, I ask what happens to prospects for a programmatic constituency as the efficiency of clientelistic mobilization declines in urban Senegal. What we observe is that parties instead turn to populist appeals, which are best classified as a charismatic linkage mechanism. While populist appeals are not typically discretionary like clientelistic appeals, neither are they programmatic. They often make vague promises to promote some group of true citizens at the expense of an outgroup but do not typically advance reforms required to pay for such policies. So while programmatic appeals necessitate broad-based fiscal contracts and clientelistic appeals necessitate narrower exchange, populism requires neither.

Voter welfare under clientelism should be lower, on average, than under programmatism. Compared to discretionary targeting, nondiscretionary programs can benefit from economies of scale and efficiency gains that are incompatible with discretionary targeting. Furthermore, some of the budget for targeted transfers must be spent on investments in the targeting itself – especially on networks needed to provide information about who the politician's electoral supporters are (or aren't). Welfare implications are also highly uneven. Loyal supporters will get more stuff than those who are perceived to be opposition supporters by the incumbent's political machine. And a small set of individuals will do very well under the clientelistic status quo because of their particular value in elections. These are the political intermediaries with informational advantages or persuasive capacity who can deliver blocs of votes to particular candidates. But while it's possible that this small set of beneficiaries prefers a clientelistic linkage mechanism, the average voter generally does better under programmatic politics.

6 Klaus, Paller and Wilfahrt (2023) argue that clientelism offers nonmaterial benefits as well as material ones, including social recognition, respect as autonomous agents, and feelings of inclusion.

So if voters could get a better deal out of using the programmatic accountability mechanism, why don't they always choose to hold politicians accountable for programmatic performance? I argue that the answer lies in weak state capacity. Voters know that providing welfare-enhancing public goods or programs requires some minimum level of state capacity. States must be able to raise revenues to provide those goods and have the bureaucratic capacity to implement them. When voters perceive the state to be too weak to do this, they know that conditioning their vote on programmatic performance will be for naught. Even well-intentioned incumbents will not be able to fulfill programmatic promises under conditions of weak state capacity. Thus, voters in these cases will settle for the second-best accountability mechanism: clientelistic exchange.

The model's main prediction is thus that when expectations of state capacity p (or the likelihood the government has a budget for public goods) are relatively high, we should expect the Public Goods equilibrium to obtain (voters discipline politicians on the basis of public goods); when expectations p are instead low, we should expect the Gifts equilibrium to obtain (voters discipline politicians on the basis of small, private transfers). The model provides the intuition for why. Even an honest, responsible incumbent would get kicked out of office too often under the public goods electoral strategy and low expected state capacity, making it more attractive for them to consume all benefits from office and get kicked out with certainty. In this case, the voter does better by employing the Gifts strategy, which at least ensures her something in every period.[7] This is a similar intuition to that in standard voter control models, where the worse the public's ability to monitor the politician, the worse the policy outcomes for the voter (Fearon 1999; Besley 2006). This is because the politician's behavior is less sensitive to their reelection probability; not only will bad behavior be less likely to be punished, but good behavior will be less likely to be rewarded.

In sum, we should expect to find at least two stable democratic equilibria: a clientelistic one where voters condition reelection decisions on the politician's ability to provide small, targeted transfers, and a programmatic one where voters condition reelection decisions on the politician's ability to provide nondiscretionary goods or programs. What distinguishes these two equilibria is a differential expectation of the

[7] In the case of a charismatic linkage mechanism, we might think of a psychic benefit to voters in the politician's ingroup.

state's capacity to provide public goods. Where the expected capacity of the state is low, the clientelistic equilibrium obtains; where it is high, the programmatic equilibrium obtains. The theory thus illustrates how the existence of clientelistic parties and electoral strategies is stable under an initially weak state.

Accountability-Capacity Equilibria Are Self-Reinforcing

In addition to generating two democratic equilibria defined by their accountability linkage mechanisms and level of state capacity, another implication of the model is that each of these equilibria is self-reinforcing. I argue that clientelistic and programmatic party competition each have very different implications for investments in state capacity. Clientelistic competition incentivizes investments in political machines that make candidates better at supplying targeted transfers, whereas programmatic competition incentivizes investments in the state's capacity to deliver public goods. To the extent that state capacity can facilitate social and economic goals in democracies, clientelistic linkages could thus serve as a drag on certain types of development (relative to programmatic ones) (Keefer 2007; Kitschelt and Wilkinson 2007).

Consider that the function of political parties is two-fold: to solve a collective action problem by pooling resources among like-minded candidates and to solve a social choice problem by more efficiently signaling to voters with limited attention spans the differences between multiple candidates (Aldrich 1995). Both programmatic and clientelistic parties solve the first problem in a similar way: by investing in the organizational infrastructure required to induce cooperation among candidates. Each party type solves the second problem in a different way.

Programmatic parties will mobilize voters by investing in what Kitschelt calls "programmatic unity building" (Kitschelt 2000, p. 848). This consists of identifying broadly appealing packages of policies or programs that they will implement if elected. Because programmatism implies competition on the basis of universalistic policies, redistribution is implemented without regard to an individual's social identity or voting background but rather on the basis of codified or rule-based criteria. And because voters are information misers, successful parties are those that can bundle policies in ways that make sense given some underlying set of values. They must also be appealing to a sufficiently broad coalition or constituency.

Clientelistic parties do not rely on interest aggregation or program formation to distinguish themselves from competitors. Instead, they create bonds of loyalty or reciprocity through direct exchange. The type and value of material resources exchanged for political support will vary by context. In "resource-rich but vote-poor constituencies," politicians dispense valuable favors in the form of contracts, subsidies, etc., in exchange for campaign finance. By contrast, in "vote-rich but resource-poor constituencies" that most resemble the cases in this book, politicians distribute selective material incentives before and after elections in exchange for the vote (Kitschelt 2000). To be successful, both cases require hierarchical political machines that allow for complex and varied local-level monitoring or targeting to be organized within a national party structure. Furthermore, informal exchange incentivizes people to invest in relationships with non-state actors rather than the state because it is those kinship networks and ethnic groups that help them claim benefits from the state such as property rights (Boone 2014, p. 50).

This discussion suggests that parties in more programmatic polities have incentives to invest in interest aggregation, so we should expect more interest-based groups to arise that might be cross-cutting with respect to region or identity. By contrast, parties in more clientelistic polities have incentives to invest in creating or reinforcing boundaries across local groups to make selective transfers more valuable.

This feature of party systems also has implications for investments in state-building: Programmatic linkage mechanisms are more likely to incentivize investments in the state compared to clientelistic linkage mechanisms. Programmatic exchange is more effective when states are sufficiently capable of implementing the promised programs or policies. Otherwise, this linkage mechanism would not be credible. By contrast, in resource-poor, vote-rich settings (like those of interest in this book), the most common type of clientelistic exchange is selective material incentives or rewards in exchange for the vote. Because votes are plentiful and the act of voting is not very costly, these material transfers can be quite small. Instead of requiring investments in state bureaucracy or infrastructure, they necessitate large investments in the machines that make individual transfers more efficient through information gathering (who is susceptible to such exchange) and vote monitoring (who followed through with their vote). These organizational investments are almost exclusively made outside the formal channels of the state.

There is also a strategic component to these incentives to invest. In largely clientelistic contexts, incumbent parties have a comparative advantage when they engage in clientelistic politics but not programmatic politics, because they can use state resources as either clientelistic transfers or investments in sustaining the machine. Fergusson, Larreguy and Riaño (2022) recognize that, in these cases, incumbents will have an electoral *dis*incentive to invest in local bureaucratic capacity because reducing the cost of providing programmatic goods, and thus increasing the opportunity cost to engaging in clientelism, gives opponents a competitive edge. Pardelli and Peveri (2025) confirm that clientelistic parties should fear state investments: They find that enhanced enforcement of labor regulations in Brazil decreases the electoral success of clientelistic parties.

The above discussion posits that democratic competition will have differential implications for incentives to invest in state-building depending on the dominant linkage mechanism between parties and voters. Chapter 6 will provide evidence for this claim. In short, in programmatic polities, there is an electoral benefit to investing in the state's capacity to provide public goods, because voters are rewarding politicians and parties along that dimension. Through electoral pressure, voters induce politicians to provide public goods and enact policies that enhance economic growth. These pressures, in turn, justify investments in state and fiscal capacity; leaders can expect to be rewarded at the ballot box. In this way, places with greater state capacity beget incentives to invest in the state through programmatic demands. But in clientelistic polities, democratic competition instead disincentivizes politicians from investing in the state. Not only are voters not rewarding politicians for their ability to provide public goods, but they are instead rewarding them for their ability to provide private goods. Given budget constraints, such investments are thus substitutive: Investments in private goods or the political machinery that makes their provision most efficient reduce the ability to provide public goods.[8]

The model thus helps reconcile divergent expectations in the literature about the relationship between democracy and state-building. Some studies show how elections can disincentivize politicians from investing in state capacity (Christensen and Garfias 2021; Fergusson, Larreguy and Riaño 2022; Martin 2023), whereas others describe how democracy can incentivize state-building (Olson 1993; Beramendi, Dincecco and Rogers

[8] As one empirical indication of how clientelism conditions state-building, De La O (2024) finds that more clientelistic parties hire more but lower-skilled workers who are better at engaging in labor-intensive distributive policies. More programmatic parties instead hire fewer but higher-skilled workers who are better at designing more sustainable economic development policies.

2019). While voters never like to be taxed, they trade off the costs of taxes for the potential perceived benefits. In order for programmatic parties to provide public goods (feasible only in sufficiently strong states), bureaucratic and fiscal capacity are required to generate sufficient revenue for widespread provision. Voters will thus be more tolerant of costly investments in state and fiscal capacity when they expect and value a return on such investment.

In the book, I refer to the clientelistic, weak-state equilibrium as a "trap" because it is stable as defined by its equilibrium dynamics, *and* because it has these self-enforcing qualities. But the term trap, in addition to connoting a situation that is hard to get out of, also has negative undertones. I defined above why voter welfare is, on average, lower in the weak-state equilibrium relative to the strong-state one, justifying one reason for thinking of the first state of the world as worse than the second. However, our normative interpretation of the weak-state equilibrium depends wholly on the counterfactual to which we are comparing it. Above, I compared voter welfare under the weak-state equilibrium relative to the strong-state equilibrium. However, I also show in the model that it is not strategically rational for voters to hold politicians accountable for providing public goods under a weak state. So, a feasible alternative to the weak-state, clientelistic equilibrium is actually a weak state in which there is little to no accountability. Under this comparison, voters do much better in a clientelistic weak state where they can hold politicians accountable for something than in an uncompetitive weak state where they cannot. This reflects existing arguments and findings that highlight the benefits of clientelist networks in meeting the needs of citizens that the state cannot (Merton 1949; Auyero 2000; Rains and Wibbels 2023). It is therefore not the case that electoral competition is bad for voters in weak states; what is at stake is simply different in weak-state and strong-state democracies.

2.3 ECONOMIC (IN)FORMALITY AND STATE CAPACITY

Having defined embedded informality and then the weak-state trap, I now turn to explaining their relationship to each other. I first discuss how weak states naturally give rise to larger informal sectors. This is perhaps self-evident. What is less obvious is whether and how the arrow points in the other direction: from informality to state weakness. To see this dynamic, we need politics. Specifically, the causal arrow between informality and state weakness (or formality and state strength) is mediated by electoral linkage mechanisms. Embedded informality constrains programmatic electoral mobilization, while an organized formal economic sector is conducive to programmatic claim-making. After discussing the logic for the first causal arrow (the effect of state capacity on economic informality), I will advance the logic for each of these reverse causal processes (the effect of (in)formality on state (in)capacity as mediated by electoral linkage mechanisms), in turn.

State Capacity Affects the Size of the Informal Sector

While state capacity is a multifaceted concept, any definition will include the state's ability to extract taxes from economically productive individuals and firms within its borders. Efficient tax extraction requires informational capacity – knowledge of what is being produced and where, as well as bureaucratic capacity – the ability to mobilize state resources to actually capture part of those economic gains. Both capacities are critical for the state to enforce fiscal policy. All else equal, we should thus expect to see higher levels of economic informality where states have lower enforcement capacity.

Enforcement, however, is not the only mechanism the state relies on for tax collection. In fact, voluntary compliance is generally the primary way the state collects taxes, reserving enforcement for a small proportion of cases (Levi 1989). State capacity is *also* critical for tax collection in the case of voluntary compliance. Economic agents face a trade-off when it comes to deciding whether or not to voluntarily declare their income and pay tax. Increased state capacity can increase the likelihood of voluntary compliance because it increases perceived benefits via the perception that other taxpayers are also paying and the belief that there will be reciprocal benefits. For example, declaring one's income makes one a better candidate for loans to increase future economic productivity (Blackburn, Bose and Capasso 2012). Benefits of formally declaring taxes (for the purposes of improved collateral in credit markets) are less valuable to the taxpayer where the cost of financial intermediation is higher, for example, the banks' overhead expenditures and net interest rate margin are higher. This is true in less advanced economies, where institutions are less established (Demirguc-Kunt, Laeven and Levine 2003).[9] In sum, the benefit of voluntary compliance is increasing with the level of financial development, which itself is related to the state's capacity to regulate

[9] Both costs of financial intermediation mentioned are higher, on average, in lower states of financial development, as exemplified by banks that operate on a relatively small scale, that hold relatively small amounts of capital, and that are subject to relatively tight regulations.

financial markets. Here, we see a direct link between state weakness and informality, defined here as tax evasion.

Informality Affects State Weakness through Non-programmatic Politics

I argue that political competition in democratic polities will be less likely to cleave along programmatic lines in the context of embedded informality. This will generate the key observable implications that I outline in the next section. Political cleavages constitute dimensions that are durable and allow voters to select among distinct parties (Lipset and Rokkan 1967). And, "when parties appeal to voters based on such cleavages, the latter become competitive dimensions" (Kitschelt 2000). While programmatic parties may have positions on a wide array of policies, "the constitutive element of programmatic political linkage is that parties solve their problems of social choice through the development of policy packages that make it possible to map issues onto underlying simple competitive dimensions" (Kitschelt 2000). So when parties offer distinct economic programs or cleave along economic lines, they are considered programmatic.

A key reason why embedded informality constrains the development of programmatic parties, and the resulting electoral competition along programmatic lines, is that it obscures the crystallization of relevant economic cleavages in society around which parties might form. This means that in places with embedded informality, we shouldn't expect to see the same class cleavages, that is, labor versus capital, that we saw emerge in so many developed democracies.

Informality can blur the traditional lines between capital and labor. Many in the informal sector think of themselves as "workers" when they are really business owners (Greven 2017). And then, even among those informal firm owners who identify as such, the often large disparity in the functioning of formal and informal firms yields very different policy preferences. Economically, formal and informal firms may look similar: "the mass of small, often unregistered craftsmen and traders in Third World cities, for whom small numbers of family members, unwaged apprentices, and waged or semi-waged employees simultaneously work, cannot easily be differentiated from much larger, undeniably capitalist enterprises exclusively employing wage labor" (Gerry 1987). But the former do not employ wage labor or sell labor-power and so hold very different preferences vis-à-vis labor regulations compared to the latter group.

When the state consistently enforces regulations and engages in a legible social contract with actors in the formal sector, it is easy to see how such interactions with the state can serve as a coordinating mechanism for both voters and parties. There will be natural economic groups with similar activities that form consistent preferences over how state policies affect them. And parties can compete over votes from these economically differentiated constituent groups by differentiating their own policy platforms.

But when the state inconsistently enforces regulations and engages in more discretionary processes of extraction and distribution, how will citizens form preferences over political parties, and how will parties compete for votes? This more irregular and discretionary form of citizen–state interaction in the economic sphere is conducive to a more discretionary form of linkage in the political sphere: clientelism. One reason for this is the value of intermediaries in both cases.

When states are unwilling or unable to interact in regularized, formal ways with groups of citizens, they still engage in the provision of goods and the extraction of taxes in informal and irregular ways, as discussed earlier. Because of their informational and bureaucratic deficits, weak states often rely on local intermediaries to facilitate these irregular forms of contact. Indeed, informal sector members often work through intermediaries to get access to public services (Krishna 2011; Auerbach 2017) or rely on non-state actors to supply them (Dercon et al. 2006; De Weerdt and Fafchamps 2011). Effective intermediaries will have information about and access to groups of citizens that the state cannot otherwise know about or reach. These non-state actors might be leaders of cultural or economic associations or nodal points in social networks that can help provide insurance in the absence of the state.

In a similar vein, intermediaries or political brokers can make clientelistic electoral mobilization more efficient. Rather than a party solidifying ties with all prospective voters, they can leverage brokers' existing social, economic, or political connections with their own followers and their subsequent information access and monitoring ability at the group level. This intermediated strategy typically manifests as collective clientelism – or the exchange of group-level benefits for coordinated group-level voting. This is good for politicians: They get blocs of votes for single transfers. But it is also good for voters: Group-level benefits often consist of club goods that people value such as wells or schools.

While collective clientelism does not require it in theory, empirically brokers are almost always responsible for helping to coordinate blocs of votes at the group level. In contrast to some older literature on clientelism focusing on individual-level targeting (Kitschelt and Wilkinson 2007), there is growing recognition of the importance of a broker-mediated model of clientelism (Stokes et al. 2013; Larreguy, Montiel Olea and Querubin 2017) in which the relevant unit of analysis is the group of voters being coordinated by brokers (Holland and Palmer-Rubin 2015).[10] The stronger the ties between brokers and voters, the better clientelism works. And because embedded informality gives rise to intermediaries whose existence is legitimated by their utility to both citizens and the state, these intermediaries become natural candidates to serve as effective brokers within a party's political machine.

A second reason that embedded informality is conducive to clientelism is the implicit particularism of each mode of citizen–state interaction. Since the informal sector is, by definition, unregulated, members of the informal sector cannot articulate demands on the state, with respect to their economic activity at least, in the form of formal policy change. Nor can they bargain for public benefits in exchange for formal fiscal revenue if they are not paying formal taxes. Instead, informal actors can offer individual or blocs of votes, and they can demand particularistic benefits to themselves or their group in exchange.[11]

Embedded informality is not the only form of informality that can support clientelistic politics. Indeed, extractive informality is defined as the exchange of forbearance for political support. But that forbearance can either be contingent, and thus targeted to specific individuals or groups of loyal voters, or it can be noncontingent. In the latter case, it can serve as a form of alternative welfare for the poor, forbearing on laws that the poor are relatively more likely to violate (Holland 2016). This illustrates the importance of whether informality is crosscutting with class; if it is, then noncontingent forbearance of this kind is less effective.

Formality Affects State Strength through Programmatic Politics

Whereas informality is conducive to non-programmatic linkage mechanisms such as clientelism, an organized formal economic sector can support programmatic competition. Writing in 1977, Martin Shefter was one of the first to try to explain where programmatic politics came from –

[10] Across seven African countries, Wahman and Boone (2018) find evidence in favor of broker-mediated bloc voting, particularly in low population density rural constituencies "that can be counted on to bloc vote per local leaders' instructions."

[11] Existing studies provide evidence of the correlation between economic informality and clientelistic electoral preferences from India and Brazil (Rains and Wibbels 2023; Pardelli and Peveri 2025).

acknowledging that young democracies often rely on patronage for electoral mobilization in their early stages of development. In answering this puzzle, he coined the term "constituency for bureaucratic autonomy," writing that programmatic politics will arise when such a constituency can beat out the "constituency for patronage" (Shefter 1977). The former type of constituency develops when, for example, external war encourages the state to develop bureaucracies or when a middle class emerges out of technological progress. Prior work has suggested that this transition is most likely under more modernized, industrialized societies because the rise in the incomes and homogeneity of voters makes patronage less efficient (Reid Jr. and Kurth 1992).

Externally mobilized parties, or ones that are not organized by members of the existing regime and thus do not have access to state resources for patronage distribution, are less likely to rely on patronage politics once in power (Shefter 1977). This is more likely to occur when there are sufficiently large and well-resourced economic groups that are independent of the dominant political class. Both insights are reflected in Geddes's (1994) rational choice treatment of the "politician's dilemma" whereby incumbents face incentives to prioritize patronage over merit in campaigning and governing. She similarly suggests that smaller parties that benefit less from patronage are more likely to prefer merit-based policies and that transitions to more merit-based politics are more likely to occur when there is widespread pressure from constituents. The US is one example of how organized economic interests can evolve into constituencies for programmatism.

The machine politics and patronage that reigned in most American cities in the late 19th and early 20th centuries eventually gave way to a more programmatic form of politics. While there were many forces at work behind this evolution, all seem to come down to organized economic pressures. One account of how political machines in the US died is that they failed to adapt to changing circumstances in their urban core, inciting new coalitions of excluded immigrant groups and excluded business groups to rally around the reform opposition due to their exclusion (Boulay and DiGaetano 1985). Another describes how corporations and the national business organizations that represented them began to push parties to adopt programmatic reforms, including investments in state capacity. As private business developed new forms of corporate management and capitalist organization, "they came to see clientelism and patronage as inimical to economic growth" (Kuo 2018, p. 80). Yet a third account describes how the rise of organized labor and the resulting, sometimes violent, struggles between capital and labor also incentivized the state to expand institutional capacities to maintain order in the private economy (Skowronek et al. 1982), thus raising the value of programmatic competition. And finally, regional and sectoral conflict between agrarian and industrial states contributed to a political compromise that expanded the country's fiscal capacity. Early pressure to implement an income tax came largely from agrarian states that would benefit disproportionately more and pay disproportionately less than the Northeastern states, but a later compromise guaranteed that Northern states would be the biggest beneficiaries of public expenditures in the navy, securing US trade, benefiting Northern shipyards, and providing pensions for union soldiers (Baack and Ray 1985).

In each of these accounts, some constituency of economic actors – independent corporations, sectoral unions, business lobbies, and regional economic interests – came to realize their material gain from the implementation of more programmatic policies. This might be because business productivity improves with investment in public goods like infrastructure and banking. Or this could be because businesses are better able to make long-term investments when state regulation is decided and implemented on the basis of rational policy rather than personalistic ties. Implicit in these mechanisms is the necessity of formal status. For businesses to demand public goods of the state, they need to finance those goods with contributions to fiscal revenue. And for businesses to eschew discretion in favor of stable, more predictable policy that universally applies to them, they need to make themselves legible to the state.

2.4 EMBEDDED INFORMALITY BLOCKS PATHWAYS OUT OF THE WEAK-STATE TRAP

So far, I have made the case that embedded informality is consistent with the non-programmatic, weak-state equilibrium, while a large, organized formal economic sector is consistent with the programmatic, strong-state equilibrium. In this last section, I outline observable implications of how embedded informality constrains transitions from the former to the latter equilibrium. To transition from one state to the other, you might imagine developments in each of the three parameters in the equilibrium shifting over time. Economic growth, for instance, could lead the formal sector to overtake the informal sector in terms of the sheer number of agents in each. Or some opposition party willing to break ties with the state and its incumbent regime could capture key constituencies interested in moving away from discretionary politics and toward greater public goods provision. Or we might imagine a positive shock to state strength big enough that it creates incentives for voters and politicians to demand and campaign on programmatic policy. I argue that each of these potential pathways out of the clientelistic, weak-state trap is inhibited by embedded informality.

Pathway 1: Embedded Informality Is Persistent

Recall that a key feature of embedded informality is that members of the informal sector still have not infrequent contact with the state. Because these citizen–state relationships are informal and unregulated, there is ample room for discretion by politicians and bureaucrats. These dynamics of particularism privilege the value of personal relationships and social identity over other types of investments. Drawing on his experiences in Nigeria, Ekeh (1975) argues for two publics: a primordial public that is identified with "primordial groupings, sentiments, and activities" but at the same time impinges on public interest; and a civic public that is based on civil structures such as the military, civil service, or police. The investments people make to succeed in each of these spheres are highly distinct.

Perhaps the clearest example of this is with respect to language and education. In the case of Senegal, a substantial proportion of the informal sector is educated in Koranic schools where Arabic is the language of instruction. By contrast, no respondents with formal-sector jobs in my survey data reported being educated in Koranic schools. The networks of religious brotherhoods in which these schools are often embedded provide access to credit and other forms of social and economic security that can improve one's economic prospects. By contrast, education in francophone public schools can be an advantage for formal economic actors who have to navigate the state bureaucracy in French, and because things like formal accounting or even numeracy are exclusively taught there. This example illustrates one reason embedded informality is so persistent. Because investments in education are long term, decisions made early in one's life are sticky, and it is difficult to change course later. There are also high levels of intergenerational transmission of education decisions, such that members of the informal sector will be far more likely to educate their children in the same way they were educated.

Another reason embedded informality is so durable is that it contributes to and is reinforced by a dualistic political system. Chatterjee's (2004) "civil society" groups that make claims on the state as fully enfranchised, rights-bearing citizens are more likely to have formal, legible economic relationships with the state. By contrast, members of his "political society" who "transgress the strict lines of legality in struggling to live and work" and are targets of electoral mobilization are more likely to have informal economic relationships with the state.

Pathway 2: Embedded Informality Constrains the Programmatic Transition

The second potential pathway out of the weak-state trap is the political mobilization of a sufficiently large programmatic constituency that will consistently condition their voting decisions on the basis of programmatic performance. I argue that embedded informality reduces the likelihood of programmatic claim-making. It affects first-order beliefs (the value of government policy to one's economic prospects) and second-order beliefs (whether other people in your sector value government policy).

To gain analytical traction, I focus on one key dimension of informality – the irregularity of the fiscal relationship between the citizen and the state. Not only is the extractive role of the state one of its primary functions, but also the formality of tax payment occurs on a spectrum, allowing for more theoretical and empirical nuance than simply considering the formal and informal sectors as dichotomous groups with internal homogeneity. By definition, informal taxation is difficult to systematically characterize. It can occur entirely outside state regulations. Or, as in the case of Senegal, the state can have legal avenues through which to tax the informal sector. But due to the undocumented nature of these taxpayers and their business activity, implementation of rules can be quite subjective, and the rules themselves can constitute a real gray area.[12]

For an informal sector businessperson, her own experience of irregular tax collection affects her first-order beliefs about tax compliance. She is more likely to expect others in the informal sector escape taxation altogether or only pay irregularly like her. The perception of lower levels of tax compliance has direct implications for beliefs about the size of

[12] Author interview with the Direction Générale des Impôts et des Domaines, May 10, 2017.

the public budget and, subsequently, voter demands. A smaller government budget is less likely to be able to fund public programs, dampening demand for public goods. The subjective or negotiated nature of informal taxation may also lead taxpayers to infer that revenues earned in this irregular way will also be spent irregularly. For instance, if taxes are extracted through negotiation and receipts are undocumented, then taxpayers may be more likely to infer that spending will also be non-transparent and subjective – characteristics associated with discretion.

We now turn to second-order beliefs. An individual's own irregular interactions with the state can generate uncertainty about how the state is interacting with other potential taxpayers. A taxpayer interacting through formal channels has a precise idea of the experience of other formal taxpayers and will be more likely to assume that formal regulations are systematically applied to others in their sector. Because she infers that the state is similarly extracting from other formal taxpayers, those citizens will be better able to coordinate reciprocal demands on the state. By contrast, informal taxpayers will form imprecise beliefs about the more idiosyncratic costs and benefits other citizens are facing in their informal exchanges with the state. In turn, beliefs about other citizens' preferences and demands will also be more uncertain. Irregular state interactions among informal taxpayers will thus impede the creation of common knowledge about the way in which other citizens like them interface with the state.[13] Common knowledge is argued to be one of the key enablers of coordination (Chwe 2001; Adida et al. 2020) when there are multiple possible outcomes that people are deciding among, and everyone does better when they act together. This can be applied to an electoral context where groups are choosing between multiple candidates, and it behooves an interest group to coordinate support behind a single candidate so that the candidate both wins and feels obligated to be responsive to that group once in office. If members of the informal sector are less likely to see themselves as part of a constituency with shared preferences vis-à-vis state policy, they will have a harder time coordinating their vote on a single candidate and extracting shared benefits for their group from said candidate.

I lastly argue that demands from the informal sector are less likely to be programmatic in nature. Because informal, often intermediated,

[13] Common knowledge is knowledge that not only you know, but you know that everyone else knows it and everyone knows that you know that everyone knows it, and so on.

relationships to the state are necessarily personal, the types of claims made by intermediaries and their constituents are more likely to be particularistic (personal) than programmatic (impersonal). Informality can foster coordination around particularistic claims while at the same time decreasing coordination capacity around programmatic ones. Workers in formal enterprises might, for example, coordinate to demand the state enforce better working conditions in their sector. Informal vendors might instead coordinate within a market to demand goods or forbearance be targeted to their specific market. Or seeing no shared economic interests, informal firm owners may prefer to coordinate with members of a shared religious or ethnic group to appeal to the state for targeted goods. Referring to those working in the informal sector, Gerry (1987, p. 118) writes that we are not "able to form any clearer picture of the economic and political position of the very heterogeneous and essentially propertyless labor working for these small producers."

This discussion yields predictions about the mechanisms through which economic informality, and the resulting irregular fiscal relationship with the state, undermines programmatic claim-making. I will test these empirically in Chapter 4:

Hypothesis 1 *Informality decreases perceived levels of income tax compliance.*

Hypothesis 2 *Informality lowers expectations of government capacity and performance.*

Hypothesis 3 *Informal taxpayers are less likely to perceive themselves as a constituency with shared preferences and coordinate demands.*

Hypothesis 4 *Informality decreases the likelihood that citizens will prefer programmatic policies.*

Macrolevel Considerations

Even if informality always shapes the political behavior of the marginal economic agent in that sector, it can have different implications for the political system as a whole based on how informality manifests in each context. If informality exists only on the margins of society, then its political implications may be relatively inconsequential for the body politic; but if the majority of citizens have an informal relationship with the state, as is the case in most low-income states, it will have meaningful consequences for mass politics. Political implications will also be affected by whether the informal sector is crosscutting with other features of the electorate. If the informal sector spans different income levels, then class-based political competition that often underlies programmatic party formation is more difficult. Finally, the political implications of a person's experience in the informal sector will be muted if she engages in both formal and informal economic activities – either at the same time or in the course of her productive life – or if members of her family are engaged in the formal sector (diversifying sectors can be a smart economic strategy) (Baker and Velasco-Guachalla 2018). But where barriers to entry to the formal sector are higher due to, for example, social status, educational background, or even language fluency, it is less likely that an individual will engage in both formal and informal economic activities either simultaneously or over the course of her life.

Pathway 3: Intermediaries Resist State Strengthening

A third and final pathway out of the weak-state trap is through an exogenous process of state strengthening, that is, if state capacity improves in spite of weak demand for public goods provision or programmatic parties. If state capacity were raised sufficiently, it could increase expectations of constituents such that they begin to find programmatic promises by candidates more credible and begin voting along a programmatic dimension. This might happen if states engage in a systematic revenue-raising campaign to meet some new revenue imperative (like fighting a war) or as a result of large external investments from donors or international agencies. This pathway out of the trap is thwarted when there are sufficiently strong local actors who have an incentive to resist state strengthening. Here, I argue that embedded informality generates actors with such preferences to remain in a weak state: The intermediaries previously described to facilitate discretionary economic and political exchange relationships between citizens and the state.

In the two equilibria described in Section 2.2, voters are better off in the Public Goods equilibrium than in the Gifts equilibrium. However, we can see why economic intermediaries in the informal sector might actually do better under the Gifts equilibrium. In a resource-poor, vote-rich context, we would expect most voters to get very small amounts of monetary or in-kind transfers in exchange for their votes. But if there are existing intermediaries who can make this exchange much more efficient by, for example, identifying likely supporters or monitoring votes, politicians will compensate intermediaries more than they do the average voter.

These intermediaries are often able to seek additional rents owing to their discretionary power in the distribution of political favors or campaign gifts. For example, in my work on the distribution of humanitarian aid in Mali, countless reports described how recipients of aid returned an implicit, informal tax to the village chief or local mayor, some portion of the cash or food aid distributed to them.

A move from a mostly clientelistic to a mostly programmatic form of political linkage would obviate the need for political intermediation and cut off this stream of relatively high particularistic transfers. Relatedly, literature on state formation has described how increases in the capacity of states to engage in direct exchange with citizens obviated the need for intermediaries with relatively greater local authority than the central state to facilitate that exchange (Mann 1984; Levi 1989). Even more directly, Tilly (2005) describes how states with expanded authority directly target what he terms "trust networks" that they see as competing with the state in an attempt to either eliminate or co-opt them.

Unlike average voters who would trade access to gifts for access to public goods, these unequally well-compensated beneficiaries under the Gifts equilibrium have no equivalent recompense under the Public Goods equilibrium, at least in the short run. As in Tullock's (1975) theory of transitional gains among groups that are favored by particular economic policies, these beneficiaries would suffer a short-term transitional loss where the discretionary access to higher private transfers under the clientelistic machine is eliminated – even if the Public Goods equilibrium promises greater efficiencies in the longer run.[14] The specter of such transitional losses generates a powerful constituency that can lobby the incumbent to maintain the status quo or resist efforts to move away from it.

While economic and political intermediaries would not constitute the electoral majority or even reflect the preferences of the median voter, they have outsized power in a democracy. Given their important role in the political machine, they likely have access to the party's top leadership and can lobby more effectively. And their role in the distribution of informal transfers may put them in a position to participate in more formal activities of the state. In that case, they may be able to personally undermine the implementation of state policies that would accompany a programmatic

[14] This application to political privilege departs from Tullock's (1975) application to economic privilege in that positions of status and brokerage confer more permanent rather than transitional gains, as they are not necessarily capitalized into assets that are required to continue receiving benefits.

transition. The resulting expectation is that clientelistic intermediaries may resist programmatic reforms even when the underlying parameters are conducive to such a transition.

2.5 LIMITS OF THE ARGUMENT

This chapter has argued that the persistence of state weakness in many low-income democracies is rooted in "embedded informality." When a large share of citizens work in the informal sector and have irregular relationships with the state, programmatic politics is unlikely to emerge because distributive cleavages are obscured, beliefs about state weakness undermine collective demands for public goods, and intermediaries dominate access to both markets and the state. In turn, non-programmatic politics (often clientelism) reinforces the weak-state trap by reducing incentives to invest in fiscal and administrative capacity. I outlined three pathways through which embedded informality sustains this equilibrium: its persistence across generations, its dampening of transitions to programmatic politics, and the resistance of intermediaries who lose from state strengthening. Before concluding, I address some of the limitations of the argument.

First, while the theory focuses on the three aforementioned mechanisms through which embedded informality can keep the state weak, there are other ways in which informality might reinforce state weakness that are not the focus of the book. For example, the informal sector may be organized around a programmatic preference for lower taxation and less redistribution, which can itself undermine state capacity through lower revenues and lower demand for public goods. We will see an example of this in Chapter 4.1, where vendors in Senegal's largest informal market organized protests against tax hikes in the 1990s. But this organized constituency fell apart soon after, as it became clear that the group's demands were more representative of the few large informal traders and less of the masses of smaller traders they mobilized.

Second, even though I argue that informality can reinforce clientelism in such a way that prevents a transition to programmatic politics, this does not imply that formality and clientelism cannot coexist. Indeed, most industrialized democracies began as largely clientelistic or patronage-based systems, in spite of having large formal sectors. There, the transition away from patronage politics did not involve a push to formalize economic relationships with the state but rather is argued to have worked through mechanisms less relevant in our empirical contexts of interest, for example, an expansion of the franchise (Lizzeri and Persico 2001), shifts in elite competition (Ansell and Samuels 2014; Beramendi, Dincecco and Rogers 2019), and increasing industrialization or modernization (Skowronek et al. 1982; Kitschelt and Wilkinson 2007). There are also contemporary cases where clientelism and high levels of formality coexist, such as those in Eastern Europe. In these cases, large state programs like workfare are used to coerce political support from voters in need of job security (Mares and Young 2019) and do not rely on intermediaries but rather substantial state capacity. This example helps illustrate the bounds of the argument: In initially weak states, I argue that informality constrains the transition from clientelistic party politics to programmatic politics that induce leaders to invest in the state. In already capacious states, we should not expect clientelism to manifest in the same way.

Third, scholars writing about more middle-income, stronger states in Latin America and South Asia have made the argument that poor and informal workers prefer non-programmatic linkages with the state because they expect they will be excluded from programmatic provision. They either prefer targeted forbearance because they expect the welfare state to pass them over (Holland 2018) or they prefer clientelistic over programmatic candidates as a means of hedging risk in a context where they expect formal insurance will not cover them (Rains and Wibbels 2023). These explanations implicitly assume that there are politicians and parties responsive to both programmatic and clientelistic preferences, whereas my argument and cases concern polities where non-programmatic parties dominate. In more mixed polities, there are still some constituencies extracting accountability for programmatic outlays, and we should expect some incentive to invest in the state to make those programs or policies more successful. My argument shows that when the state is weak enough – as it is in much of sub-Saharan Africa – it may be rational for most voters (including some in the formal sector) to engage in non-programmatic linkages with parties and politicians, making it even harder to escape from the weak-state trap.

Appendix

2.A MODELING ACCOUNTABILITY UNDER UNCERTAIN STATE CAPACITY

In moral hazard models of electoral control (Barro 1973; Ferejohn 1986; Fearon 1999; Besley 2006), voters discipline politicians by conditioning electoral decisions on their performance in the previous term. As in standard principal–agent models, politicians will perform better when there are smaller information asymmetries between voters (principals) and politicians (agents) about incumbent performance in office. In these models, state capacity to carry out policies and fiscal capacity to finance them are assumed. To better describe true variation in such capacities, I extend the standard electoral control model to accommodate contexts in which the capacity to raise fiscal revenue and implement public works projects may not be available in every term. When it is not, uncertainty among voters about capacity becomes another information asymmetry that has strategic consequences. I formalize this argument in a simple model below.

To reflect the context of many new democracies, there is a nonzero probability that the government will not have the capacity to provide public goods in that term – either because fiscal capacity to raise funds and/or state capacity to spend them is too low. In each term, the government knows for sure whether such capacity exists, but voters only have a probabilistic expectation of whether it exists. In other words, voters have rational beliefs about the expected value of government capacity, but are uncertain about whether the government has such capacity at its disposal in a given period. (Politicians can only provide public goods if the capacity is currently available.) Politicians can also provide smaller, targeted transfers for which government capacity is not necessary.

Another key difference between this model's setup and standard electoral control models is that the representative voter has a choice to either condition reelection of the incumbent on the receipt of particularistic gifts or on gifts *and* the provision of public goods. This choice is motivated by the real variation in linkage strategies employed by parties from mainly particularistic to mainly programmatic, overcoming the problematic "simplifying assumption that above all, programmatic linkages matter for democratic accountability and responsiveness" (Kitschelt 2000, p. 846).

Setting Up the model[15]

The intuitions of my argument are formalized in an electoral model that takes into account voter uncertainty about the state's capacity to provide public goods, which is represented here as whether there is a budget for public goods. This can either represent the state's fiscal capacity to collect sufficient taxes to provide public goods or sufficient bureaucratic capacity to actually implement the provision of such goods.

Consider a polity that either has a representative voter or can be assumed to all vote as one. The polity votes whether to keep or drop the incumbent politician in successive elections at times $t = 1, 2, \ldots$. The politician gets $w < 1$ every period he is in office, which includes both a wage and other informal benefits to office. With probability $p \in (0, 1)$, the politician has an available budget of size 1 (relative to w) that would provide a universal public good in the polity, such as a health insurance scheme or better wages and working conditions for teachers.

There is asymmetric information about the budget for public goods: The politician knows if the funds are available, while the voters do not. This is justified in contexts where voters know there is a budget that can fund public goods, but they may not know if there is enough in any given period to support such a nontargeted public good project or policy.

The sequence of the game is as follows. In each period t, the politician observes whether funds are available (recall: Funds of size 1 are available with probability p). He then chooses whether to build the public goods project and how much to dispense in campaign gifts, $k \leq w$. After observing the amount of gifts dispensed, k, and whether a project is built, the voter chooses to keep or drop the incumbent.

[15] I thank James Fearon for his help formalizing the model.

The incumbent's period payoff is $w - k + 1$ if funds are available, but he does not build a project and $w - k$ otherwise. Future payoffs are discounted by $\delta \in (0, 1)$ each period, assuming for simplicity that a politician receives zero each subsequent period after getting kicked out of office.

The voters' period payoff is $g + k$ (shared equally among voters in the polity) if a project is built, and k otherwise. $g > 1$ is the voters' value of the public good, reflecting its positive externalities and assuming the voters prefer the project to having the money to spend on other things.

Equilibria

Consider Markov equilibria in which voters use the same rule in each period and can condition reelection on observed gifts, public goods, or both. This gives the voter essentially two feasible "electoral control strategies": the *Gifts* strategy, in which the voter conditions her vote only on the receipt of campaign gifts, and the *Public Goods* strategy, in which the voter conditions her vote on both gifts and the public good, voting against the incumbent if either the public good or sufficient gifts are not provided.

Both strategies assume retrospective voting using a cut point or threshold. Since the voter observes k_t in period t, suppose the voter conditions reelection on whether $k_t \geq \overline{k}$, where $\overline{k} > 0$ is the cut point. (For simplicity, assume the incumbent is liquidity constrained and so cannot provide more than w_t in gifts in each campaign.)

In the Gifts scenario, the voter's strategy is

$$a_v^G(\overline{k}) = \begin{cases} \text{reelect} & \text{if} \quad k_t \geq \overline{k} \\ \text{sanction} & \text{if} \quad k_t < \overline{k} \end{cases}.$$

Let V_I^G be the equilibrium expected payoff for a politician who has a probability p of having the funds to build a public goods project, who decides to provide gifts k but not to provide public goods, and who acts optimally in each period.

$$V_I^G = (1 - p)(w - k_t + \delta V_I^G) + p(w - k_t + 1 + \delta V_I^G).$$

At the cut point $\overline{k}$,

$$V_I^G = \frac{w - \overline{k} + p}{1 - \delta}.$$

For certain values of the parameters, the incumbent will prefer to shirk and get kicked out of office. The incumbent will only provide $\overline{k}$ in gifts if what he can get from holding office in the future is greater than what he can get by shirking. In other words, the incumbent will have an incentive to provide voters with gifts rather than keep $\overline{k}$ for himself if

$$IC^G\colon \delta V_I^G \geq \overline{k}.$$

Substituting for V_I^G and solving for $\overline{k}$,

$$\overline{k} = \delta(w + p),$$

and because it is not feasible for the politician to provide more than w by the illiquidity assumption,

$$\overline{k} = \min(w,\ \delta(w + p)).$$

So, the maximum the voter can get each period in this Gifts equilibrium is the smaller of w and $\delta(w + p)$. The expected equilibrium payoff for the voter is then

$$V_v^G = \min(w,\ \delta(w + p)).$$

Note that while some accountability is possible here in the form of private transfers, no public goods are provided even when they are available – the voter ignores the incumbent's record on public goods and votes only according to whether he provides sufficient campaign gifts.

Alternatively, the voter can employ the Public Goods strategy, voting against the incumbent if he fails to distribute $k_t \geq \overline{k}$ in gifts *or* if he fails to deliver a public good. In this scenario, the voter's strategy is

$$a_v^{PG}(\overline{k}) = \begin{cases} \text{reelect if } k_t \geq \overline{k} \text{ and } g > 0 \\ \text{sanction otherwise} \end{cases}.$$

In this incentive scheme, the incumbent loses office with probability $1 - p$ in each period, even if he is complying, making it harder to motivate him to provide public goods. This is the cost of the moral hazard problem arising from the voter's uncertainty about the size of the public budget.

Let V_I^{PG} be the equilibrium continuation value for a politician who has a probability p of having the funds to build a public goods project, who decides to provide a public good g and gifts k, and who acts optimally in each period.

$$V_I^{PG} = (1 - p)w + p(w - k_t + \delta V_I^{PG}).$$

At the cut point $\overline{k}$,

$$V_I^{PG} = \frac{w - p\overline{k}}{1 - \delta p}.$$

Incentive compatibility requires that the incumbent's payoff from providing the gifts and project in a period when the project is available is at least as great as what he could get by providing zero gifts, consuming the project money, and losing office. Thus,

$$IC^{PG}: w - k_t + \delta V_I^{PG} \geq w + 1,$$

substituting for k_t and solving for $\overline{k}$ at the point of inequality,

$$\overline{k} = \min(w,\ \delta(w + p) - 1).$$

In this Public Goods equilibrium, it is impossible for the voter to set a nonzero cut point $\overline{k}$ when $\delta(w+p) - 1 \leq 0$. In such a case, the voter cannot extract any campaign gifts from the politician, and because the incentive compatibility constraint is not met, the politician prefers to shirk on the provision of public goods as well. When $\delta(w + p) - 1 > 0$, however, the expected equilibrium payoff for the voter is

$$V_v^{PG} = \delta(w + p) - 1 + pg.$$

Comparative Statics

In the Public Goods equilibrium, the politician prefers to shirk when $\delta(w+p) \leq 1$, or $p \leq \frac{1}{\delta} - w$. This is more likely the lower is p, or the belief that the budget is sufficient to fund a public good. The problem here is that the public good is thought to be rare enough that if the voter were to condition on it, the politician would almost always do better to shirk or not provide either gifts or public goods and get kicked out of office. In this case, the voter does better employing the Gifts electoral strategy, which at least ensures them gifts in every period.

In the Gifts incentive scheme, politicians have the ability to consume any available funds for public goods, unlike their counterparts in the Public Goods scheme, who have incentives to always provide such goods when the capacity is available. This ability to consume public funds is implicitly used to give politicians a stronger incentive to provide gifts to voters. Intuitively, the equilibrium level of gifts is higher under the Gifts electoral strategy than the Public Goods strategy. The theory thus provides a new rationale for an empirical regularity that more gifts are provided to voters under clientelistic politics than under programmatic politics.

Figure 2A.1 shows the equilibrium outcomes for different values of p and $\overline{k}$. At low values of p and middling values of $\overline{k}$, the voter is better off employing the Gifts incentive scheme. At higher values of p and lower values of $\overline{k}$, the voter is better off employing the Public Goods strategy.

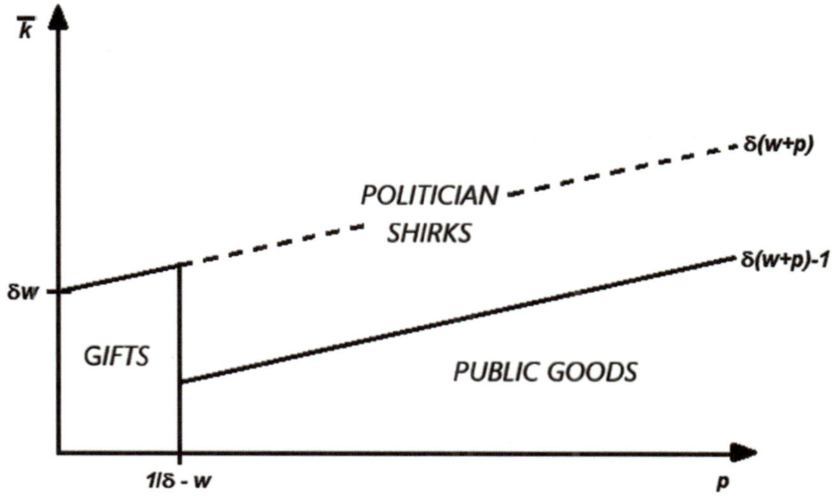

FIGURE 2A.1 Equilibrium outcomes for different values of p and $\overline{k}$.

Even though fewer gifts are distributed under this scheme, the voter is better off in expectation because of the better probability of getting the higher-valued public good. At high values of $\overline{k}$, the politician will always shirk.

When it is possible for the voter to discipline the politician to provide public goods, that is, when $p > \frac{1}{\delta} - w$, the voter's relative value of being in the Gifts or Public Goods incentive scheme now depends on g, or their value for public goods. When $p > \frac{1}{\delta} - w$ and $pg > 1$, the voter's expected equilibrium payoff is higher in the Public Goods incentive scheme. But when $\frac{1}{g} > p > \frac{1}{\delta} - w$, the voter's expected equilibrium payoff is higher in the Gifts incentive scheme. This indicates that there may be some low values of g at which the voter would do better to condition on gifts even when they *could* incentivize the politician to deliver public goods. This leads to the intuitive insight that the Public Goods equilibrium is more likely when voters value public goods more.

A less obvious intuition yielded by the model is that if a representative voter's expectation of state capacity, p, is sufficiently low, then she will employ the Gifts electoral control strategy in which she conditions only on gifts; she cannot then induce the politician to provide any public goods with the threat of electoral sanction. The problem here is that the capacity to provide public goods is believed to be sufficiently unlikely that if the voter were to condition on the provision of these goods, the politician would almost always do better to shirk – to provide neither public nor private goods – and get kicked out of office.

3

The Origins and Persistence of Embedded Informality

Considering the political implications of informality becomes especially important when the majority of citizens operate in this sector. In Figure 3.1, we see that this is the case in much of the Global South – in Africa, South and Southeast Asia, Central America, and northern South America. This may not be surprising as these contexts are also among the poorest, and a large informal sector is associated with lower economic productivity (La Porta and Shleifer 2014).

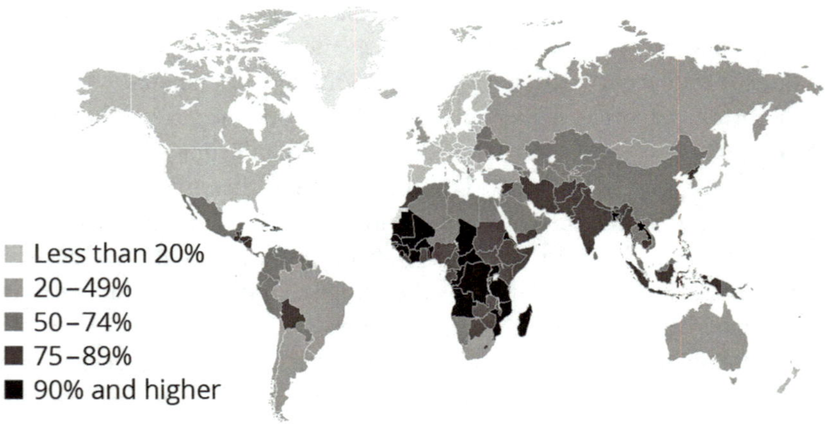

FIGURE 3.1 Share of informal employment in total employment, by country. *Note*: Based on International Labour Organization's national household survey micro datasets from 147 countries (2022 or latest available). Values for countries with missing data are estimated.[1]

[1] Produced by Statista at www.statista.com/chart/30349/map-of-informal-employment/.

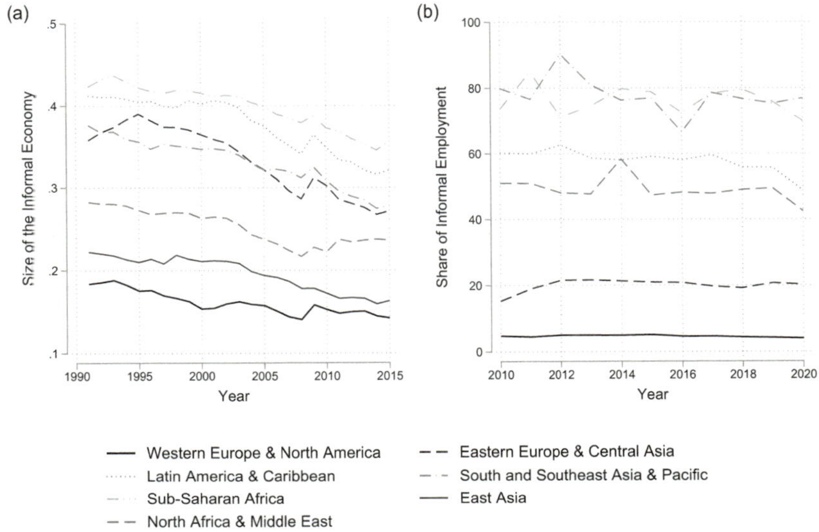

FIGURE 3.2 Informality over time.

Note: Panel (a) measures informality using Medina and Schneider's (2018) indicator of the size of the informal economy as a percent of GDP. Panel (b) measures informality using ILO's indicator of the rate of informal employment in total employment. Both figures take the mean of the available data for each region in each year for which the relevant indicator is widely measured.

Given the strong correlation between GDP and the size of the informal sector (both in terms of employment and the proportion of the economy), it would be easy to conclude that "as an economy develops, informality shrinks" (La Porta and Shleifer 2014, p. 119). But the size of the informal economy has remained large and persistent in much of the developing world. Figure 3.2(a) shows a slight global downward trend in the size of the informal economy over a recent 25-year period for which we have data. But we also see that the differences across regions have remained intact rather than converging.[2]

If we instead measure informality as the share of employment in the informal sector rather than the share of the economy (Figure 3.2(b)), the recent downward trend is even less apparent and the regional divergence more stark. This is not simply a function of having only more recent data for the rate of informal employment. While the ILO has only been consis-

[2] We only see Eastern Europe switch ranks briefly with South and Southeast Asia in the period directly following the collapse of the Soviet Union.

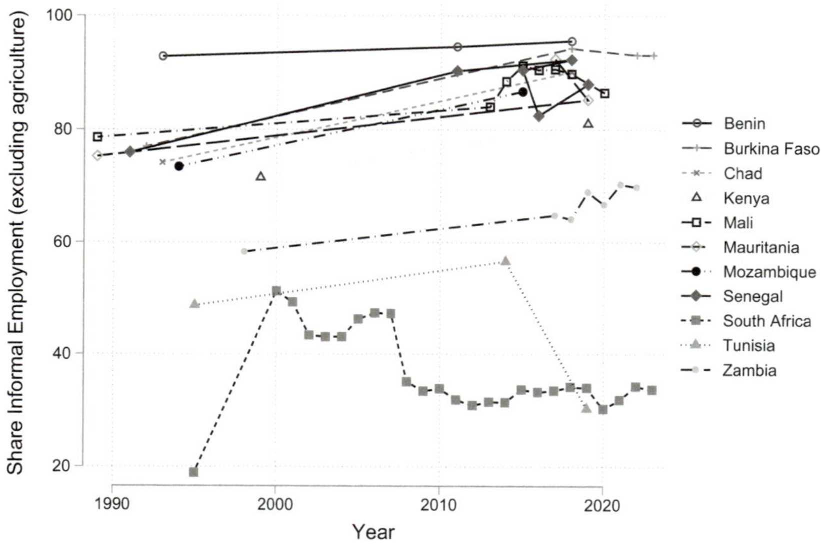

FIGURE 3.3 Change in informal employment over time in 11 African countries. *Source:* Data prior to 2000 are from Charmes (2000); remaining data are from the ILO.

tently reporting on this measure of informality since about 2010, Charmes (2000) collected data on 11 African countries going back to 1989. As we can see from Figure 3.3, in every case but the two middle-income countries of South Africa and Tunisia, the share of informal employment has not only been stagnant but has also been *increasing* over time.

I argued in the last chapter that informality can take on several forms depending on the state's capacity and motivation to enforce. While the stylized fact that informality decreases with economic development may be true for some categories of informality (La Porta and Shleifer 2014), it appears not to hold in many of these sub-Saharan African countries, where informality persists and even strengthens in spite of relatively stable economic growth. In this chapter, I investigate the origins of embedded informality in the Global South to help us better understand its persistence today.

3.1 INFORMALITY IN THE GLOBAL SOUTH

Even the definition of informality changed in response to its unique manifestation in the Global South. The origin of the ILO's present definition is attributed to Keith Hart (1973), who, in doing research in postindependence Ghana, noticed a prevalent type of economic activity that took place outside the reach of state regulations and thus posed a problem to many economic models.[3] The ILO first operationalized the term "informality" in its 1972 employment report on Kenya, broadening Hart's term to capture the entire urban working poor and "economic activities which largely escape recognition, enumeration, regulation and protection by the government" (Leys 1973). The motivation for defining the term thusly was to highlight the need for a new approach to development policy beyond conventional industrialization strategies that recognized "the growing problems of rural–urban migration, underemployment, and inequality" (Gerry 1987, p. 110).

Migration, underemployment, and inequality are not themselves new or specific to the Global South. What is new about the ILO's definition of informality is the reference to "locally produced inputs" (Leys 1973) and the "reliance on indigenous resources" (Peattie 1975). This recognition of indigenous capital as a key feature separating the informal from the formal sector is one consequence of colonialism and globalization. As Gerry (1987, p. 111) notes, these indigenous entrepreneurs "previously had been restricted to the poorest end of a limited market by a history of state and foreign capital collusion and monopoly."

Indeed, historical phenomena have produced different patterns of informality in the Global South relative to the Global North. Early industrializers in Europe and North America were initially able to absorb more labor than today's more capital-intensive form of industry. The large swaths of the population engaged in regular and regulated employment helped generate collective action for labor rights and the rise of the welfare state (Lipset 1959; Huber and Stephens 2001). The resultant social contract provided incentives for labor, capital, and the state to invest in the formal economy.

When some labor became redundant in the Global North in the nineteenth century, one escape valve was settlement in colonies in the Americas. For excess labor in the Global South, the reverse trajectory is not similarly available to them. The economic prospects of European colonial settlers a century ago were incomparably better than those of economic

3 Hart's contribution was impactful also because "he focused on the complex, organized, and dynamic income generating activities of informal enterprises [and] found that informal activities were not a mere extension of traditional subsistence strategies and that participants in these unregulated activities were not universally condemned to poverty and marginality" (Yusuff 2011, p. 626).

refugees from the Southern hemisphere (Breman 2023), leaving a larger segment of employable labor in the Global South that is willing to tolerate the more precarious conditions of informal employment.

Colonialism and Legal Dualism

While the colonial period was relatively short, lasting one-half to three-quarters of a century on the African continent, it contributed not only to the larger size but also to the embeddedness of the informal sector today. In particular, it created a dual legal system that applied one set of rules to indigenous economic activity and another to European commerce. While this line was blurred at independence, vestiges of this dual system remain today, as I will soon illustrate in the case of Senegal.

Imperial powers created these dual legal systems, in large part, to restrict capital accumulation among colonial subjects. Although some aspects of legal dualism are present elsewhere, it is most apparent in African colonies. The African colonial legacy is an even more extreme version along several dimensions because it came at the end of a dying era of imperialism and because there were multiple claimants competing for territories in such close proximity (Young 1997, 278–280). Competition made the forcible demonstration of dominance more critical while meeting revenue imperatives in a short amount of time. Racism and technological advances in weaponry, communication, and transport further exacerbated the style of dominance and repression practiced in these colonies. While large populations of *Mestizos* blurred the lines between Europeans and indigenous populations in Latin America, for example, such mixing was rare in Africa (although more common in Portuguese colonies).

To control the local population while meeting their extractive goals, colonizers used a combination of direct and indirect rule. Direct rule was a way of excluding local people from the civil rights and freedoms guaranteed to citizens in a civil society. To the extent that a select few were granted authority under indirect rule, such authority was recognized only under a state-enforced *customary* order. And, even though the French are better known for direct rule, they, like the British, relied on intermediaries and indirect rule, especially in the later colonial period (Austin 2010).

Contrary to its name, customary law was not grounded in tradition. While no single tradition can be ascribed to all precolonial polities, one common feature of local leadership was its ability to be restrained by peers or the people (such as a village council). The colonists removed these traditional restraints so that the only power a local authority was beholden to was the central colonial power – a practice referred to as "decentralized despotism" (Mamdani 1996). Another benefit of this practice to the colonists was that it prevented coordinated resistance. As customary authority was bound up in a single group and its leader, colonial subjects were effectively "containerized." Colonialism thus left a legacy of institutions set up to fractionalize and disenfranchise, to rule in a discretionary manner without turning subjects into citizens.

The delineation between formal and customary authority created a legal dualism that also had implications for the economy. Customary law not only applied to political power but also governed one of the most precious economic resources: land. Unlike in prior colonial experiments such as India, where local landholding was possible, land in Africa was a communal and customary possession that was controlled but not owned by customary authorities (Boone 2014). For the local population, land was outside the scope of the market. Even though peasant households were often in customary possession of land, without the right to alienate it, they could not take advantage of the economic benefits of property rights, such as access to collateral or security to invest (Mamdani 1996). While colonists created and profited from a market for local products on the continent, Africans were essentially excluded from it.

To illustrate how these phenomena affect the formation and persistence of embedded informality, Section 3.2 turns to a historical narrative analysis of a specific country context, Senegal. The deep dive uncovers key general phenomena that the rest of the chapter then takes on. Section 3.3 considers how two factors – linguistic barriers and social networks – contribute to the persistence of informality. Section 3.4 evaluates the scope conditions of the argument, and especially how and why nonsettler colonialism created a context of legal dualism and high informality that is conducive to the formation of a weak-state trap. Together, Sections 3.2–3.4 justify the book's focus on postcolonial Africa and explain how the first pathway out of the weak-state trap, a slow shrinking of the informal sector, is unlikely in cases of embedded informality.

3.2 ORIGINS OF INFORMALITY IN SENEGAL

To understand the origins of the vast informal sector in Senegal, we must also look to the origins of the indigenous corporate sector and ask why it is so small, leaving room for extensive informality to arise. Here, I tell the story of how colonial powers systematically crushed autonomous, well-resourced groups that could have formed the corporate class at independence. In the words of Amin (1969, p. 40), writing shortly after independence: "After having known half a century of brilliant development, [Senegalese commerce] was completely liquidated by colonization." I then describe how the lack of a vibrant corporate class at independence had economic and political implications postindependence.

One legacy of colonialism is that the foreign–local divide in the economy overlaps with the formal–informal divide such that much of the corporate sector is foreign-owned and much of the informal sector is locally owned. This has two related consequences, both of which reinforce the weakness of the local corporate class. First, the pro-business preferences of largely foreign corporate interests were not captured by local political parties that might have otherwise served as a check on the venality of the state. Second, since the state was the locus of economic power, it was able to buy off emergent business interests and was motivated to do so to protect its political stability.

Colonization Crushes Senegal's Indigenous Bourgeoisie

Senegal's precolonial context has features that pushed against and toward the development of an indigenous corporate class. On the one hand, Senegal's economy was centered on peasant production of an export crop and resulting trading networks rather than local production or industry that would lead to greater capital accumulation. However, Senegal's indigenous bourgeoisie has a longer history than almost anywhere in Black Africa due to its early roots in the slave trade. But as this historical narrative suggests, the forces of imperialism largely destroyed the prospect of a strong local bourgeoisie by the end of colonization.

In the first half of the nineteenth century in coastal Senegal, a thriving local commerce developed primarily around the exportation of gum arabic (essential to the expanding European textile industry) and some gold. While French merchants from Bordeaux and Marseilles settled in the port towns of Saint-Louis and Gorée Island, local bourgeois families (Black and mixed-race) also amassed wealth alongside them. The latter were often descended from families that had been involved in the slave trade as military or commercial agents. This Senegal River trading network constituted France's most important sub-Saharan establishment, comprised up to 95 percent of West African exports to France, and was the only navigable route to the interior (McLane 1986).

In addition to these relatively few local bourgeois families acting as licensed overseas exporter-importers, there was also a much larger network of local middlemen or *traitants*. Interestingly, the name "traite" was given locally to the period of commercial activity after the peanut harvest. This French word is not the typical one to describe trade or exchange but rather a holdover from the slave trade, which was called in French, "traite des esclaves" (Roubaud 1918). These Senegalese traders carried goods being exchanged between the merchants at the ports and the seasonal upstream markets. While some French companies sent their own agents to conduct this trade, the local middlemen had a competitive advantage in terms of loyalty and trust, as they had established ties to merchant families living in the interior of the country through marriage and lines of credit (McLane 1986). Traitants also facilitated the growing economy because they were able to give loans to cultivators to increase their production. Loans were based not on collateral from land, but rather on gold or silver jewelry that would be held by the traitant until the trade was completed (Roubaud 1918).

Economic growth in the region benefited these indigenous economic agents in the second half of the nineteenth century. The railway from Saint-Louis to Dakar, completed in 1885, gave rise to an active peanut trade which would dominate the French West African export market until the rise of Ivoirian coffee and cocoa in the 1950s (Cogneau 2023, p. 108). The annual production of peanuts multiplied by a factor of 10 between 1870 and 1914, which also had an effect on the number of active traitants. At the start of the second half of the nineteenth century, Amin (1969) counts about 250 of these Senegalese middlemen. By 1900, about 800 Senegalese traders were counted as paying "patente" or tax. Often, these middlemen came from local notable families themselves. *Traitants* were mostly Black Africans (two-thirds), and otherwise descendants of secondary branches of mixed-race families.

Governor Faidherbe, who ruled the colony during the 1850s and 1860s, imagined Senegal to be like the settler colonies of the Antilles, where the bourgeoisie would be assimilated and mixed-race (he had a mixed-race son himself), and he even prohibited Europeans from seeking commerce along the river to the advantage of Senegalese middlemen (Amin 1969). Faidherbe also implemented policies that undermined the Moorish hold on trade in the interior to the advantage of both French and Senegalese merchants of Saint-Louis since both stood to gain by having their own trading posts along the river (McLane 1986). But that all changed around 1900 with the new colonial strategy of direct rule.

The number and competitiveness of both the Senegalese merchants and middlemen shrunk after 1900. There was a crash in the gum arabic trade, which disrupted existing commercial relationships. Because better-resourced Europeans were better able to pivot than the local merchants, French trading posts expanded from the coast into the interior of Senegal, capitalizing on the growing peanut trade. In little over a decade, the Bordeaux trading posts came to dominate trade in the interior. Further driving the Senegalese middlemen out of business, the French importers could sell goods at the same price irrespective of location along the trade route.

Following World War I, France could no longer afford to send its own bureaucrats to administer the colonies in large numbers and began to rely more on local leaders. While an obvious choice for local administrators would have been those educated in the French school system in Senegal, they posed a greater threat to the metropole because of their high expectations for access and redistribution. Many were disillusioned by the inequality they faced in the French colonial system relative to their European counterparts, and by the decline in their economic position for those who hailed from the once-wealthy commercial families of Saint-Louis (Cogneau 2023, p. 182). Instead, France turned to the more compliant religious and traditional leaders to execute colonial policy. Chief among these were the Mouride marabouts in the center of the country, whom I discuss more fully later.

By 1920, the number of taxpaying Senegalese traders had halved relative to 1900. Senegalese merchants attempted to hold onto their economic position in the face of the economic crisis and changing landscape. They sought direct relationships with European exporters to be able to buy goods at more competitive prices, but failed for two reasons directly related to their inferior economic and political position in the colonial empire. First, their European competitors used political clout to quash such attempts. Second, local merchants could not get credit at internationally owned banks.

An important impediment to the development of local capital was thus the inability of Senegalese to obtain formal loans. Here, the exception proves the rule. Sectors that did not require loans like meat wholesaling, or that exceptionally allowed loans like construction, were those in which indigenous businessmen succeeded. But the capital accumulation that was possible in these smaller internal markets paled in comparison to the accumulation potential in international markets, which remained dominated by foreign capital. Another comparative advantage of the imperial powers was their economic diversification. This allowed them to withdraw from the least profitable sectors, leaving them to the newly independent states that often nationalized them (like the peanut sector) because the state was the only actor that could afford such slim margins (Amin 1969).

Another global phenomenon further reduced the role of indigenous Senegalese in these trading networks. The influx of Lebanese after World War I led to a new hierarchical commercial structure in which the Lebanese were placed above local Africans. Lebanese could be more competitive as traders price-wise because they did not have big families to support. They were also favored by the French colonists as economic intermediaries because they were less likely to pose a political challenge than the indigenous colonial subjects. By the 1940s, the Senegalese traders "were reduced to a subordinate role of grain collectors for the Lebanese accounts and the colonial trading houses" (Amin 1969, p. 36). While the most successful Lebanese merchants eventually rose to the status of direct importer from Europe after World War II, the Senegalese traders saw no such economic advancement.

By the late colonial period in Senegal, the income differential between the French and the Africans in the formal economy was staggering. Alfani and Tadei (2019) recreated social tables of the different classes and sectors of workers from historical sources. They found that from 1939 to 1954, European settlers received from 23 percent to 42 percent of the total income of the colony (on average 29 times their proportional share) despite accounting for only 0.8–1.5 percent of the working population in the formal sector. And the average prices paid to Senegalese (and other sub-Saharan African) producers were about one-fifth to one-third of what they should have made on the global market (Cogneau 2023, p. 275).

This discussion of the preindependence bourgeois class in Senegal illustrates the initial promise of local merchants benefiting from access to international trade and then their demise at the hands of imperial policies that privileged metropolitan interests at the expense of peripheral ones. Not only did French commerce marginalize the economic position of indigenous elite merchants and traders, but the colonial administration also empowered traditional and religious authorities at the expense of these more cosmopolitan elites. France was not alone in this approach. For example, Power (1992) describes how the British in Malawi strengthened the power of the traditional tribal authority to crush the "petit bourgeoisie."

But it is also true that the nascent indigenous bourgeoisie in Senegal existed, in large part, thanks to the forces of globalization that provided a market for local goods. So it is hard to know what the fate of Senegal's local economy would have been in the absence of both globalization and imperialism. But what is indisputable is the small size of the indigenous formal sector at independence. The next section discusses how that sector fared in the postindependence period.

Postindependence State-Led Politics

The postindependence period in Senegal did nothing to revive the local bourgeoisie. The nationalization of the peanut trade and creation of a marketing board put an end to the utility of the old "traitants" who would stock peanuts and serve as intermediaries between producers and the colonial trading houses. The distribution of rice quotas by the state gave rise to a new local commercial sector – both companies and individual traders. But private local capital remained confined to a few sectors: trade, transport, and construction. There was practically no industry other than peanut processing, and even there, the Senegalese firms accounted for only one-third of the market (Amin 1969).

While the state monopolized the peanut export business, European trading companies monopolized the legal importation of consumer goods. Even the Senegalese business associations of the immediate postindependence period were dominated by French colonial and neocolonial interests. The Dakar Chamber of Commerce, which worked with the government to set economic policy, was controlled by European trading houses. As a direct legacy of the colonial economic structure, most larger formal firms in the less lucrative commercial, transport, and real estate sectors were owned by businessmen of Lebanese origin (Thioub, Diop and Boone 1998).

The state-led development model common to postindependence economies meant that capital accumulation in this period was enriching the state and party members rather than contributing to the rise of an autonomous economic class. Furthermore, former colonial powers that had benefited from exclusive access to the formal economy in colonial times continued to maintain a privileged position in the postcolonial economies. In the decades immediately following independence, the local private sector was weak and subordinate to the emergent state and foreign capital. State leaders saw private interests in maintaining this status quo and "protect[ed] and promote[d] foreign capital in light industry, the import trade, extractive industry, and services" (Thioub, Diop and Boone 1998).

The example of Dakar's short-lived prosperous textile industry demonstrates how constituencies that primarily owned capital (foreigners) were distinct from the constituencies ruling the state (locals), leading to divergent interests. Boone (1992) describes how the textile industry's prosperity in the 1960s and 70s was driven by foreign industrialists' monopoly over the sale of staple textile goods on the local market. But when the state stopped enforcing this monopoly, parallel markets developed in which powerful members of the political and economic elite became importers and circumvented restrictions and taxes, leading to the decline of the industry. Whereas local corporate interests may have successfully disciplined the state's venal tendencies or at least advocated policies in line with economic productivity, foreign corporate interests were not a priority for the postindependence Senegalese regime trying to consolidate its power.

There was eventually growth elsewhere in the local business sector, but rather than engaging in the kinds of state reform that would have been more conducive to economic productivity, the state instead bought off local business interests. This is a common clientelistic tactic in vote-poor, resource-rich polities (Kitschelt 2000), a description that can be applied to Senegal in this period before real multiparty competition. By 1975, Senegal had 70 parastatal corporations that comprised 40 percent of the formal sector and employed a third of its workforce (Diouf 1993). The state's new access to foreign capital and the interests of international trade in maintaining privileged access to local markets lent the newly independent state both drive and capacity to co-opt local business interests. It did this successfully throughout the 1960s and 1970s, responding to challenges from the local business elite with preferential access to rents generated by control over the commercial sector (Boone 1994).

The most successful Senegalese traders in the more formal, quasi-legal domains of the economy owed their prosperity to close ties and access to the ruling party, and in the more informal, illicit domains, to forbearance from taxation and regulation. Neither group would be expected to comprise a constituency for bureaucratic autonomy or to lobby the state for nondiscretionary policies, as we saw in the cases of successful programmatic transitions. Boone (1992, p.8) highlights the resultant inability of a bourgeois class to discipline the state: "Because local capital was so weak, African capitalists could not ensure that state power would be used on their behalf, much less at their behest." Instead, upon decolonization, the new powerholders did not own important local capital nor represent indigenous capitalist interests. Postindependence leaders restructured institutions to contain elite infighting and suppress "the potential development of any autonomous source of power" (Diop 1993, p. 5).

In addition to explaining the absence of a powerful indigenous economic class at independence, this historical trajectory also helps explain the absence of economic class cleavages in early political competition. As the social status of local entrepreneurs rapidly declined, the old Senegalese bourgeoisie began directing their sons toward the civil service rather than into faltering local commerce. The major postindependence political party was thus comprised of "French-educated bureaucrats, technocrats and teachers" (Topouzis 1989).

The large informal sector that persisted postindependence was an outgrowth of colonial and neocolonial policies that gave preferential treatment to foreign capital and allowed for local market activity to go unregulated. According to Thioub, Diop and Boone (1998): "From the time of independence (and before), the vast majority of the African businessmen have operated in the 'informal-sector' transport and internal distribution networks, outside the tax and regulatory net of the state." The state turned a blind eye to contraband trading networks that had the political advantage of employing many and ensuring a supply of cheap consumer goods (Thioub, Diop and Boone 1998). These illicit networks were often tightly linked to Islamic brotherhoods whose existing networks and relationships of trust gave them a comparative advantage in trade.

In the 1990s, Senegal, like most of its neighbors, underwent political and economic liberalization. These reforms were intended to decrease the state's ability and motivation to undermine independent local business interests. Indeed, they created "both threats and opportunities for . . . Senegal's business sector," fracturing the "political and economic elite into unstable factions" (Thioub, Diop and Boone 1998). We might have expected steady growth in the formal economic sector as a result of the decreasing economic power of the state. But even as the macro conditions changed in Senegal, the relative size of the informal sector remained very large.

One reason for weak growth in the local formal sector is the continued prominence of foreign capital. When states privatized their companies as part of structural adjustment programs, many state-owned firms were sold in part or in full to foreign entities, further undermining the development of a domestic business class. In Senegal, there was no restriction on the participation of foreign investors in the privatization of state-owned firms. When the government privatized the national telecommunication company, Sonatel, in 1997, France Telecom purchased 42 percent of Sonatel's capital. Today, French-owned companies account for 25 percent of GDP in Senegal (and 30 percent in Côte d'Ivoire) according to the French government.

Later in the chapter, I describe some of the other contributing factors to the stability of informality in the period following structural adjustment and political liberalization, namely, language and strong social networks. But first, I delve into a case within a case: the Mouride, one of Senegal's main religious brotherhoods. This group epitomizes the ways in which a cultural or religious identity and its associated social networks contribute to the maintenance and growth of the informal economic sector.

Religion, Economy, and Politics in Senegal

One cannot write a historical narrative of Senegal without talking about the influence of religion on all aspects of society. I briefly describe Senegal's main religious groups and their influence, which extends beyond the spiritual life of their followers and into economic and political life. Section 3.3 will then reflect on the implications of that influence for the persistence of informality.

Today, Islam is practiced by about 97 percent of Senegalese, the majority of whom belong to one of the two main Sufi orders or brotherhoods – Tidjane (49 percent) and Mouride (32 percent) (ANSD 2002). While the Mouride are not the most populous brotherhood in Senegal, it is the most politically important due, in part, to its centralized organizational structure and the economic benefits it has brought its followers (O'Brien 1971). The more numerous members of the Tidjane brotherhood have a more fractionalized structure with different branches of religious families throughout the country. Both Sufi brotherhoods are organized around religious teachers or shaykhs, also called *marabouts* in French West Africa. "The Senegalese maraboutic model is characterized by its extraordinary presence in public life…for the vast majority of the Senegalese population, relations with a marabout are an integral component of an individual's life" (Villalón 1999, p. 134).

While Islam has been present in West Africa since the eighth century, the leaders of the Wolof states – the medieval kingdoms (1350–1890) in what is now Senegal – did not initially convert and mainly relied on Muslim clerics for counsel (Levtzion and Pouwels 2000). Although the extent of Islamic diffusion among the Wolof prior to French conquest is disputed, it was the incursion of French colonial forces against these kingdoms that triggered a mass conversion to Islam (O'Brien 1971). Lat Dior, king of the Wolof state of Cayor, is a celebrated national hero for his resistance to French conquest. But his defeat in 1886 for opposing the extension of a railway line through his territory demonstrated to the Wolof people that French rule could not be opposed by force. The Mouride brotherhood, founded only three years earlier by Shaykh Amadou Bamba, offered a more promising alternative with its policy of adaptation.

Here again, colonialism has important implications for the development of Mouridism – as a collective response to French conquest (O'Brien 1971). With the collapse of the Wolof states, the brotherhood provided an alternative authority structure created by that vacuum. In particular, the dissolution and disarming of the Wolof states and their social hierarchies of patron–client relationships left slaves and low-caste clients of the old nobility searching for a new way of life. They were then easy targets for religious leaders looking to expand their followership, and those leaders "took over the status and many of the functions of the discredited chiefs" (O'Brien 1971, p. 15).

Mourides were key to the expansion of peanut cultivation in the Wolof zone, the cash crop that accounts for the largest source of export revenue, as described earlier. The colonial government saw the power of a centralized hierarchical organization to propagate new agricultural methods and attract people to farming and so worked with Mouride leaders to increase cultivation (O'Brien 1971). In turn, the Mouride leaders were granted large tracts of land and found easy access to loans and other economic support from the French. While much of the peanut production is generated by individual families, the Mouride leaders are able to use their position in the brotherhood to become some of the biggest producers of groundnuts in Senegal. At the time of independence, over two-thirds of the country's "great producers" were Mouride notables.

A key feature of Mouridism is the relationship between work and faith. Manual labor is of spiritual value, and followers of Mouride notables work on collective farms called *daras* (O'Brien 1971). Not only do leaders benefit from free or very cheap labor, but they also benefit from material contributions from disciples or followers with their own production. Unlike the majority of their countrymen, Mouride leaders are thus able to accumulate and invest capital.

These independent sources of wealth help shape the role of Mouride leaders as political intermediaries which we will discuss in Chapter 5. Their involvement in politics predates independence. In fact, intense electoral competition prior to independence "enormously increased the power of the religious leaders – who at times appeared to be virtually the arbiters of Senegal's destiny" (O'Brien 1971, p. 4). Foreshadowing the evidence of resistance by intermediaries to transitions that would result in losses to them, Mouride leaders who benefited from French rule "forced the hand of the Senegalese national leaders in 1958 to ensure the postponement of independence" (O'Brien 1971, p. 4). The collaboration between marabouts and the state continued well into the postindependence era; up until the period of multiparty democracy, they would issue *ndigals* or pronouncements of support for the ruling party (Villalón 1999).

The Mouride social hierarchy and the economic dependence and reciprocity between followers and religious leaders were developed in rural agrarian relations of production. Changing economic circumstances, including land scarcity and the price of cash crops, led to mass migration to urban centers starting in the mid-twentieth century. While the primary religious leaders remained in their rural homelands, they developed networks of intermediaries in cities to connect them with their followers, some of whom were more independent from the original leaders than others (O'Brien 1971). While not as powerful as the original rural leaders, these urban networks of Mouride intermediaries remain economically valuable to migrants for a social safety net and for finding employment in the informal sector. Successful Mouride businessmen, for example, often provide young migrants with work as street vendors as well as goods on credit and assistance with food and housing (Golub and Hansen-Lewis 2012).

Upon arrival in cities, the majority of Mouride migrants worked as petty traders and artisans. (Not much has changed today.) As evidence of the continued link between religion and economic activity in this new setting, Mouride disciples congregated in markets for religious purposes (O'Brien 1971). Followers continue to seek loans from their marabouts or religious leaders, whom they see at least once or twice a year when they visit their leader's village or the spiritual capital, Touba, for religious ceremonies. And migrants continue to give material offerings to the leaders, even though the amount and form change with the changing circumstances.

While the economic version of the agricultural *dara* described earlier did not transfer to the urban setting, the educational version did. Many Mouride families sent their children to *dara* schools where students live with the marabout, receiving Koranic schooling and, in turn, contribute the proceeds from begging back to the marabout (O'Brien 1971). This practice remains incredibly common today. A recent study found that over half of girls and 60 percent of boys attended a Koranic school for at least one year (André and Demonsant 2009).

Another religious institution with more economic implications also took hold. The *daaira* are religious associations that unite followers of individual marabouts into organized groupings (Villalón 1999) and generally meet once a week for religious singing and discussion. These organizations are not specific to the Mouride, but the Mouride were more likely to use them to raise money for their religious leaders (O'Brien 1971). They take on even more of an economic character when they are organized, which they often are, among members of an economic sector, occupation or market. Mutual aid is a key function of these groups.

For Mourides in particular, *daaira* meetings are conducted exclusively in Wolof, the language of religious expression more generally. While the vast majority of Mouride are Wolof by origin, those who are not adopt Wolof as their language (O'Brien 1971, p. 242). This is consistent with the fact that Senegalese commerce, especially in cities, is conducted primarily in Wolof – partly to facilitate communication between the many different language groups.

The "cohesiveness of the Mourides and their deep relations of trust have proven to be extremely valuable in fostering their informal commercial network" (Golub and Hansen-Lewis 2012, p. 178). Mourides dominate not only domestic commerce, but are also prominent in transport and real estate – all informal enterprises. There is also an international component to Mouride commercial activity. The consolidated Mouride neighborhoods and *daairas* of Senegal are replicated in cities of Senegal's trading partners around the world. Trade is made efficient by family and kin ties linking the cities, usually headed by a wholesaler in the prominent Sandaga market of Dakar. There was even an informal money-exchange mechanism started in 1991 by a Mouride trader in New York that allowed merchants to travel internationally without carrying large sums of money (Tall 2004).

3.3 FACTORS CONTRIBUTING TO THE STABILITY OF INFORMALITY

I argue that embedded informality will be more likely to persist when there are higher barriers to leaving the sector and greater advantages to staying. In this section, I review two such features of informality in Senegal revealed by the above historical narrative.

The discussion of the role of religion, and especially the Mouride brotherhood, in economic life illuminates one key advantage of the informal over the formal sector. The Mouride came to dominate informal commerce thanks to their solidarity, belief in a higher purpose, and mutual trust. "Mourides almost never default on loans or commitments to other Mourides, as to do so would be viewed as a breach of religious as well as commercial bonds" (Golub and Hansen-Lewis 2012, p. 178). This can make trade in the informal sector more efficient than in the formal sector as costly formal institutions of contract enforcement are not necessary – reminiscent of the story of the success of Maghribi Traders in the eleventh century (Greif 1993). Indeed, "Mourides have outcompeted European and Lebanese commerce because they have been able to escape full payment of internal taxes" (Boone 1994, p. 460).

We also saw evidence of a barrier to exiting the informal sector in the form of language. Religious and economic life is conducted primarily in Wolof for the Mouride and many others in the informal sector. Not only is there little economic utility to speaking the administrative language of French in this sector, but there is also a push to send children to a Koranic school where Arabic is the language of instruction.

Language

When I asked Senegalese researcher of the informal economy, Ibrahima Dankoco, about the relationship between colonization and informality, his first response was about language and the written tradition. He pointed to the large proportion of Senegalese citizens who are not sufficiently fluent in the language of the administrative state to conduct formal interactions. He also pointed to the colonial imposition of a written society that many still feel alienated from. If the informal economy defines economic activities that happen outside the purview of the state – unknown to or unregulated by the state – then there similarly exist noneconomic activities of citizens that are not seen or regulated by the state. These might be births or deaths that go unregistered, nonprofit associations or groups that go unseen, or services that get accessed or provided without passing through the state. The coexistence of colonial and indigenous languages helped to create and reinforce this informality with respect to the state. And it is an enduring feature of society that did not change with the liberalizing reforms of the 1990s.

Why did often nationalistic postindependence leaders in Africa choose to run their states in colonial languages? One rationale is that it was an attempt to substantiate their legitimate claim to power by teaching these languages in schools and adopting Western political structures (Ekeh 1975). These leaders often came from a bourgeois class that emerged under colonialism, a class that acquired Western education from the colonizers and thus was the most exposed to European ideologies and institutions. But this class often lacked legitimacy because it was not created out of pre-existing cultural capital or an extension of precolonial institutions. Indeed, it was sometimes just the opposite. In Senegal, chiefs of administrative units were "chosen by the colonial rulers in consideration of their submissiveness and their literacy in French rather than their traditional qualifications" (O'Brien 1971, 14). In Mali, traditional chiefs, in an act of resistance, would send the children of slaves to French schools, protecting the children of nobles from imperial reach. This created friction at independence when subordinate classes rose in the administrative ranks and upper classes faced barriers to entry in the new regime.

So not only did a new elite class that formed under colonialism take the reins of power at independence, their very origin that sapped them of local legitimacy incentivized them to perpetuate the distinction between them (the ruling class) and everyone else. This helps answer the question of why, at independence, new forms of government that were more closely tied to the people (through language) and to older forms of local governance were not tried. Ekeh (1975) argues that this dynamic created two publics: a primordial public that is identified with "primordial groupings, sentiments, and activities" but at the same time impinges on public interest; and a civic public that is based on civil structures such as the military, civil service, or police. This dualism has persisted since independence, in part, because state language policies often prioritized communication with the outside world, especially with the former metropoles, rather than local employment (Djité 2020). And unlike in former colonies with a high proportion of settlers such as those in the Americas, the formal economy and population structures have evolved in such a way that indigenous populations have felt little pressure to shift to European languages as their vernaculars (Vigouroux and Mufwene 2020).

In sub-Saharan Africa, for example, citizens overwhelmingly use indigenous languages in interactions associated with the "primordial public" sphere. These are the languages through which social groups constitute and express themselves. They are also more fit to adapt to the changing and complex environment of informal economic exchange: "this complexity is mitigated through the indigenous languages lexicon and idiom, which over time – in a classic manifestation of reciprocity and symbiosis – have evolved to accommodate informal economic transactions" (Mwaniki 2016). The preference for using indigenous languages in social groups reinforces their use in the informal economic sector because such groups tend to distribute and consume goods and services produced in the informal economy. Mwaniki (2016) even describes it as a "captive market" in which "the informal economy is almost the exclusive supplier of goods and services and owing to the consumers' socio-economic statuses that curtail access to formal schooling with the resultant illiteracy and semi-illiteracy, consumers inevitably resort to indigenous languages for economic intercourse."

The colonial legacy of indigenous languages dominating the informal economy and European languages dominating the formal economy contributes to the stability of economic dualism. It increases the competitiveness of the informal sector relative to the formal one by sheer necessity of being able to cater to end-consumers, and at the same time increases the stability of each of these two economies and their reliance on each other. Mwaniki (2016) highlights how informal traders also act as language facilitators when they source goods from distribution networks in the formal economy using the country's dominant language and then provide those goods or services back to customers in indigenous languages. The existence of these "broker-agents" reduces incentives of ordinary citizens to invest in the language of the formal economy. Their existence also reinforces intermediated forms of political exchange, at the same time enhancing the legitimacy of brokers who serve both purposes.

Social Networks

As described in the previous section, the pervasiveness and strength of Islamic brotherhoods in Senegal facilitated informal trading networks. Their preexisting relationships of trust gave them a comparative advantage. The state tolerated them because they provided benefits to the masses in the form of employment and cheap goods. With political and economic liberalization, these social networks did not disappear. The state's political calculus changed from one that aimed to appease the masses enough to prevent popular revolt to one that aimed to appeal to a majority of voters. But this change did not result in a more rigorous approach to regulating these socially embedded trading networks. Instead, as we will see, multiparty politics may have offered an even greater incentive to invest in them.

The economic autonomy of Senegal's religious brotherhoods from the state can be traced, in part, to their role in the colonial project. France relied upon the maraboutic clergy to collect taxes, garner support for policies, and win the submission of subjects (Diop 2011). We saw in the last section how marabouts gained land and other economic benefits in exchange. Postcolonial leaders did not deviate from this clientelistic strategy of reliance upon religious leaders; this is how Léopold Senghor, a Christian postindependence leader, came to rule a Muslim-majority country so effectively. He went and solicited the support of the leaders of the Mouride and Tidjane Muslim brotherhoods and of the Lebou, the ethnic group indigenous to the capital city, who maintained a strong hierarchy there.

As a prelude to the role that religious and traditional intermediaries play in clientelistic exchange today, Senghor's constituent base was made up of religious marabouts and their disciples, traditional chiefs and their followers, and the big informal businessmen – particularly those in the peanut trade. The opposition's constituent base consisted primarily of intellectuals, workers in formal industries dominated by France, and civil servants. This pattern has continued in spite of more competitive elections. Religious brotherhoods and their intermediaries today often still support incumbents. They do this in the face of party transitions by switching parties, as I further describe later.

The 2000 elections in Senegal saw the first alternation in executive power from the long-ruling Socialist Party (PS) to Abdoulaye Wade's Social Democrat Party (PDS). While there were free elections in 1993, they were not particularly fair. The opposition "continued to cry fraud, refused to accredit the official results, and called for the establishment of an independent national election commission" (Gellar 2005, p. 82). And up until 1991, elections were not particularly free either: "the administration controlled the entire electoral process, discouraged the secret ballot, and excluded representatives of opposition parties from verifying the vote tally" (Gellar 2005, p. 81).

For the next couple of decades, Senegal was often touted as the most stable democracy on the continent. The move to more competitive politics pushed parties to establish stronger linkages with voters. But as in most developing democracies, parties in Senegal have not typically been distinguished by ideological commitments. Diop (2011, p. 388) classifies the party system into the "party of the president" and the "parties that eat." The latter refers to opposition parties that are purely motivated by the search for profit and material goods and define themselves with respect to their relationship with the party in power. The search for electoral support by these smaller party leaders is often motivated by the negotiating power that comes with electoral clout: Once they prove themselves sufficiently popular, party leaders can negotiate with the ruling party to gain access to coveted state posts that then serve as a source of rents.

In this transactional environment, it is difficult for any party to differentiate itself on the basis of ideology or to make credible programmatic promises. According to the 2008 DALP data, Senegal scores second lowest on the continent on its measure of programmatic party structure. Electoral expert Ababacar Fall said that political parties in Senegal displayed some programmatic differentiation early in the country's postindependence political development but that today's parties are mostly patrimonial in style, built around a single person who financed and created the party. He says contemporary vote choice in Senegal is affective, not ideological; people do not vote by conviction, but rather by how well they know or are connected to the person.[4]

Even though today's party system is far more fractionalized than in Senghor's time – there are now 343 registered parties – traces of the original constituent divides remain. Religious and traditional leaders, along with informal business leaders, are more likely to side with the government, while civil servants, intellectuals, and workers in the formal sector are more likely to side with the opposition – even in the face of party transitions. When former opposition leaders have come to power, constituencies have often switched allegiances upon getting there. Whereas Abdoulaye Wade spent more than 30 years in the opposition, when he came to power in 2000, he too courted religious and traditional leaders. They, for the most part, quickly engaged in what the Senegalese call *transhumance*: They migrated from backing Senghor's party (now run by his predecessor) to backing Wade shortly after the election. A similar phenomenon occurred in 2012 when Macky Sall first came to power.

The most iconic brokers in Senegal – Mouride marabouts – have systematically switched to supporting the incumbent, whoever it may be (Osei 2012). For example, President Wade's first mandate was marked by a favoritism toward his own brotherhood, the Mouride; his reelection

4 Interview with the author, July 13, 2022. Dakar, Senegal.

was then aided by top religious leaders who gave clear instructions to vote for him and by leaders lower down in the political machine who helped mobilize followers (Diop 2011, p. 430). Whereas the 2000 elections were thought by some to mark the end of this religious clientele, Beck (2002) instead described Wade's win as beholden to clientelism. His old and new supporters were not voicing a rejection of the status quo but rather banking on access to future clientelistic access.

As further evidence of vote switching, Horacio Larreguy and I used village-level data on elections to show that over the span of the first three multiparty presidential elections (2000, 2007, and 2012), very few villages that bloc vote remain loyal bloc voters to the same party over time (Gottlieb and Larreguy 2020). Namely, less than three percent continued to bloc vote for the PS after the 2000 change in the incumbent party. Many more villages shifted to bloc voting for a different party in a later election. Such a pattern is consistent with transactional political brokers trying to extract targeted benefits from the state in exchange for loyal support.

Experience with multiparty politics thus demonstrated to incumbents that investing in local social networks like the Sufi brotherhoods and traditional leaders could be electorally beneficial. The continued relevance of these networks in the political sphere would, in turn, facilitate their persistence in the economic sphere.

Summing Up

Motivated by the case of Senegal, I argued that linguistic dualism and social networks contribute to the persistence of informality. The former serves as a barrier to exiting the informal sector, while the latter increases the comparative advantage of remaining in the informal sector. There is some evidence that this insight travels outside Senegal. Across African countries, informal employment rates are negatively correlated with literacy rates in the inherited colonial language (and language of the formal sector).[5] And, informal employment rates are positively correlated with the strength of social networks as measured by trust in informal leaders.[6]

5 Share informal employment and literacy rates are based on averages between 2010 and 2023 to account for missing data, sourced from the ILO and the World Bank, respectively.

6 Strength of informal leaders is an average index comprised of three measures from the 2022 Afrobarometer: trust in traditional leaders, trust in religious leaders, and the perceived influence of traditional leaders in local governance.

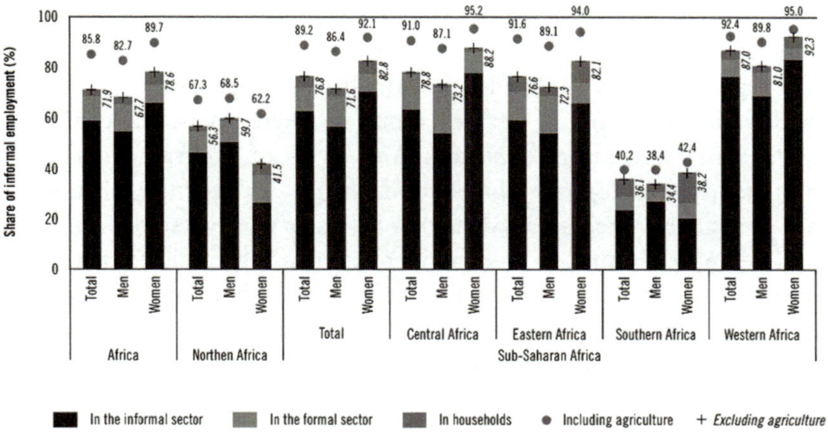

FIGURE 3.4 Informal employment across African regions.
Source: International Labour Organization (2018).

3.4 SCOPE CONDITIONS OF THE ARGUMENT

In this final section of the chapter, I reflect on some of the particularities of Senegal as our motivating case to help inform where else we might expect embedded informality to contribute to keeping the state weak. West Africa, Senegal's regional home, is exceptional in that it experienced the benefits of a cash crop boom even before colonization. Trade in gum arabic and peanuts in Senegal and in rubber, palm oil, and mahogany in forested areas such as Guineé enriched both European and local merchants. West African producers were selling on internal and overseas markets as early as the first decade of the nineteenth century (Austin 2010). So we might expect the indigenous bourgeoisie in other regions to be smaller at the start of colonization. And, we might have expected to find a somewhat larger formal sector in West Africa today. But this is clearly not the case as illustrated in Figure 3.4; West Africa has the highest rates of informality on the continent (87 percent), more than twice as high as that in Southern Africa (36.1 percent).

One explanation I advance below for these regional trends in contemporary informality considers settlement patterns during the colonial period. From the Senegalese narrative, we saw the different ways in which the French commercial and political interests shaped the informal sector. Settlement patterns were themselves not exogenous but rather responded to existing opportunities and constraints for economic development. Rather than making a causal argument about the effect of settlement on our outcomes of interest, I instead aim to set out some of the scope conditions for my argument about the intractability of the weak-state trap in contexts of embedded informality. This phenomenon is most concerning in a specific set of countries where we see a confluence of factors: large informal sectors, low levels of programmatism, and particularly weak states. This section illustrates that these phenomena are particularly likely to arise in colonial states without settlers.

To empirically analyze this claim, I rely on Easterly and Levine's (2016) original dataset, which documents the European share of the population during colonization. They use a variety of primary and secondary sources dating back to the sixteenth century and are thoughtful about how they choose the date at which to report settlement numbers. Their analysis inductively produces a threshold at which to consider a colony a *settler colony*. Estimates indicate that "once European settlement is above 4.8 percent, the small colonial European settlements have a positive effect on development today compared to no colonial European settlement" (Easterly and Levine 2016). I thus define *minor settlement* as countries with less than a 4.8 percent share of European settlers, and *nonsettler colonies* as those having no record of European settlement.

Before turning to the argument about settlement patterns and informality, I want to highlight that Senegal also has some peculiarities even within the West African region that should inform how we think about the typicality of the case. First, it was the capital of French West Africa and the origin of colonial expansion on the continent in the mid-nineteenth century. So any effects of colonial policies might be expected to be more pronounced here than elsewhere in francophone Africa. Second, Senegal's partially mixed-race indigenous bourgeoisie, partially a function of early French commerce based out of Saint-Louis, was also somewhat rare. Another example of this is the Afro-Brazilian elite in Dahomey (today's Benin) who met a similar fate (Cogneau 2023, p. 182).

While these two factors may lead us to expect a larger indigenous formal sector in Senegal today, a third distinctive characteristic generates the opposite prediction. Senegal's postindependence government was particularly bad at managing the economy. Its francophone neighbor, Côte d'Ivoire, experienced economic growth at an average rate of about eight percent from 1960 to 1975, thanks to the liberal policies of the state (Woods 1988), whereas Senegal averaged a growth rate of two percent during that same period (The World Bank). And cocoa producers in Ghana appear to have survived colonization better than the Senegalese traders. Hill (1997) characterizes cocoa farmers in colonial Ghana as capitalists and accumulators whose economic productivity and profits grew during the colonial period and afterward.[7] Perhaps as a result, contemporary Senegal has a substantially larger informal sector (representing about 90 percent of total employment) than does Ghana (with 78 percent of employment in the informal sector) (Labor Force Survey, ILO 2015).

Variation in Colonial Settlement and Informality

Earlier in the chapter, we learned how imperial powers were sometimes incentivized to restrict African competition in trade, thus pushing local commercial activity into the informal sector. But this was not the only way in which colonial policies affected levels of informality. In other cases, colonial policy instead restricted exit options into the informal sector to keep labor costs low, thus decreasing the size of the informal sector. These latter policies were common to settler colonies where Europeans were directly involved in economic production.

Apart from simply having citizens from the metropole choose to reside permanently in colonial outposts, one of the main distinctions between settler and nonsettler colonies in Africa is economic. In "peasant" colonies, land remained overwhelmingly controlled and worked by indigenous people (even though land was not alienable). In "settler" colonies, Europeans appropriated land for their own settlers or for plantations, which not only provided European investors and settlers with cheap land, but also obliged locals to sell their labor to European farmers, planters, or mineowners (Austin 2010, p. 14). Africa is the

7 Why the cocoa producers in Ghana did not face the same fate as the Senegalese bourgeoisie may have to do with the fact that they are producers rather than traders. The colonists in French West Africa could more easily compete with Africans in trade but not in rural production, since the model of colonization there did not include large-scale settlements or plantations. Or it could have to do with the politics of peanut expansion pushed by the French through Mouride marabouts and their followers. Mouride disciples who accounted for a large proportion of peanut production were actually poor cultivators. O'Brien (1971, p. 220) attributes this to "the fact that they were drawn from those strata of Wolof society (warriors, traders, artisans, slaves) which had little experience of, or interest in, cultivation." One consequence of this inexperience is the shorter time horizons of Mouride cultivators who were more interested in "quick cash return" at the expense of preserving the sustainability of the land and soil. Part of the incentive to over-farm for quick returns comes from the desire for the disciples to contribute cash to their spiritual leaders. This depiction is very much at odds with the way Hill (1997) describes the efficiency and adaptability of cocoa farmers in Ghana.

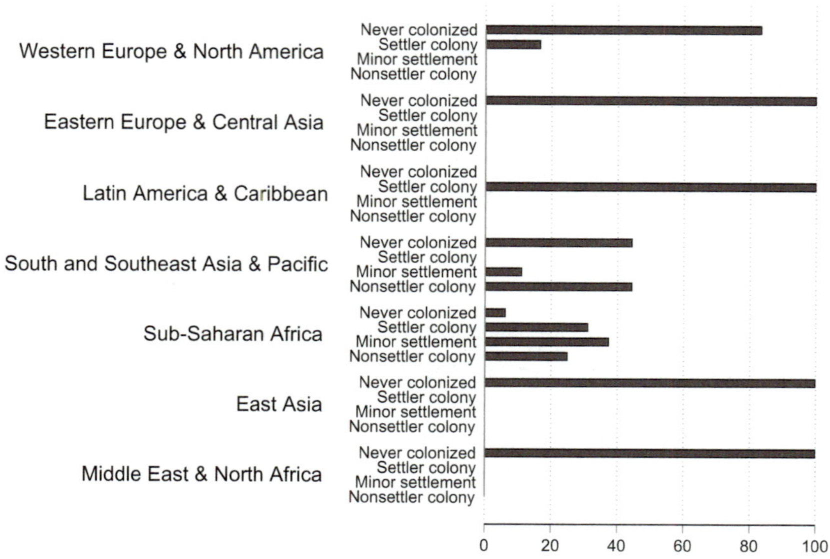

FIGURE 3.5 Proportion of post-colonial democracies by region.
Note: Settler colonies are defined as having at least 4.8 percent share of European settlers, following Easterly and Levine's (2016). *Minor settlement* indicates countries with less than 4.8 percent share of European settlers; nonsettler colonies have no record of European settlement according to Easterly and Levine's (2016) data.

only region with substantial variation in colonial settlement patterns across contemporary democracies as seen in Figure 3.5. Former colonies in Latin America have a high degree of settlement, whereas almost all former colonies in the Asia-Pacific region had no European settlement.[8]

Given the distinction with respect to labor and property rights, there are two reasons we might expect greater colonial settlement to increase the size of the formal sector relative to that in peasant colonies.[9] First, there is a greater likelihood that small- to medium-size enterprises emerge in the formal sector, with all the attendant institutional developments (even if they, at first, are excluded Africans). Second, the property rights and economic securities afforded to European settlers allow for the accu-

[8] While there was colonial settlement in the MENA region, none of those countries is currently considered democratic.

[9] Koehler-Derrick and Lee (2023) provide a third, more indirect, reason: that higher levels of settlement increase the bargaining power of military conscripts to demand public goods after fighting wars. They find that communes in Algeria with higher levels of French settlers relative to Algerian subjects experienced greater increases in state spending after wartime.

mulation of capital that remains in the colony and is protected by, but autonomous from, the state. I discuss each in turn.

First, in settler economies that required vast reserves of cheap, indigenous labor, colonial powers tried to block alternative sources of income. Such alternatives would compete with wage labor in White-owned mining and plantation agriculture, driving up wages. Europeans thus restricted exit options into the informal sector by disrupting peasant agriculture, controlling migration and settlement, and criminalizing informal activities. Thus, small enterprises that would have been the informal sector in other contexts "were formalized and reserved for whites, and were thus registered and subjected to taxation" (Mkandawire 2010). As a result, the capacity to tax and regulate small businesses developed early in settler colonies.

Second, settlers formed a unique class in colonial polities that had access to property rights and economic opportunities, including the ability to accumulate capital. In particular, banking and access to credit in the colonies were mostly reserved for Europeans. On the African continent, banks would accept Africans' savings but were loath to give them loans. This was a direct result of legal dualism and the exclusion of Africans from the ability to get titles to their land (Austin 2010). Colonization also undermined capital accumulation among indigenous entrepreneurs by pushing them lower down the chain of intermediation between shippers and farmers as more lucrative positions were taken by European merchants, as seen in the Senegal case.

While the colonial powers got out of the business of administering colonies at independence, some European settlers stayed behind with their capital. The decision to stay or leave often came at the end of a conflict between the militant indigenous independent movements and the settlers. In some colonies such as Algeria, Mozambique, Angola, and Kenya, settlers mainly left the country after decolonization. In others, like today's South Africa and Zimbabwe, settlers remained, but their political power eventually diminished. In the former, they became a tolerated minority, while in the latter, they were more explicitly under threat.

This raises the question of whether the implications of colonial settlement for the size of the formal sector would endure past independence. On the one hand, settlers themselves were unlikely to comprise a large formal sector in terms of the number of formal sector employees or local businesses (even if much of their capital remained). On the other hand, the institutional features favoring the productivity of the formal sector were more long-lived (Sokoloff and Engerman 2000; Easterly and Levine

2016). For example, Boone (2014) suggests that some of the largest variation in macro-level property rights institutions across African countries today is explained by whether or not they are former settler colonies: The state is more involved in regulating land ownership in former settler colonies relative to informal institutions that dominate in nonsettler colonies.

Economic institutions developed for settlers continued to provide investment opportunities and protections at greater rates in former settler colonies (Acemoglu, Johnson and Robinson 2001). And the postcolonial state often maintained restrictions on informalization in these colonies even as Black Africans gained greater access to economic opportunities in the formal sector. Similarly, postcolonial states continued to engage in extractive practices that largely resembled colonial ones. For example, largely agricultural states set up marketing boards (or continued their colonial equivalent) with a monopoly over the purchase and export of major crops. Because they were state-owned and not subject to market pressures, and since they were not paying market prices and keeping the difference, these boards led to the enrichment of the state at the expense of a thriving market (Bates 1981).

Consistent with the idea that settlement had long-lived implications for the size of the informal sector, we see a large discrepancy in contemporary formal employment between the primarily labor reserve economies of Southern Africa and the primarily cash crop economies of West Africa. Figure 3.4 from the International Labour Organization shows that the vast majority of employment is in the informal sector in Western Africa (80 to 92 percent depending on whether you include informal employment in the formal sector), while the majority of employment is in the *formal* sector in Southern Africa (around 60 to 70 percent).

The theory suggests that the mutually reinforcing effects of informality and the weak-state trap are more worrisome in contexts where all three parameters coincide: embedded informality, low levels of programmatic politics, and an initially weak state. We just explored an explanation for why we see a larger informal sector in colonies that had lower levels of European settlement. Figure 3.6 illustrates that the extent of colonial settlement is also positively correlated with the extent of programmatic linkages in the party structure according to DALP data from 2008. And, Figure 3.7 shows how (1) programmatism and state capacity are positively correlated across sub-Saharan African countries, and (2) how the stronger, more programmatic states are all found in former settler colonies with the exception of Botswana which I return to below.

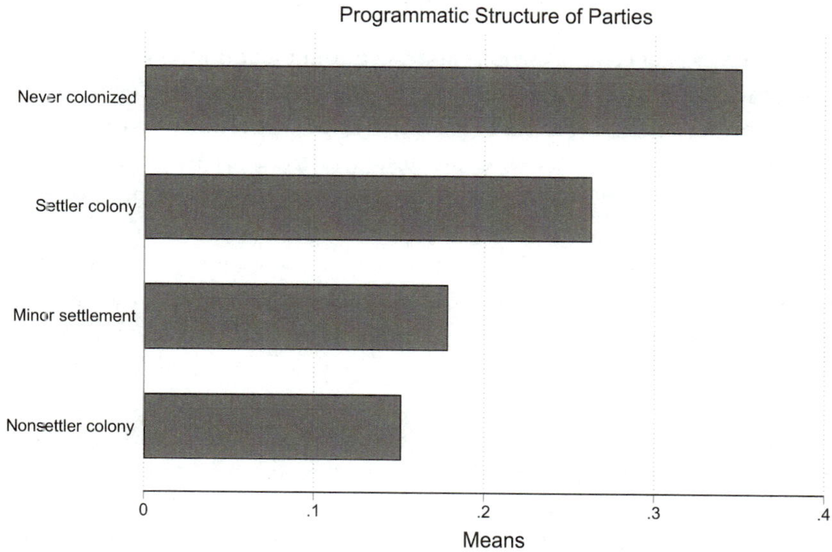

FIGURE 3.6 Programmatism by colonial status.

Note: The summarized data are averages of an index of questions about the extent to which parties advocate for state-led, universalistic social policies from the DALP dataset collected in 2008 (Kitschelt 2013). Categories are constructed according to colonial settlement data from Easterly and Levine (2016).

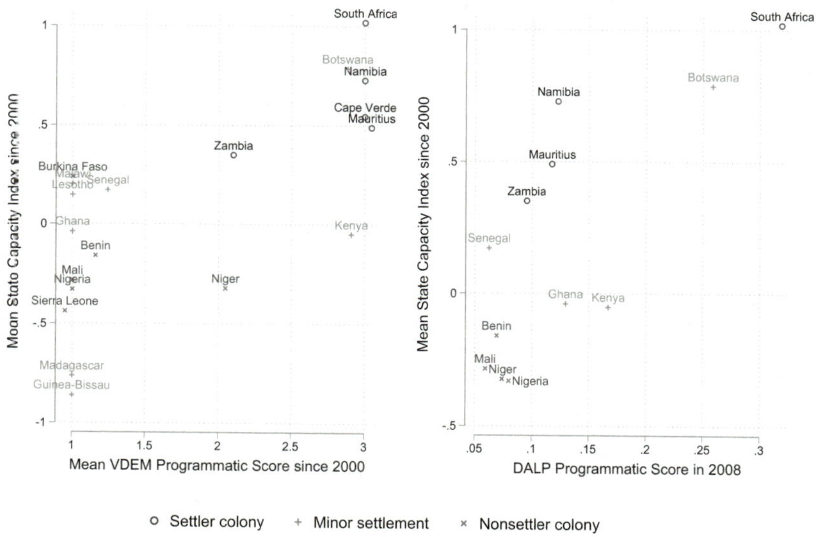

FIGURE 3.7 Programmatism and capacity by settlement patterns in Africa.

Former Colonies with Constituencies for Programmatism

While the existence of a broad-based economic coalition with political power was rare in Africa's largely nonsettler ex-colonies, the same is not so for former settler colonies. In a comparative case study of when we see state-building in postcolonial countries, Saylor (2014) shows that countries that had exporters as constituent members of the majority political coalition granted more public goods during the boom times in favor of the exporters. By contrast, in countries where the majority coalition was led mostly by political elites without such an economic base, increases in public goods provisioning did not take place. Instead, increased demands were either quashed through material side payments or pacified via means of coercion or co-optation.

Consistent with Shefter's (1977) emphasis on the importance of a constituency for programmatism, these "export-oriented" coalitions consistently implemented policies that contributed to the growth of state capacity, for example, new transportation infrastructure and credit accessibility to help maximize profit from export opportunities. Notably, Saylor's (2014) successful cases were mainly settler colonies: Argentina, Chile, and Mauritius. The two failed cases in Africa were nonsettler colonies: Nigeria and Ghana.

Botswana is an exception that helps prove the rule.[10] Within Africa, it is the only nonsettler ex-colony[11] with both a highly programmatic electoral linkage mechanism and a relatively capacious state. While others have discussed historical reasons for Botswana's anomalous status among other nonsettler ex-colonies,[12] this produced two particularities of relevance to my argument: preexisting institutions (not destroyed by colonization) that encouraged restraint and imbued political actors with

[10] I thank an anonymous reviewer for the helpful suggestion about framing the Botswana case in this way.

[11] Easterly and Levine (2016) code it as having 0.8 percent European settlement compared to 1.2 percent in Senegal.

[12] Historical features contributing to Botswana's uniqueness include (1) precolonial institutions were relatively strong with both deliberative and accountability features, (2) precolonial conflict to defend against a common enemy (the Afrikaners) both united the disparate ethnic and linguistic groups and prevented large-scale precolonial European settlement by the Boer, (3) the British were relatively uninterested in the colony blunting the impacts of colonization, and (4) the postindependence party made an unusual decision to keep a considerable number of expatriate European staff in the bureaucracy until the local cadres were sufficiently prepared to take over, contributing to a more autonomous and professionalized bureaucracy from the outset (Robinson, Acemoglu and Johnson 2003).

longer time horizons because of expectations of stability, and autonomous economic actors holding political power.

First, while nominally democratic, Botswana's ruling party from independence until 2024 had a strong hold on power and the long time horizons needed to invest in the state that other African leaders in more competitive places lack. Chapter 6 provides evidence to support the claim that political competition reduces investments in state capacity. In this way, Botswana doesn't meet the scope conditions of the puzzle that motivate the book: why *competitive* elections are not incentivizing leaders to invest in the state. Second, most of Botswana's economic activity is heavily concentrated in just a few sectors, and formal owners of capital were integrated into politics from the independence. The theory suggests that these initial conditions should have made it relatively easier for voters to coordinate around, and the state to respond to, coherent programmatic policy demands.

Early economic development in Botswana focused on the rural sector, and cattle ranching in particular, contributing to a "rising rural capitalist class" that was compared to the "settler political elites" in Rhodesia (modern-day Zimbabwe) and their government by farmer-politicians (Good 1992, 73). This developing economic class was directly integrated into politics; in the early years, two-thirds of the National Assembly consisted of large- to medium-size cattle owners. This can be contrasted with the urban elite who drove much of the rural policymaking elsewhere on the continent (Bates 1981). This phenomenon of government by property owners was less possible elsewhere on the continent, where property rights for local economic actors had been explicitly removed during the colonial period. While marketing boards elsewhere were controlled by elites without an economic basis in agriculture, cattle ranchers controlled the market board for beef. It thus invested in subsidies like veterinary and extension services as well as cattle fencing that increased productivity in their sector.

Botswana's postindependence trajectory thus more closely resembles that of European states where legislatures were primarily formed from among local barons, for example, wealthy aristocrats or property owners, who could effectively check the chief executive's power because of his dependence on these local elites for material resources. Opalo (2019) notes that this institutional process was often thwarted in postcolonial Africa, where local leaders had been stripped of their ability to accumulate independent wealth and exercise autonomous power. This is not to say that powerful local elites do not today exist in Africa, but rather that the power balance between the postcolonial elites that inherited executive power in the capital and local elites in the periphery was far more skewed toward the center compared to European cases of institution-building – except in rare cases like Botswana.[13]

Summing Up

In this final section of this chapter, I posited that we should be particularly likely to see embedded informality emerge in contexts of nonsettler colonization. The Senegal case illustrated how colonial powers found it economically advantageous to reduce competition from indigenous populations and how restricting formal market access to Europeans was an effective way to do this. A different logic emerged in settler colonies, where indigenous labor was required and so local populations were welcomed rather than barred from entry into formal markets. Contemporary data is consistent with the prediction that nonsettler colonies should see larger informal sectors, lower levels of programmatism, and lower state capacity. These contexts are thus of greatest relevance to the book's argument about the weak-state trap and informality's contribution to keeping it weak.

13 Robinson, Acemoglu and Johnson (2003) are careful to point out that other postcolonial African countries had political elites with strong economic interests, such as in Ghana and Côte d'Ivoire, but the difference was that the political base of those elites was narrow, so investing in productivity that would generate broad-based development was politically threatening and resulted in distortionary policies.

4

Informality as a Constraint to Programmatic Claim-Making

If embedded informality is indeed persistent – closing off a first pathway out of the weak-state trap that would involve a growing formal sector, I argued that a second potential pathway out is an increase in programmatic claim-making. In this chapter, however, I provide evidence from a variety of sources that embedded informality constrains programmatic claim-making. First, historical evidence from Senegal illustrates the rarity of organized claim-making by the informal sector and why any attempts have been short-lived. Second, an original in-person survey of formal and informal sector members in Dakar from 2017 directly tests implications of the argument that informality reduces expectations of state capacity and the ability to coordinate around shared preferences for public goods. Third, a phone survey of formal and informal firms in the run-up to the 2022 local elections provides evidence that the informal sector is less likely to vote for candidates who have a more programmatic platform.

Others have argued that democratically elected leaders will be motivated to invest in state development when the majority group has an "encompassing" interest in the market (Olson 1993). In other words, the majority of citizens benefit from increasing market productivity; therefore, they will also support investments in state capacity to provide the public goods necessary to facilitate such increases. But do all groups of economic agents have an "encompassing" interest in the market? Consider some of the members of the informal sector in this book's primary case, Senegal.

There is a tailor working in an informal market in a large, enclosed stall. His success depends little on the state. When he needed a loan for a sewing machine to start his business, he did not go to a formal bank but rather a peer-to-peer savings group. He was able to start and run his business with only an elementary school education, and he plans to send his son to a non-state Koranic school like many in the informal sector. He pays some tax on his profits, but they are collected irregularly; the amount and timing vary according to the whims of the collectors. When he and fellow vendors in the market have a common need, they do not demand it of the government; they instead rely on each other to respond to the need themselves. For instance, they all contribute to a common fund to pay for security at the market. This doesn't mean he's disinterested in politics. He voted for Macky Sall in 2019 because of promises to decrease the price of rent and rice. While that promise was initially kept after reelection, the price reductions were only temporary.

In another part of town, a small business shows its success with a permanent, fixed shop location on a regular city street (not inside an outdoor market). This multiservice shop meets the office needs of clients, ranging from printing to collating to selling office supplies. The younger brother of the shop-owner runs the shop. He doesn't speak French but considers himself an intellectual. They pay tax on their turnover, but he says the amount of tax you pay in his type of work is based on who you know. Because his older brother is friends with someone in the mayor's office, his tax burden is reduced. His vote choice is also based on personal connections. His older brother is in the incumbent's party and close to the general secretary, so he voted for the incumbent.

An owner of another brick-and-mortar store, a *quincaillerie* or hardware store, considers himself a member of the middle class because he eats enough and is never indebted. He tries to pay tax in the legal way by declaring his revenue in person at the Treasury (rather than waiting for collectors to come assess). But when he goes, they ask him to wait for an agent from the mayor's office to come because they want to get their percentage. He said he doesn't think there's any bloc voting among members of the middle class like him; they are individually targeted by parties like everyone else during elections. However, he thinks that salaried workers are more listened to than informal firm owners like him because they pay more in taxes; they also have direct benefits from the state like health insurance and pensions.

One commonality across all three of these members of the informal sector is that they said they would rather pay tax and have those taxes fund public services than to not pay tax at all. This suggests a latent willingness to pay tax among an under- or irregularly taxed sector. All are also self-proclaimed members of the "middle class," either because they say they are able to satisfy their needs or because they are satisfied with their station in life.

Now let's look at some members of the formal sector. One public sector employee has worked in a number of posts in his long career, including an elementary school teacher, a school inspector, and even in the state agency for preschool education. He always paid tax through monthly deductions on his paycheck. But he thinks taxes on salaried people like him are too low, and that taxes on enterprises are also too low, not sufficiently progressive, and collected too irregularly – favoring some for personal reasons. He doesn't vote because he says all the parties are the same and do not have the potential to change the system in ways that are needed.

A private sector employee working at DHL also sees himself as a member of the middle class which he defined as having a salary that allows you to pay rent, education, food, and support family members – but not necessarily enough to save. He votes on the basis of past performance and compared the public goods delivered by the past two presidents. One built infrastructure, gave health care to the elderly, and created a park. The other has done less well attracting foreign investment but built a new port and infrastructure, including a high-speed train. He thinks taxes are too high relative to what the government provides, though. Education quality and teacher pay are declining, and there is not enough support for small businesses to make markets more competitive.

Now, let's return to our question of whether these citizens would be considered as having an "encompassing" interest in the market that could produce support for investments in productivity-enhancing public goods. The informal sector enterprises often seem to be successful in spite of rather than because of any government actions. Goods like education, security, and credit access are provided informally, and shop-owners do not seem to expect anything different from the government. This chapter shows that these divergent relationships to the state have implications for political preferences and electoral behavior.

In particular, I study how variation in the regularity of citizen-state interactions in the economic sphere conditions political attitudes. Some citizens interact with the state in regularized ways that reflect the implementation of written policy and that are carried out by state bureaucrats. Others interact with the state in highly irregular ways that might include discretion over payments or services, the use of non-state intermediaries, or exchanges that have no legal or policy backing. These differential experiences affect whether people believe that the state has the capacity to provide public goods, and whether they expect gifts from politicians in exchange for votes or support.

The chapter provides two types of evidence for this claim. First, it uses a narrative case of the major informal business association in Senegal, UNACOIS, to explore whether, historically, the informal sector has been able to coordinate to make programmatic demands on the state. There is little past evidence of this; instead, the case highlights how the demands of a largely informal business sector differ from those of formal business lobbies like those in the US and Britain that were instrumental in pushing the state toward programmatic politics (Kuo 2018). Second, the chapter uses novel survey data from urban Senegal to directly test the implication outlined in Chapter 2 that the informality of one's relationship to the state affects expectations of state capacity and the value of public goods, with consequences for whether voters discipline politicians along a programmatic dimension.

The history of business interests in Senegal described in the previous chapter exposed how a large proportion of indigenous capital accumulation independent of the state is currently occurring in the informal sector. It also provided a concrete example of how the colonial project drove indigenous capital into the informal sector with policies that implicitly made Senegalese firms and entrepreneurs unable to compete with foreign ones. This raises the question of whether the informal sector or an *informal* bourgeoisie can serve as a driver of a transition to programmatic politics in the same way that formal corporate interests have sometimes played this role in the West. To address this question, I thus examine two constituencies within the informal sector: large and small informal firms, studied using the more historical case narrative and original survey data, respectively. Each group of firms has distinct preferences with respect to state engagement, but neither has incentives to demand that the state invest in capacity-building.

Large informal business owners have coordinating capacity and political capital that small business owners lack. But when they mobilize to make demands on the state, the demands tend to be state-undermining rather than state-reinforcing. In particular, the comparative advantage of large informal firms is precisely their informality – the fact that they can escape regulation and taxation. They thus primarily demand forbearance from the state, as paying their true fiscal burden would be very costly.

Small informal business owners benefit much less from forbearance. They are subject to informal forms of taxation, and the taxes they would or do pay formally are relatively low. They do not mobilize around forbearance or make negative claims on the state in the same way as the large informal firms. However, they do not tend to mobilize around positive claims on the state either. I show in Section 4.2 that this lack of mobilization is rooted in low expectations of state capacity.

4.1 DEMANDS FOR A WEAKER STATE IN THE INFORMAL SECTOR

The informal sector was largely politically unmobilized during the initial postindependence decades. Then, structural adjustment policies of the 1980s and 90s would incentivize the state to increase taxes on the informal sector. As we will see, this has the effect of mobilizing large informal firms to demand lower taxes and forbearance from the state.

During this time, the entire economy is also growing more competitive. As the state relinquished control of the economy, capital in the informal sector was more competitive and broke up trading monopolies held by ex-colonial firms (Boone 1994). Lebanese firms were one beneficiary; Senegalese members of the Mouride Islamic order, in particular, were another. Business interests linked to the Mouride brotherhood that initially grew wealthy from the rise of contraband commercial circuits in the 1970s, eventually came to dominate the commercial sector in Dakar by the 1990s. But while Mouride networks may have been at the forefront of this growing informal sector, there was a continued diversification of the origin of its members (Thioub, Diop and Boone 1998).

At the same time as liberalization policies were making informal sector business interests more competitive, they also created new pressures for the state to increase revenue. This led to state attempts to capture the informal sector in the fiscal net, something which the state had long been loath to do as it relied on the mass base of the informal sector for political support and on "Mouride leaders to rally or calm their followers at times of political crisis" (Boone 1994).

The Case of UNACOIS

New fiscal pressure by the state was a "catalyst for the political mobilization of informal-sector business" (Thioub, Diop and Boone 1998). Such mobilization was mainly organized through UNACOIS, the Union Nationale des Commerçants et Industriels du Sénégal, which itself was born out of traders' resistance to a 1989 state policy of fiscal strengthening. Distinct from the way that Mouride leaders had previously intermediated the relationship between the informal sector and the state,

UNACOIS "eschewed a political strategy that rest[ed] on the personal brokerage of big religious leaders" (Thioub, Diop and Boone 1998). UNACOIS's founding leaders, who were younger and rose to prominence in the informal sector, were thus different from the first generation of Senegal's postcolonial business class that "was dependent on state promotion and imbricated in the ruling party's political networks" (Thioub, Diop and Boone 1998).

Inspired by labor movements elsewhere, UNACOIS used direct action and mass protest throughout the 1990s to make collective demands such as a reduction in taxes or distortionary quotas. When the government attempted to increase the VAT rate and customs duties by 5–6% in 1989, traders in Dakar closed their shops and halted business in protest. Throughout the 1990s, UNACOIS continued to bargain with the government along two major points of contention: the government's import and distribution monopolies and its attempt to raise taxes on the informal sector. It did this, in part, through its role as the leading business association in the Dakar Chamber of Commerce (after winning the 1991 elections) and other consultative organizations. But when these negotiations were frustrated, UNACOIS resorted to threats such as withdrawing bank deposits, suspending import–export activities, and even strikes. These actions not only won UNACOIS popular legitimacy, but they also worked to some extent to stave off fiscal increases like the extension of the VAT tax.

While this evidence of mass protest and ability to influence policy appears to signal the rise of consolidating informal business interests, it rests on a shaky foundation. First, there is an inherent paradox in the two major demands of the organization. On the one hand, UNACOIS sought "equal treatment under the law" for entrepreneurs seeking access to state-controlled commerce, while on the other hand, it defended the fiscal privileges of its members (Thioub, Diop and Boone 1998). Second, the organization is led by a handful of the biggest informal merchants who amassed their wealth through a combination of commerce, migration, and contraband trade, but it relies on the masses of smaller ones for political legitimacy. That these two sets of actors have very different preferences and demands is another source of instability. The masses of smaller-scale traders in the organization do not have as much to gain by preserving tax forbearance, but follow the larger merchants due to ties of credit and business relationships. And finally, the organization vetoes government actions, but provides no feasible alternative economic plan. A policy of continued fiscal forbearance is not sustainable.

Writing in the 1990s, Thioub, Diop and Boone (1998) predicted the downfall of UNACOIS, stating "the organization may not outlive the circumstances that promoted its rise." Indeed, in the decades since, UNACOIS has fractured multiple times, its membership has declined, and it has lost its credibility with the government. The first fracture occurred in 1997–1998 when the organization splintered into two – UNACOIS-DEF and UNACOIS Association – as a result of a governing dispute among founding members (Dabo 2018). The groups reunified in 2007 under the banner UNACOIS-JAPPO, *jappo* meaning "togetherness" in Wolof. One struggle during this time was over the question of how to handle the influx of cheap Chinese imports, reflecting the divergent interests of the large importers seeking to maintain their competitiveness in the market and the small distributors valuing low-priced goods as well as more open access to distribution channels controlled by the large traders (Marfaing and Thiel 2013).

The second fracture occurred in 2007 following a protest by street traders decrying their eviction from Dakar – a direct action among smaller traders from which UNACOIS was notably absent. UNACOIS was even reported to have supported the evictions in a letter to the mayor (Brown, Msoka and Dankoco 2015). This lack of support led to the formation in 2009 of new profession-based vendor associations and several umbrella groups (Greven 2017). During this time, the number of members in UNACOIS-JAPPO receded from 100,000 to 70,000 (Bak 2024). The year 2017 marked yet a third fracture with a group of members leaving to create UNACOIS-YEESSAL due to continued disputes over governance (Bak 2024).

Whereas UNACOIS's early bargaining with the state appeared to successfully negotiate the divergent interests of the large and small traders within the organization, later state interactions more clearly promoted the interests of the larger merchants.[1] For example, UNACOIS bargained with the state in 2006 to alter the details of a recently instituted tax scheme – the *Contribution Globale Unique* (CGU), a lump-sum tax on commercial actors with a turnover below 50 million CFA.[2] UNACOIS successfully demanded that the state lower rates for the highest tax brack-

[1] Meagher (2011) exposes similar examples from Nigeria where the interests of the poorest actors within informal business associations are consistently marginalized.

[2] UNACOIS was also involved in the creation of the CGU, which replaced the earlier *forfait* and could potentially have lowered the effective tax on this sector, in addition to requiring less paperwork and bureaucracy (DGID official, Dakar, July 14, 2022). Indeed, average tax collected per firm fell in the first years of the CGU even as more firms were paying it (Bak 2024).

ets (by as much as two-thirds) and raise them for the lowest brackets (Bak 2024). In a second example, UNACOIS bargained with the government to undermine the monopsony on sugar importation held by the Compagnie Sucrière Sénégalaise (CSS), the largest private employer in Senegal. But only a few large traders benefited from the newly expanded access to this market (Mbaye, Golub and English 2018).[3]

UNACOIS's leadership thus walked a fine line. They sought to advance their own interests, which often diverge from those of their members. But their expansive membership was what provided them with the legitimacy to bargain successfully. UNACOIS's declining will or ability to negotiate these countervailing interests led to its decline in membership and in its perceived legitimacy as the voice of the informal sector. One focus group member[4] highlights this growing divide by stating a clear contrast between "us" and "UNACOIS." When asked who constituted "us," he answered "the informal sector," explaining that UNACOIS is for big people and not for them. He elaborated that UNACOIS makes noise but does not participate or "come down here." He wouldn't mind throwing in his lot with UNACOIS, but they do not play "their true role." Even the state tax office, the DGID, recognizes that UNACOIS leaders are speaking only on behalf of themselves and several large firms and not the masses of smaller vendors. One DGID official said that it is only the big firms that have access to negotiations with the state, and that UNACOIS represents only a small group of these.[5]

This has had clear implications for UNACOIS's ability to bargain with the state. For instance, they denounced a new tax instrument implemented in 2012 that was meant to encourage informal importers to register and pay tax. The *Acompte BIC* is a three percent advance payment on profits that is deducted from tax liabilities after declaring tax each year that would make it harder for informal importers to escape their fiscal burden. UNACOIS has been unable to change the new tax policy and even declined an invitation by the state to engage in dialogue (Bak 2024).

[3] UNACOIS and CSS continued to make opposing demands on government over the next decade with policy swinging back and forth between the two camps. Interestingly, though, UNACOIS-YESSAL broke from UNACOIS-JAPPO in 2018, aligning with the protectionist claims of the local sugar industry (Baba 2018).

[4] These focus groups were led by Dr. Ane Karoline Bak Foged in 2022 as part of a different project. The information contained here is based on email communications with Foged on July 7, 2023.

[5] Interview with the author. Dakar, July 14, 2022.

Lessons from the Case

The UNACOIS case is an example of successful coordination and political mobilization within the informal sector. On the one hand, it exposes the types of collective demands that might be typical of an organized informal sector constituency. On the other hand, its evolution demonstrates some of the key challenges to coordination within the sector, stemming largely from disparate interests across large and small firms.

Some of UNACOIS's initial demands could be construed as calls for bureaucratic autonomy. The government monopoly on rice importation created a system of patronage based on the granting of rice quotas that generated "enormous rents for marabouts, politicians, traditional notables, and other strategic political allies of the regime." UNACOIS, initially comprised of a broader constituency of informal entrepreneurs with varying levels of connectedness to the regime, thus supported liberalization policies demanding "that those at lower levels of the rice distribution circuit be allowed to bypass the rent-collecting intermediaries at the top" (Thioub, Diop and Boone 1998).

Other demands went in the opposite direction: Calls for member firms to remain sheltered from taxation and regulation instead had the effect of undermining the state. These distinct demands reveal differences across the constituencies that would benefit from state strengthening. The elimination of rents from intermediaries would most benefit the smallest traders, while tax forbearance is of most benefit to the large merchants.

From this discussion, it is not clear whether a large informal sector is necessarily antithetical to programmatic claim-making. Indeed, as liberalization policies undermined the prominence of businessmen whose wealth was propped up by a dependence on the state, there was a hope that informal merchants whose prosperity was independent of the state could serve as an autonomous and robust counterpoint to the state's venality. But because the informal sector's success – at least for the larger merchants – relied upon forbearance by the state rather than on some version of fiscal exchange, the resultant political pressure undermined rather than promoted state strength. In other words, it is not that informal firms are incapable of coordinating to exert pressure on the state and its economic policies. Instead, the value of the state to some informal firms derives from its absence. Formal firms may want limited taxation, but are generally willing to pay something in exchange for the spending on infrastructure, security, and other public goods that make markets secure.

A revision then to the argument is that economic informality is antithetical to the kind of programmatic claims *that require state strength*, claims based on some notion of a social contract rather than on forbearance. The possibility of forbearance as a programmatic claim is more likely to arise in this context of a bifurcated economy where the formal sector pays into state coffers, and the informal sector cannot be excluded from the public goods they finance. Were the economy to be completely informal and non-taxpaying, informal traders would want roads, electricity, and some measure of public security that are all necessary for business. So to the extent that informality breeds demands for forbearance, the existence of a formal sector makes these demands possible.

4.2 LOW EXPECTATIONS AMONG SMALL FIRMS IN SENEGAL

In this section, I test Hypotheses 1–3 articulated in Chapter 2 about the mechanisms through which economic informality undermines programmatic claim-making.[6] I argued that one's relationship to or experience with the state conditions the perceived expectation that the state has the capacity to provide a public good. A citizen who experiences informal or highly irregular interactions with the state will perceive the state to be less able to provide public goods relative to a citizen who has a regular or more formal relationship to the state. This variation in one's relationship to the state also has implications for how you perceive others in your economic sector, and for your ability to coordinate with them. To directly test these hypotheses, I conducted an original survey among a population of formal and informal economic actors in urban Senegal. I constructed a sample that was intended to maximize variation across the dimension of interest: the regularity of one's relationship to the state.

I measure this construct by focusing on one of the most important interactions an individual has with the state: taxation. While I expect this construct – regularity of interactions with the state – to covary with informal status, definitions of informality can be highly context-specific and too stark to capture other interesting variation outside the formal/informal binary. I thus include informal and formal actors in the sample and examine within- in, addition to cross-sector, variation in one's relationship to the state. Outcomes of interest to the theory include expectations of state capacity, the ability to coordinate with others in your sector, and preferences for a programmatic politician.

[6] These and other analyses were originally presented in a published paper (Gottlieb 2024).

Data Collection: Taxpayers in Urban Senegal

The main data I describe in this section is from an in-person survey conducted in Dakar in 2017 that asked questions about experience with taxation, demands on and expectations of government, and other political beliefs. Thirteen of Dakar's 43 urban communes, each with its own local government, were sampled first on the basis of eligibility – having sufficient concentration of informal sector businesses – and then on the basis of representativeness with respect to local political competition. To maximize variation in type of experience with the state, the survey targeted two distinct samples of participants drawn from the informal and formal economic sectors. Among private businesses, wealth is highly correlated with formality, so sampling only among private businesses would have risked conflating informality with wealth level, which can have its own independent effect on political beliefs. I thus targeted samples of participants from the formal and informal sectors likely to be closer in wealth level.

To construct the "informal sector sample," I recruited small, street-level business owners who largely tend to be informal. They include people selling wares and providing services such as tailors, carpenters, metalworkers, and hairdressers. To avoid sampling individuals who would consider themselves poor rather than middle class, I targeted businesses operating inside a physical storefront and thus with some measure of stability. (This excluded market or ambulatory vendors.) Confirming the effectiveness of this strategy in recruiting informal vendors, the vast majority of participants (96 percent) were unable to provide a NINEA – a national identification number received upon registering a business or association with the state.[7] Additionally, when asked which of the small businesses declared business revenues to the Tax Office in the preceding year (the procedure for formal tax payments), only six percent of respondents said they did. And, only six percent of respondents among the small business sample had ever heard of the CGU – the tax code that would apply to these businesses based on their small size.

To construct the "formal sector sample," I recruited salaried workers with jobs in both private and public sector institutions, such as bank tellers and teachers (about 1/4 private sector and 3/4 public). While there

7 Analyses in the next section are robust to excluding the 4 percent of vendors who had a registration number from the "informal sample".

are important differences in these economic sectors, for example, in mean level of education, the vast majority of participants in both consider themselves members of the middle class (91 percent in the formal sector and 84 percent in the informal sector).

Different sampling strategies were used to recruit participants of each type. Due to lack of availability, salaried participants were recruited purposively and using a snowball method from local public functions (e.g., teachers, police officers, public transport workers, nurses) and from larger formal businesses (e.g., banks, insurance agencies). For the small businesses, enumerators randomly sampled street-level businesses in sample communes using a random walk method among a subset of neighborhoods that were themselves selected randomly using a grid.

Though almost equivalent proportions of respondents in the formal and informal sectors say they pay tax on their income (salary or revenue), their interactions with the regulatory and fiscal arms of the state are quite distinct. For most salaried workers, the fiscal relationship with the state is systematic: Expected amounts of tax are deducted from their paychecks in the same way and on a regular basis. By contrast, informal businesses often pay income tax but do so on an irregular basis and in unsystematic ways. I now turn to examining whether such variation in the fiscal experience with the state correlates with programmatic demands on the state and citizens' capacity to coordinate demands.

To provide evidence of the ways in which economic informality can weaken the incentive and ability of citizens to coordinate to make programmatic demands of the state, I rely on two measures. I use both a dichotomous measure of informality that compares the almost entirely informal small businesses to the almost entirely formal salaried workers and a continuous measure. Motivated by the theory's emphasis on irregularity of the relationship to the state, the latter is constructed using measures of the regularity of tax payment as a proxy for one's formal fiscal relationship to the state and the signals it sends about fiscal capacity. Among salaried workers, 74 percent said they were paid by direct deposit, which requires both a formal bank account and a taxpayer ID, evidence of compliance with fiscal regulations. Among the 19 percent of salaried respondents who instead are paid in cash, only about half said they pay income tax. The remaining few who are paid by check look more like the direct-deposit group than the cash group, paying income taxes 80 percent of the time.

In spite of infrequent tax payment through the formal channel, 71 percent of small business owners said they still paid income tax on their business.[8] Among these participants, there is variation in both when, where, and how income tax is paid. Only 60 percent paid the total amount asked on the spot. About 10 percent paid the amount asked but over time, and more still said they paid multiple times per year – some up to once a month. In terms of where they paid, 55 percent of small businesses said they paid taxes to agents who came to their place of work, 21 percent said they went to the town hall to remit their tax payment, and 14 percent said they paid to the Treasury. Among those who were visited by agents, the vast majority said the agents were from the local government, although 26 percent said the agent was accompanied by a member of the federal government (the Tax Office or Treasury) and 13 percent said they were accompanied by a police officer.[9] And even though the presence of national bureaucrats is supposed to ensure that regulations are followed and tax payments get deposited into the Treasury, about 34 percent of informal businesses said they negotiated tax payment with the tax collector.

Informality Lowers Expectations of Government

To test whether those who have a more informal fiscal relationship with the state also have lower expectations of government performance (Hypothesis 2), I examine differences across respondents in answers to the following two survey questions.

I. *If the Commune Government wants to improve all of the roads in the commune, it will do this quickly and without problems.*

II. *Let's say the Government of Senegal (local government) received 1.8 billion USD (18 million USD) in tax receipts last year. What proportion of this will be put to good use, on things like public goods and services, for example?*

8 Suggesting this is not an artifact of response bias, self-reported compliance for real estate tax (paid by owners and renters) is only 15 percent. Under an expectation of response bias, some individuals should be more prone to dissembling than others, but self-reports of these two taxes are uncorrelated (the correlation coefficient is actually negative).

9 While formal legislation indicates that a team of four agents – from the local government, Treasury, Tax Office, and police – is supposed to collect taxes from informal vendors, survey data indicate this team is rarely complete.

To increase power in the within-sector analyses, I collapse the categories of how informal firms pay tax into two. I consider firms as paying in a *more* formal way when they either declare their taxes (this is rare) or pay everything asked on the spot. *Less* formal ways of paying thus include negotiating with the tax collector and/or paying over a period of time. Comparing responses to Question I shows that firm owners who pay in a more formal way indeed have higher perceptions of local government capacity in that they are significantly more likely to agree that the government will improve roads in the commune if it wants to.

I now investigate how answers to Question II vary across the sample. Depicted as the dependent variable in regression models in Table 4.1, a more formal fiscal relationship with the state is associated with higher expectations of (national and local) government performance. This is true both across (Panel A) and within (Panels B & C) samples of survey respondents. Within the informal sector sample, this relationship is stronger for perceptions of the local government relative to the national government, which is not surprising given the implication of local governments in actual tax collection. The reverse is true for formal sector participants. Columns 2 and 5 show that simple correlations with the main independent variables are robust to controlling for observable respondent characteristics that might produce omitted variable bias. This relationship is robust to adding commune-level fixed effects, mitigating an additional concern that the relationship of interest is instead driven by variation in commune-level capacity to provide services.

As I describe more fully in a companion paper (Gottlieb 2024), there are two complementary mechanisms that reinforce the negative relationship between informality and programmatic demands. First, one's own experience of irregular tax collection should lead to inferences that other taxpayers are more likely to escape taxation altogether or only pay intermittently. The perception of lower levels of tax compliance has direct negative implications for beliefs about the size of the public budget, supported by the evidence above. A larger government budget is more likely to be able to fund public programs, potentially inciting more demand for public goods that citizens previously thought were infeasible.

Second, an individual's irregular interactions with the state can generate uncertainty about how the state is interacting with other potential taxpayers. Because formal tax payment is based on written policy and undergirded by bureaucratic process, a taxpayer interacting through formal channels has a precise idea of the experience of other formal taxpayers. When they themselves interact in a formal way, they will be more likely

TABLE 4.1 *Formality of tax payment and expectation of government spending on public goods*

	National government			Local government		
Panel A: Comparing salaried workers to small businesses						
Salaried worker	5.471*	7.213*		5.040*	10.090**	
	(2.156)	(3.650)		(2.212)	(3.734)	
Constant	59.603**	61.699**		53.541**	56.254**	
	(4.482)	(6.234)		(4.592)	(6.371)	
Observations	461	459		461	459	
Controls for education, gender, age, & association	No	Yes		No	Yes	
Panel B: Comparing within small businesses						
More formal taxpayer	5.615	6.956		13.441+	14.597+	
	(7.026)	(7.699)		(7.038)	(7.700)	
Proportion group paying tax			0.147			0.185+
			(0.097)			(0.097)
Constant	54.769**	74.838**	78.935**	51.210**	78.899**	74.571**
	(9.109)	(22.330)	(16.572)	(9.125)	(22.333)	(16.608)
Observations	81	80	112	81	80	112
Controls for education, gender, age, association, & weekly profits	No	Yes	Yes	No	Yes	Yes
Panel C: Comparing within salaried workers						
Paid by direct deposit	15.078**	14.648+		6.424	10.683	
	(5.506)	(7.685)		(5.318)	(7.449)	
Paid by check	16.225	16.264		4.103	6.519	
	(9.784)	(10.552)		(9.420)	(10.143)	
Proportion group paying tax			0.168+			0.176*
			(0.085)			(0.080)
Constant	43.187**	36.427+	35.079	51.193**	57.176**	38.070+
	(9.552)	(21.498)	(21.230)	(9.204)	(20.690)	(19.929)
Observations	104	102	99	104	102	100
Controls for education, gender, age, association, & monthly salary	No	Yes	Yes	No	Yes	Yes

OLS models with enumerator fixed effects. $^{+}p < 0.10$, $^{*}p < 0.05$, $^{**}p < 0.01$. Smaller sample sizes in Panels B and C are due to the fact that tax questions needed to construct key explanatory variables were only asked among a random half of the sample, and then among those in Panel B who said they paid business taxes. The base category in Panel C is "Paid in Cash."

to assume that formal regulations are systematically applied to others in their sector. Because they infer that the state is similarly extracting from other formal taxpayers, those citizens will be better able to coordinate reciprocal demands on the state.

By contrast, informal taxpayers will form imprecise beliefs about the more idiosyncratic costs and benefits other citizens are facing in their informal exchanges with the state. In turn, beliefs about other citizens' preferences and demands will also be more uncertain. Irregular state interactions among informal taxpayers will thus impede the creation of common knowledge about the way in which other citizens like them interface with the state. Defined as a fact that everybody knows and that everybody knows that everybody knows, common knowledge is said to be one of the key enablers of coordination (Chwe 2001; Adida et al. 2020). Due to their lower levels of common knowledge, members of the informal sector should thus be less likely to see themselves as part of a constituency with shared preferences vis-à-vis state policy. I test both mechanisms – about compliance beliefs and coordinating capacity – in the next two sections.

Informality Reduces Perceptions of Tax Compliance

Let's investigate how informality conditions perceptions of tax compliance (Hypothesis 1). Lower perceptions of tax compliance have several important political implications. First, when perceived tax compliance is low, the perceived budget for public goods is necessarily lower – assuming that some tax revenue funds public goods provision. Second, when perceived tax compliance is low, perceptions of the state's enforcement capacity are also lower. And third, perceptions of low compliance can affect beliefs about whether there is a sufficient constituency of taxpayers who can credibly demand reciprocation from the state.

To evaluate perceptions of tax compliance, members of the formal and informal sector survey samples were asked the proportion of "salaried people" and "small businesses" they believed paid income tax. Consistent with Hypothesis 1, informal vendors perceive significantly lower rates of compliance in the formal sector than do salaried workers (66% vs. 74%). By contrast, salaried workers perceive significantly lower compliance in the informal sector than informal vendors themselves (35% vs. 54%) – likely because they are less aware of the irregular taxation that goes on in the informal sector.

A more convincing test examines how variation in contact with the state *within* each sector moderates perceptions of compliance in that same sector. Providing additional support, Figure 4.1 illustrates that as respon-

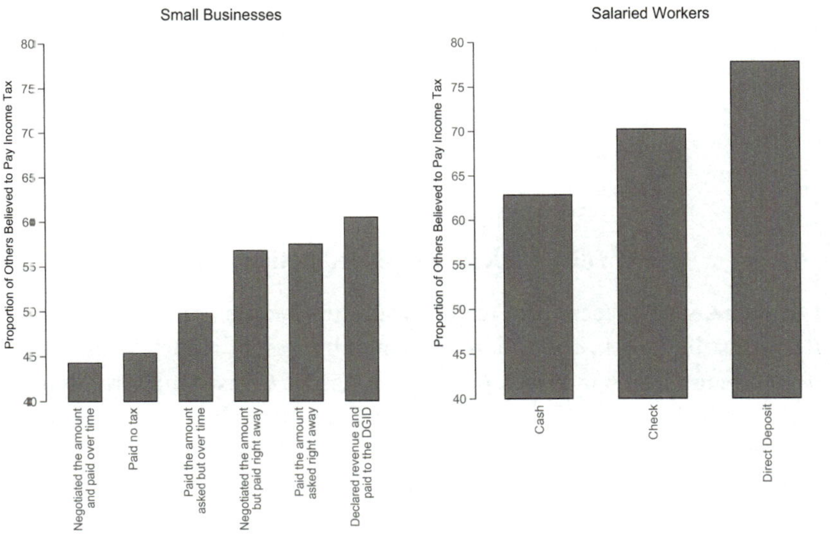

FIGURE 4.1 How people pay tax moderates beliefs about tax compliance.
Note: As respondents pay income tax in a more regularized way, their perceptions of tax compliance increase.

dents pay income tax in a more regularized way, they are more likely to believe that a greater number of other people in their sector also pay income tax.

Respondents in the informal sector are much more likely to underestimate the level of income tax compliance in their sector. While the data indicate that 71 percent of the informal sector pays income tax on their business, 70 percent of the respondents in this sample guessed less than this. By contrast, 87 percent of the formal sector sample report paying income tax, and only 49 percent of that sample underestimate this figure. Interestingly, informal sector respondents who paid no tax on their business, on average, had the same belief about the degree of tax compliance as those who paid in the most irregular way (negotiated the amount and paid over time).

This variation in beliefs about tax compliance should also contribute to higher expectations of government. To test this, Columns 3 and 6 in Panels B and C in Table 4.1 include the respondent's belief about other group members' tax compliance as an explanatory variable. Again, this is measured by asking respondents the proportion (out of 100) of others in their group (small businesses or salaried workers) who they believe pay income tax. Beliefs about higher levels of tax compliance are indeed positively and significantly correlated with expectations of government performance.

Informality Undermines Coordinating Capacity

For citizens to successfully make programmatic demands on the state, they must be able to coordinate with members of a distinct social or economic group that has shared policy preferences. Consistent with Hypothesis 3, which states that informality reduces the ability to coordinate, survey data shown graphically in Figure 4.2 illustrate how those in the formal sector have greater coordinating capacity.

First, coordination requires some shared sense of who is in your group. When asked the extent to which small business owners (salaried workers) thought their fates were linked to others like them, those in the formal sector were statistically significantly more likely to say their fates were linked. Second, the coordination of demands is facilitated by discussion with others to identify and recognize shared preferences. While the vast majority of members of the formal sector say they meet with people in their line of work to discuss problems, those in the informal sector do so much less frequently. And finally, participation in formal economic associations not only institutionalizes these types of discussions but also demonstrates a group's coordination capacity to the government. While more than half of formal sector workers are involved in an economic association, less than 10 percent of small business owners are.

While informality can restrict the development of common knowledge about others' interactions with the state, discussing problems you face in your work with others in your sector could potentially overcome this constraint. We saw in the above analyses that informality was associated with more inaccurate perceptions of tax compliance in one's own sector. Among the one-quarter of the informal sector sample who say they meet often with others in their line of work to discuss a problem, the prediction for the number of other informal sector vendors who pay tax is 6 percentage points higher – bringing it closer to the true estimate of taxpayers in this sample. This suggests that increasing coordination capacity in the informal sector could occur both by increasing the regularity of citizen-state interactions and by increasing communication and exchange within the informal sector.

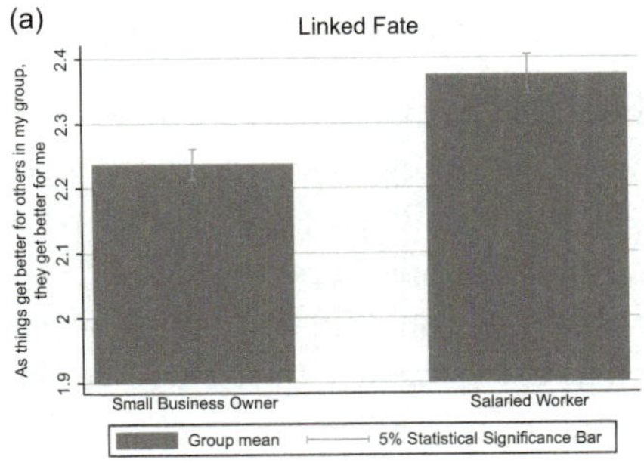

(a)

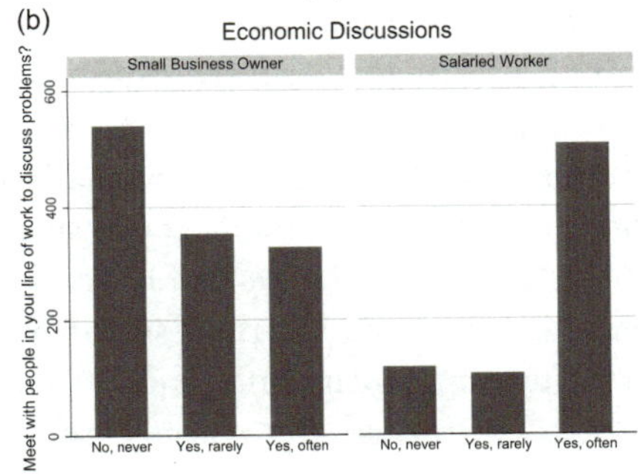

(b)

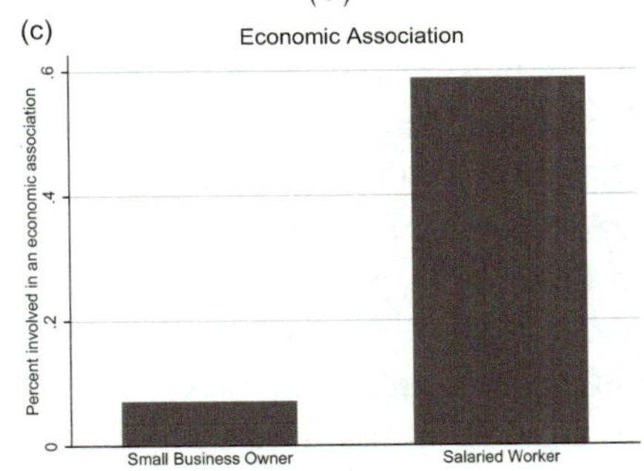

(c)

FIGURE 4.2 Formality is positively associated with concentrated preferences, perceptions of linked fate, economic discussions, and involvement in economic associations.

Note: Panel (a) shows that those in the formal sector are statistically significantly more likely to say their fates are linked with members of their economic group compared to respondents in the informal sector. Panel (b) shows that respondents in the informal sector are much less likely than formal sector respondents to say they meet with people in their line of work to discuss problems. Panel (c) shows that members of the formal sector are also much more likely to be involved in an economic association.

4.3 FORMALITY INCREASES PROGRAMMATIC PREFERENCES

In this section, I show that formal sector members not only have higher coordinating capacity, but they also are more likely to prefer programmatic policies (Hypothesis 4). As one way to illustrate variation in preferences for public goods across economic sectors, Figure 4.3, depicts responses to the question, "Of the things the national government could be doing, what is the most important?" It shows that informal and formal economic actors have qualitatively different preferences over what the national government should be doing with its budget. Salaried participants from the formal sector are much more likely to say the government should prioritize a universalistic program – education than the mostly informal small businesses (69% vs. 28%). Conversely, small businesses are more likely to say the national government should prioritize personalistic or locally excludable goods such as personal help, clean streets, or local security (20% vs. 7%). Employment, especially youth employment, and aid to the informal sector were unsurprisingly mentioned far more often among the informal sector (48 and 43 times, respectively) relative to the formal sector (only twice each). Given the different average education level across these samples, this is perhaps unsurprising.

Another data collection exercise lends additional credibility to the idea that members of the formal sector are more likely to support programmatic candidates. A separate survey conducted in 2022 evaluated the electoral preferences of informal and formal business owners just prior to local elections in Senegal. In particular, we asked participants about their support for a relatively new politician and his coalition that was credibly campaigning on programmatic issues, Ousmane Sonko. Shefter (1977) would likely consider Sonko's party to be externally mobilized, and thus more likely to reject patronage as an efficient means of vote mobilization.

Sonko, then a tax inspector, blew the whistle on government corruption in 2016 and was subsequently fired from his job by President Macky Sall. This experience gave Sonko the credibility he needed to build a political movement around a new vision of social justice and transparency (Monks 2019). In the 2019 elections, Sonko campaigned on specific economic policies, including moving away from the country's colonial era currency – the CFA franc, and reducing tax evasion and unfair expropriation by foreign firms. But Sonko only won a majority of the vote in his home region of Zinguinchor. That said, he got a respectable 20 percent of the vote in Dakar (relative to 16 percent nationally), which is consistent with the idea that voters in the formal sector (who reside primarily in the capital city) would be most likely to support him.

To better understand the relationship between formality and voter preferences for Sonko's coalition, we surveyed members of both economic sectors by phone prior to the 2022 local elections. This survey was conducted jointly with Abhit Bhandari, which allowed us to expand our sample by using participants of formal and informal sector vendors we had both recruited separately for previous studies in 2017. We surveyed more than 1,000 private business owners (about 41 percent formal and 59 percent informal), asking about support for one of the mayoral candidates and a likely 2024 presidential candidate, Ousmane Sonko.

Confirming our intuition, when asked which of the six main political coalitions best represented programmatic politics, 53 percent of survey respondents said Sonko's coalition, compared to only 22 percent saying that of the incumbent president, Macky Sall. Notably, Sall had increasingly been eroding democratic governance as evidenced by his launching criminal cases against key political rivals, repressing public demonstrations, and arbitrary arrests (Diop and Absa 2021).

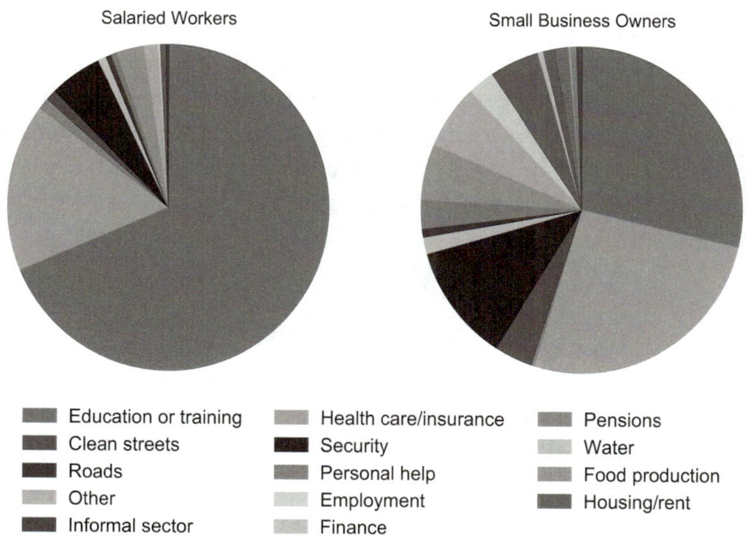

FIGURE 4.3 Priorities for the national government, by sector.
Note: The figure depicts responses to the question, "Of the things the national government could be doing, what is the most important?" Preferences in the informal sector are more fractionalized than those in the formal sector.

Comparing informal respondents to formal ones, we see several indications that informal sector respondents are less likely to support the more programmatic candidate and his coalition. Among business owners reporting party membership, formal ones were far more likely to align with Sonko's party than informal ones (43% vs. 17%). While Sonko was not himself a mayoral candidate in Dakar, formal sector respondents were more likely to say they would vote for the candidate from Sonko's coalition relative to informal sector respondents (50% vs. 38%). By contrast, informal sector respondents were more likely to say they would vote for the mayoral candidate from the incumbent coalition (BBY). And formal sector respondents say they will vote for Sonko in the 2024 elections with a significantly higher probability than informal sector respondents (59% vs. 49%). These large and significant differences in political preferences between sectors are robust to controlling for a key potential confounder, the businesses' level of revenue.

Kitschelt (2000) writes, "a rising urban white-collar and professional middle class is the first to defect from clientelism . . . The rise of professions, often associated with an expansion of a universalistic welfare state, spells the demise of clientelism." The Senegal data show that in the case of an economy with a large informal sector, we even see formal workers in nonprofessional jobs and small firms turning away from clientelism and toward programmatic candidates. While not inconsistent with the above claim that is based on modernization theory and the growing affluence of these white-collar constituents, I argue that the reasoning behind the formal sector's greater attraction to programmatic politics is somewhat different. It is not only about preferences for public goods, but it is also about expectations that the state actually has the capacity to provide them.

4.4 SUMMING UP

If we look back at Figure 3.7, we see that Senegal has a relatively middling level of state capacity among African countries but has one of the lowest levels of programmatism. So, state capacity must have reached this level in spite of, rather than because of, programmatic electoral competition. The evidence in this chapter helps to explain why this might be.

Senegal's state capacity has grown slowly over time, like that in most African countries that have not experienced major internal conflict. But this growth in capacity is likely experienced differently by the majority of economic actors who reside in the informal sector. Whereas formal sector participants may perceive these secular increases in state capacity and update their beliefs accordingly, informal sector participants should not. So the original clientelistic bargain between citizens and politicians is sustained as politicians have nothing to gain by campaigning on programmatic platforms.

Politicians may have nothing to lose either. Recall from the discussion in Chapter 2 that politicians' continuation payoffs are equivalent in each equilibrium as long as they can ensure reelection on the basis of their performance along the relevant dimension. In the next chapter, I describe one reason that politicians may be deterred from campaigning on a programmatic platform, even if it is feasible to do so and get reelected (because the probability of having a budget for public goods is sufficiently high). Politicians may face resistance from a constituency of clientelistic intermediaries who unequally benefit from the status quo.

5

Informal Intermediaries Impede Investments in the State

The third pathway out of the weak-state trap is a substantial increase in state strength, setting off a virtuous chain of events. Voters would update their beliefs about the likelihood of the state providing public goods, making them more likely to condition their vote on programmatic performance. This, in turn, would incentivize politicians to invest more in the nondiscretionary provision of public goods and services. Seeing this, members of the informal sector may find formalization more appealing in that they would have access to greater state-provided benefits. Such large increases in state capacity, however, are rare and have often been in response to exogenous shocks. The most prominent example of this in the literature is the impetus to invest in building military capacity in response to external threats, which has historically induced states to increase fiscal capacity to fund wars and bureaucratic capacity to improve investments in human capital (Tilly 1990; Downing 1992; Ertman 1997).

While such military threats are less likely to be motivating factors for today's weak states (Herbst 2014), there are other sources of exogenous pressure that could improve state strength. The World Bank and other international donors recognize the drag that state weakness can have on economic development and have, in turn, paid more attention in recent years to investing in state capacity. For example, the World Bank committed 80 million USD to a project to help the Government of Senegal map and digitize land registration to improve property rights and land tenure management. Just in the area of digitizing property registers to enable greater tax revenue collection, one report cites similar projects in 16 other countries, many supported by international donors (Knebelmann 2022).

But when the impetus to develop capacity comes from external pressure, like from these multilateral institutions, there may be limited domestic political will for governments to ensure the proper implementation of projects and, importantly, there may be powerful local actors with incentives to undermine the implementation. In particular, if there are intermediaries who benefit from their role in the discretionary allocation of goods and application of regulations, then those intermediaries would have something to lose from a transition to a more rule-based system implied by many of these capacity-increasing programs. For example, researchers studying the aforementioned World Bank-funded property tax project in Senegal randomly assigned whether bureaucrats would set property values using discretion (the status quo) or an algorithm based on newly digitized information from the project. They find that bureaucrats using discretion dramatically undervalued properties, especially more expensive ones, leading to a more regressive and less efficient outcome (Knebelmann, Pouliquen and Sarr 2023).

This chapter empirically tests the claim that embedded informality constrains the third pathway out of the weak-state trap by strengthening intermediaries: A constituency that will resist moves to make the state more programmatic and rule-based, so it can preserve a status quo based on personalism and discretion. Generating evidence for this claim requires us to leave Senegal and visit several of its neighboring countries. The reason is that we need a real or intended shock to the state's ability to implement rule-based governance in order to observe the reactions of intermediaries. I was not able to identify such a shock in Senegal, but in some of my related fieldwork, namely in Mali and Nigeria, I found useful terrain to test this conjecture. In Mali, the state was seeking to amend its policy of intergovernmental transfers to local governments to include a performance-based funding model. Local social and cultural leaders would be given an opportunity to report on the performance of local elected officials as part of the state's performance measure. In a coauthored study, we show that some of these local intermediaries are more willing to move to this programmatic performance model while others prefer the more clientelistic status quo (Bleck, Gottlieb, and Kosec 2023). In Lagos, Nigeria, the state government was seeking to induce informal market vendors to move to a formal fiscal relationship with the state. In a project with Adrienne LeBas, we study a large representative sample of Lagosian market vendors to understand whether one key intermediary, marketplace associations, is a credible partner in this formalization campaign (LeBas and Gottlieb 2025).

Before turning to these theory-testing cases, I begin the chapter by describing how embedded informality gives rise to a class of intermediaries who are necessary to link citizens to the state and the variation therein. For this descriptive exercise, I rely on qualitative fieldwork from Lagos, Nigeria and from Senegal. Some intermediaries are defined by their role in informal economic activity, such as market associations that govern informal marketplaces. Other intermediaries primarily serve political or cultural functions, such as village chiefs or religious leaders, but become important to informal economic actors as they can be a resource for credit or social insurance. What these actors have in common is coordinating capacity and access to information about members of the informal sector. The former asset makes them valuable to their members in the informal sector when making demands for particularistic transfers from the state. The latter asset makes them valuable to the state when they want to extract resources or information from those members. Not only are intermediaries valuable for discretionary distributive and extractive relationships between citizens and the state, these same intermediaries can be exploited by political parties to increase the efficiency of clientelistic electoral exchange. The chapter continues by describing and providing evidence of this key role of intermediaries in facilitating vote mobilization with the case of marketplace associations in Lagos. Especially when intermediaries serve these dual purposes of linking the bureaucratic and political state to citizens and voters, they have bargaining power they can use to extract rents from the state.

Illustrating this variation in types of intermediaries suggests that they might differentially benefit from their role in facilitating citizen–state exchange. But it is not immediately clear what might make some intermediaries value their position more than others. To generate intuition about this, I describe some of my prior research on political intermediaries in Senegal. I show that variation in capacities and communities conditions the types of strategies political intermediaries can use to mobilize citizens. Some, for example, are able to use coercion while others rely on persuasion or reciprocation. These capabilities, in turn, allow them to extract relatively more or less value from their role in state-citizen exchange.

This motivates the first empirical exercise in which I exploit within-country variation to examine one observable implication of my argument: Those who benefit more from their intermediary status will be more resistant to transitions away from the discretionary status quo. I turn to a context similar to Senegal, the neighboring country of Mali, where coauthors and I have collected data on both constructs of interest: variation in intermediary strength and willingness to transition to a less discretionary institution (Bleck, Gottlieb, and Kosec 2023). Using survey evidence from over 1,000 local civil society leaders, we show that more embedded local leaders both benefit more from their close relationship with the local government and are less willing to participate in a more rule-based policy that could curb their ability to collude.

This chapter began by motivating the idea that policies to strengthen the state might be undermined by intermediaries. The chapter concludes with case evidence in which intermediaries have done just this. I describe three country cases, starting with Lagos, Nigeria, in which intermediaries who benefit from the status quo resist policies that would result in a stronger, less discretionary state. To describe the additional cases of the Democratic Republic of Congo and India, I leverage my involvement in a coordinated field experimental research project across several country contexts – a *Metaketa* organized by EGAP.[1] In each context, researchers studied the effect of a new policy to formalize some relationship between citizens and the state. While the main goal of that multicountry research project was to understand the conditions under which citizens comply with formalization, I instead use this opportunity to test whether clientelistic intermediaries, observing these policy changes, react by resisting or impeding efforts at formalization. In at least three of the project's six country cases, we find that they do.

5.1 EMBEDDED INFORMALITY CREATES A NEED FOR INTERMEDIARIES

In a society marked by considerable legal dualism, citizens with a more formal relationship to the state make claims on the government on the basis of impersonal justiciable rights or with respect to de jure changes in law or policy (Chatterjee 2004). By contrast, citizens with a more informal relationship to the state make claims on the basis of how government largess is distributed de facto through individualized negotiation. Without recourse to a formal social contract, this latter type of citizen cannot easily make claims on the government for some of the public goods needed for their businesses, or even for their own survival. As a result, non-state

[1] See https://egap.org/our-work/the-metaketa-initiative/roundtwo-taxation/ for more information.

actors often fill the void and serve important functions usually reserved for the state, such as the provision of services or the extraction of taxes.

For example, most rural villages in Africa have some form of traditional authority structure that wields influence over important social functions like birth, marriage, and even land distribution. These authorities are frequently seen as separate from formal political authority, even if they are beholden to the state. In other cases, non-state actors take on state-like roles completely autonomously from the government. A wide range of non-state actors provide or facilitate the provision of welfare in contexts of weak states, that is, political parties, faith-based organizations, community-based organizations, family networks, and private firms (Cammett and MacLean 2014).

So one way that state weakness and its attendant economic informality can give rise to legitimate non-state actors is through a substitution effect: The legitimacy of non-state actors grows as they undertake extraction and provision of resources in the absence of the state (Dercon et al. 2006; De Weerdt and Fafchamps 2011; Auerbach et al. 2018; Lust and Rakner 2018). A second way is through a complementary effect: Intermediaries can help link the state to citizens.[2] Some linkages are political in nature, whereby intermediaries help organize collective action, lobby the government, and distribute patronage (Krishna 2011; Auerbach 2019). Other intermediaries are located principally in the economic sector, such as unions, cooperatives, and vendors or market associations (Awuah 1997; Hummel 2017; Grossman 2020). Some, as we will see, play both roles – political and economic.

Recall that a defining characteristic of embedded informality is that citizens in the informal sector interact with the state but in irregular ways. The state may take advantage of one-off opportunities to extract revenue from some informal sector members, and citizens may take advantage of ad hoc coordinating capacity or personal connections to make one-off demands for themselves or on behalf of their group. For example, most small entrepreneurs in Senegal are illegible to and unregistered with the state. The state does not have the capacity or political will to bring all unregistered businesses into compliance, but instead collects taxes in a more spontaneous fashion; in periods after holidays, when they know vendors are flush with cash, a group of state agents visits some subset of

[2] Henn (2023) shows that both types of relationships emerge with traditional leaders in Africa and that variation is explained by the extent to which these leaders are integrated into formal government structures.

street-level businesses demanding a tax on their profits. In the same way that these small businesses do not engage in formal accounting, neither does the state. Tax receipts from this type of extraction are not digitized or aggregated.

Since the formal-legal code governing taxation of small businesses does not accord with the reality of how small businesses interact with the state, it is difficult to imagine how an organized group of small businesses would lobby for formal policy change. Indeed, in the survey data from Dakar, formal sector respondents were twice as likely as respondents from the informal sector to say they contacted a government official in the previous month to discuss a problem affecting their community, discuss taxes, or demand something from the government. Instead, informal firms are more likely to seek recourse in social networks than in the state (Bhandari 2023).

Because of the inherent irregularity of their relationship with citizens in the informal sector, the state can use discretion in extraction and provision of resources. And that discretion often involves a political logic: the exchange of targeted benefits for political support. In other words, clientelism. While much of the modern scholarship on clientelism focuses on electoral relationships – the exchange of material benefits for votes – an older literature also uses the word to describe patron-client relationships of dependency that exist outside the context of vote mobilization. In both cases, however, the role of intermediaries is paramount.[3] Because patron–client ties are based on an individual's relationship with a specific leader, they tend to be very localized; there is a limited number of personal ties any single leader can accumulate. These clusters of relationships become more powerful when they are organized in a larger pyramidal structure. A single leader at the top, for example, might have personal relationships with multiple mid-level leaders who then each support their own cluster of ties to individuals at the bottom. These intermediate links in the pyramid themselves are dependent on the top-level patron but also have many individuals who are dependent on them.

Intermediaries in these networks of dependency can help the state or other political patrons solve information problems. Because the provision of goods is targeted (and sometimes revocable), patrons need to know who among the potential clients are most likely to proffer political

[3] In 1972, James Scott canonically described the multitier pyramidal structure of patron–client relationships (Scott 1972).

support. The best intermediaries are those who have access to information for a large group of potential clients. Obvious intermediaries are thus those who already serve a coordinating or leadership role and thereby have easier access to information about their members or followers. These might be village chiefs who are typically involved in local dispute resolution and community-level redistribution. They might be religious leaders who are granted legitimacy and deference on the basis of their spiritual role in a follower's life. Or they may be association heads who coordinate activities among an economic group.

As we saw in Chapter 3, religious and traditional leaders are often enmeshed in relationships of economic informality even if their primary role is not an economic one. Their legitimacy and coordinating role can make them an obvious resource for accessing credit or social insurance or for networking, all important for informal economic activity. Those leaders can, in turn, be potential mediators when informal sector members make claims on the state. Here, I will provide a more straightforward example of how explicitly economic leaders in the informal sector directly mediate relationships between members of that sector and the state. The example comes from Lagos, Nigeria, where I worked with my colleague Adrienne LeBas on a related project about informality, the state, and social intermediaries (Gottlieb, Lebas and Magat 2025; LeBas and Gottlieb 2025).

Marketplace Associations in Lagos, Nigeria

Marketplace associations in Lagos are an example of a non-state actor with all of the qualities discussed earlier. First, they provide necessary functions of governance and service provision to allow for the conduct of economic activities. Second, they mediate economic relationships between member citizens and the state. Third, they actively facilitate political clientelism. While intermediaries active in the informal sector may exhibit one or two of these characteristics, these marketplace associations exhibit all of them. I discuss each in turn.

Marketplace associations have played important social and political roles in Lagos since the colonial period. The Lagos Market Women's Association boasted 8,000 members in the 1920s (Kamm 2016). The association engaged in self-governance and organized collective action against the state, such as during tax protests in 1939. Today, marketplace associations governing each market are collectively represented at the state level by the Lagos Market Women and Men Association. The former hold meetings with members within markets, while association leaders hold weekly meetings at the state capital with executive members of the umbrella organization which, incidentally, is led by the daughter of former Governor Bola Tinubu, a role previously held by his mother.

Marketplace associations continue to serve these dual functions of self-governance and intermediation with the state. They protect vendor interests by outlawing underselling, regulating methods of attracting customers, providing appropriate sanitation facilities, and ensuring security (Olukoju 2005). Associations wield heavy sanctions in the face of rule or norm violations in the marketplace – suspensions or "lockouts" lasting up to several days. In a survey of 3,248 vendors in over 178 markets across Lagos, Gottlieb and LeBas (2022) find further evidence of the market association's role in self-governance. About half of the vendors report active involvement in their own marketplace association. Two-thirds say they would go to their marketplace association or its leader to solve problems in the market, compared with only 2.5 percent who said they would go to a government actor. Among vendors who said there was an unavoidable tax or fee they had to pay in the market, a plurality of 43 percent said that it was paid to the marketplace association.

Marketplace associations mediate relationships with the state and its members in both formal and informal ways; tax extraction is the most telling. In the past, the Lagos Internal Revenue Service (LIRS) provided a pathway to business formalization through the marketplace association. Informal sector registration drives issued tax identification cards linking the individual vendor to their association. The tax office was recently interested in establishing a direct link with vendors, thus limiting this collective pathway to formalization. However, in recognizing the importance of market associations to the economic life of vendors, they tasked our research team with understanding whether and how these associations could more informally persuade vendors to formalize their relationship to the state (Gottlieb, Lebas and Magat 2025). Currently, when the LIRS visits individual markets to promote formalization and tax compliance, they first establish stakeholder agreements with the leadership of the local market association. The Informal Sector Director of the LIRS said that each market association has their own social code and a quote that they say; she learns the quote in advance and recites it when she gets there to earn their respect. She said she's not afraid to get down and kneel before the market mother, speak to them in Yoruba, and do their dances.[4] There are also examples of the marketplace association extracting benefits from the government. Olukoju (2005) describes an incident in Agege whereby the marketplace association leaders negotiated with the local government to reduce the price of market stalls from an originally inflated number.

Finally, market associations in Lagos are highly political. That the highest leader of the market associations, the *Iyaloja General* is directly related to the political "godfather" of Lagos, Bola Tinubu, reveals the partisan nature of the organization. In addition, members of the market associations "hold regular meetings of *Afenifere*, the pan-Yoruba cultural organization that produced the ruling Alliance for Democracy party ... Leaders and members of the associations have reaped political patronage in the form of government contracts and other largesse as a compensation for their incorporation into the prevailing political order" (Olukoju 2005, p. 163).

Intermediaries Are Leveraged for Electoral Mobilization

Much of this section focused on the role of intermediaries in connecting informal sector members to the state. Especially in a democracy, these intermediaries can additionally be leveraged to connect political parties with potential voters. The logic of intermediation is largely the same: The access to information, legitimacy, and trust enshrined in intermediaries can be incredibly valuable to political parties campaigning on particularistic appeals. And voters will feel more assured that political discretion will be marshaled in their favor when their own intermediaries have close ties with the likely incumbent.

Barnes (1986, p. 146) puts it well when she says (of Lagos) that parties could "[exploit] the many close ties that already existed among leaders and their clients" and put to use their "reliable, redundant control". Writing about Senegal, Beck (2008) agrees that existing dense social networks with established legitimacy and social authority outside the state are instrumentally useful to political parties seeking to mobilize votes (Beck 2008). Organizations and community leaders can use immaterial resources (existing legitimate status, bonds of trust, or social sanctions) unavailable to most parties, making them efficient political brokers.

4 Interview with the author, March 14, 2022, LIRS office.

Doing fieldwork in rural Senegal in 2012, I was struck by a common feature of every village I visited. When I asked people in the village to identify the local *intermédiare politique*, the person who served as a link between political parties and residents in the village, I was immediately given an answer. And that answer was almost always the same person, irrespective of whom in the village I asked. Even though this role was informal – neither elected nor appointed – there was unanimity in each village about who their intermédiare politique was.

The ubiquity of political intermediaries in Senegal speaks to the prevalence of collective rather than individual-level clientelistic exchange. When political parties visit villages to mobilize voters, they work through the political intermediary. Often, the intermediary has ties to a particular political party (although these ties may change over time). And when people decide who to vote for, they often take into account the advice or preferences of the political intermediary.

Clientelistic exchange – when parties trade favors or gifts for votes – does not require the presence of these intermediaries; parties can distribute directly to voters. But such exchange is far more efficient when effective brokers are in the picture. Rather than a party solidifying ties with all prospective voters, they can leverage brokers' existing connections with their own followers and their subsequent credibility or monitoring ability at the group level. The stronger the ties between brokers and voters, the better clientelism works for the party.

This intermediated strategy typically manifests as the exchange of group-level benefits for coordinated group-level voting. Such collective clientelism is good for politicians: They get blocs of votes for single transfers. But it is also good for voters: Group-level benefits often consist of club goods that people value, such as local wells or schools.

While collective clientelism does not require it in theory (small groups could spontaneously coordinate votes without the direction of an intermediary), empirically, brokers are almost always responsible for helping to coordinate blocs of votes at the group level. In contrast to some older literature on clientelism focusing on individual-level targeting (Kitschelt and Wilkinson 2007), there is a growing recognition of the importance of a broker-mediated model of clientelism (Stokes et al. 2013; Larreguy, Montiel Olea and Querubin 2017) in which the relevant unit of analysis is the group of voters being coordinated by brokers (Holland and Palmer-Rubin 2015). Across seven African countries, Wahman and Boone (2018) find evidence in favor of broker-mediated bloc voting, particularly in low population density rural constituencies "that can be counted on to bloc vote per local leaders' instructions."

This last study suggests there might be something attractive about rural areas for broker-mediated clientelism. Coordinating bloc votes works best for parties and voters when transfers are targeted at the same level at which electoral outcomes are available because the allocation of a locational good is contingent on the coordination of voters in that area (Smith and De Mesquita 2012). Polling results at a well-defined group level enable inexpensive monitoring of bloc voting (Chandra 2007; Kitschelt and Wilkinson 2007). Rural villages often fit this description well. Polling stations tend to overlap with village boundaries, and excludable goods like wells or clinics or schools can be targeted at the village level as well.

Urban spaces pose a greater challenge for collective clientelism. Polling station catchment areas tend to constitute less obvious political or social units. And because of higher population density and increased mobility, it is harder to target excludable goods to a limited constituency of voters. Intermediaries can help solve this problem if they have a particularly strong hold on voters and can ensure coordination and compliance without the added benefit of being able to monitor polling station results. As we will see in Chapter 7, such intermediated clientelism has indeed declined in its utility in rapidly urbanizing spaces like Senegal's capital, Dakar.

One counterexample is the marketplace associations in urban Lagos. Barnes (1986, p. 133) writes that parties were able to consolidate their base by seeking "support from organisations that contained large blocs of voters ... market organisations were especially important". Adrienne and I find more recent evidence of their involvement in vote mobilization which we describe more fully in our book (LeBas and Gottlieb 2025). We conducted a phone survey of our initial sample of market vendors after the 2019 gubernatorial elections in Lagos state. Prior to the election, we had randomly assigned some market vendors to receive a message delivered by the market association that emphasized potential penalties for tax evasion.

The results of our survey are striking. Relative to vendors who did not receive a tax appeal from their marketplace association, those who did reported significantly lower turnout rates in the election held one week earlier. We infer from these results that the message from the market association primed respondents to think about the negative inducements these brokers might apply during election campaigns. With this in mind, opposition voters known to the market association and who received the message were more likely to stay home on election day rather than turn out and risk being sanctioned.

We have so far seen the different ways in which informal economic and political relationships with the state are facilitated by intermediaries. We can presume that one reason these intermediaries agree to engage in this work of connecting states to citizens is that they materially benefit. In the next section, we will actually measure variation in how much intermediaries benefit from this role and observe one of the consequences of this variation for state-building.

5.2 VARIATION IN INTERMEDIARIES: TRANSITIONAL COSTS AND WILLINGNESS TO CHANGE

We have seen examples of different types of intermediaries according to their functions; some coordinate economic organizations, some are spiritual guides, and others are traditional leaders. This chapter ultimately aims to produce evidence for the argument that intermediaries will resist moves away from the status quo that imply immediate costs to them. Given the substantial variation in intermediary types illustrated above, one observable implication of the argument is that intermediaries who benefit relatively more from their role in citizen–state intermediation will be more resistant to transitions away from the status quo. In this section, I first describe the type of variation that might matter to the relative benefits intermediaries derive from their position. I then provide evidence of this variation from a survey of over a thousand potential local intermediaries in Mali. Results of the survey also show that those respondents who benefit more from their personal ties to local government are more likely to resist a programmatic intervention intended to constrain discretionary governance.

Variation in Clientelistic Intermediaries

The preceding section highlighted the wide range of actors that might serve as intermediaries between the state and citizens. More importantly to the theory, intermediaries also differ in the extent of their bargaining power with and value to the state. In particular, they vary in their autonomy from or relative dependence on their communities (Beck 2008) and this, in turn, affects the likelihood that they will be co-opted by the central state (Boone 2003). In earlier work, I argued that these social and economic characteristics of intermediaries and their communities also affect the strategies political intermediaries employ to mobilize votes for their preferred candidates (Gottlieb 2017). In particular, I showed how (1) egalitarian versus hierarchical social organization of communities affects the competitiveness of selection of political intermediaries and thereby the ability of these brokers to use *persuasion*, and (2) the economic autonomy of brokers from their community conditions the relative use of *coercion* versus *reciprocation*.

Here, I make the case that variation in an intermediary's social or economic status, and the clientelistic strategies available to them as a result (persuasion, reciprocation, or coercion), affect the extent to which they benefit from their position as an intermediary between voters and parties. Benefits to one's intermediary status may be material or affective. If brokers mobilize followers by persuasion alone, they may benefit from respect or higher reputational status in the community. If brokers mobilize followers through reciprocity – you vote for my candidate and I give you part of the targeted goods in return, they may benefit from increased trust and legitimacy that improves their ability to achieve other goals. And if brokers mobilize followers through coercion – you vote for my candidate or else you will suffer social sanctions or withholding of transfers, they may benefit from rents they have access to through their privileged relationship with the winning party.

During fieldwork visits to rural villages in 2012, I observed some of the monetary advantages that intermediaries can derive from their status. In the Diourbel region, home to the Mouride brotherhood, political intermediaries are often connected to well-resourced religious leaders called marabouts. In one village, for example, the individual reported to be the political intermediary by a majority of the community was a marabout's son; in another, the intermediary was a marabout's disciple. Even in these poor rural villages where nearly everyone lives in homes with mud walls, these two intermediaries lived in large concrete houses with electricity and multiple cars. This observation is consistent with accounts of Mouride marabouts controlling large amounts of money and access to land, facilitating its distribution through networks of economic exchange (O'Brien 1975; Villalón 1995). There is a debate, however, over whether these resources are acquired through more coercive means – using religion and the core idea of submission in Mouridism to extract from followers (Copans 1980; Fatton 1987), or whether such economic exchange is more reciprocal due to the marabout's ability to offer insurance in times of need (O'Brien 1975; Villalón 1995). Results of my own research are more aligned with the former than the latter interpretation; voters in Mouride areas were less likely to follow the vote preference of their political intermediary when their vote was anonymous (Gottlieb 2017). In either case, the benefits derived by the Mouride intermediaries in the above communities were visible and material in nature.

In another village visited during my fieldwork – this time outside the influence of the Mouride brotherhood – the traditional village chief, rather than a religious figure, was cited as the primary political intermediary. The reason for my visit to this village was to pilot a voting game that studied whether and how people coordinated with each other when it came time to vote. What happened next illustrates the village chief's implication in the vote coordination process and how his legitimacy and status could improve by serving the role of political intermediary.

The game assigned half of 16 randomly selected villagers to a yellow team and half to a green team. The participants were given a ballot with which they could cast a vote for either yellow or green. The outcome of the vote implied different payoffs for each group. If the voters coordinated on green (at least 12 out of 16 votes), the green team got 3,000 CFA each (~ 5 USD), and the yellow team got 1,000 CFA each. If voters coordinated on yellow, the payoffs were the opposite. If the vote was not coordinated (less than 12 votes for each color), no one got paid. In this particular village, where the chief was the political intermediary, the participants coordinated successfully on green (14 to 2). This is how it happened.

The night before the votes were counted, the chief told the participants in the game to convene a meeting in the public square and come to a consensus. He also suggested that green be the color that they coordinate on. Twelve people participated in the meeting, and the remaining four were visited in their homes to pass on the information. The two people who voted for yellow were women who attended the meeting, one of them a member of the chief's household. A member of the research team suggested this might be to make it look like there was some opposition in the village.

When we left the village after the election results were announced and the payoffs distributed according to team color, the participants were all sitting in the courtyard of the chief's compound with their envelopes in hand. Why? The research team discovered that it was so that the chief could redistribute the money evenly among the participants, that is, the 8 participants who won 3,000 CFA would give 1,000 CFA to those who only won 1,000 CFA. The village chief would not tax the participants because his ability to obtain a good result for the village is a good deed he can benefit from later on – when it comes time for elections. In other words, his greater ability to coordinate votes at the village level promises future benefits for him and the community. But unlike in the case of the Mouride village, the economic status of the village chief did not appear as disparate from that of his fellow villagers, suggesting that the benefits to his intermediary status are not necessarily material in nature.

This latter example more clearly highlights how the strategy of reciprocity implies a different kind of benefit for intermediaries who employ it. In this case, the resource-constrained traditional chief benefits from the status and legitimacy conferred by being the political intermediary. Unlike the marabout-connected intermediaries in the first villages described, the chief does not have the financial resources to buy votes or the economic power to threaten retribution or material costs. His strategy for mobilizing voters for his preferred party in the prior election was instead to remind villagers of the good things he had done and could do for them. Investing in a long-term reciprocal relationship with villagers makes him a more effective broker. And being a broker can yield communal or personal benefits from the party in power.

In polities where brokers are so ubiquitous, they comprise a powerful constituency that is invested in the clientelistic status quo. As these examples illustrate, brokers benefit from their position as intermediaries in the relationship between voter and party. But they also expose variation in the extent to which intermediaries benefit – and how contingent those benefits are on the clientelistic status quo. For example, we might expect intermediaries with clear financial benefits to be especially invested in maintaining their position under the status quo. If political parties were to change their linkage strategies and to start mobilizing support on the basis of programmatic policies, these brokers would have the most to lose from the disappearance of clientelistic exchange.

Within-Country Evidence from Mali

Measuring transitional losses or an intermediary's valuation of the clientelistic status quo is difficult because they tend to receive benefits informally and may be unwilling to admit to payoffs that could be perceived as illicit or corrupt. In a study with colleagues Jaimie Bleck and Katrina Kosec in one of Senegal's neighbors, Mali, we were able to systematically measure these transitional costs (Bleck, Gottlieb, and Kosec 2023). What we find in that project is that variation in expected benefits of the clientelistic status quo indeed correlates with the willingness to transition to a more formal, programmatic institution. Here, I describe our fieldwork and what we found.

One reason that Mali serves as a useful country case for this empirical inquiry is that, in my previous work, Malian citizens have proven to be more forthcoming relative to Senegalese citizens about experiences with informal transfers. When asking about the valuation of the status quo, we would want respondents to be as honest as possible in their reporting of whether and what they might have received in terms of clientelistic benefits from politicians or government officials. In a survey of Malian citizens in 2011, about one-quarter reported that they would be willing to change their vote (for a hypothetical candidate) for some amount of money. The questionnaire first gave respondents a choice between two candidates: one more programmatic and one more clientelistic. For the 74 percent of respondents who voted for the more programmatic candidate, I asked a series of questions about whether they would change their vote if the more clientelistic candidate offered them increasing amounts of cash – essentially assessing their willingness to accept payment in exchange for a vote. If they refused the first amount offered (about 1 USD), I asked if they would change their mind for slightly higher amounts, up to about 20 USD. In this exercise, about one quarter of the respondents who were offered the choice to change their vote for cash said they would do so at one of the values offered.

I repeated the same exercise in Senegal in 2017. Exactly zero respondents said they would change their vote if offered any amount of cash; this time, the highest cash amount was much higher (about 100 USD) to reflect the higher standard of living of some of the respondents. While some of this difference in response patterns may be attributable to actual differences in levels of vote-buying or differences in the samples (one being more rural and one being more urban), widespread anecdotal reports of vote-buying in Senegal lead me to believe that at least some Senegalese respondents were dissembling or failing to report a willingness to accept money in exchange for their vote. This may be due to much clearer norms against vote-buying in Senegal (even though it happens regularly), or to a greater awareness of the socially desirable answer. In any case, the weaker social desirability bias in the Malian context makes these more sensitive questions easier to ask and to get truthful answers.

In spite of these differences in reporting behaviors, I would expect that lessons about real behavioral patterns from the Malian case should extend to Senegal and other contexts with clientelistic democracies. Mali has a similar colonial history to Senegal; indeed, they gained independence as a single polity that then quickly divided into two nations. Mali and Senegal share many administrative and political features, both borrowing a lot from the French model. And Mali's first multiparty election in 1992 coincided with Senegal's move to more free multiparty elections in 1993. In spite of these similarities, Mali is a poorer and less developed country compared to Senegal. A string of coups over the last decade has also destabilized Mali's democracy and economy. However, the data we collect in Mali is at the level of the commune or local government, which have continued to function as democratic entities with a somewhat regular electoral calendar in spite of the institutional challenges at the central level.

Setting for Data Collection

The Mali study leverages the introduction of a new policy that would imply a shift from a more informal or discretionary mode of redistribution to a more formal, nondiscretionary form. Mali's decentralized governance system, like Senegal's, puts the onus to provide local public goods like primary schooling and health care on locally governed districts called communes. Due to difficulties in raising sufficient internal revenue for financing the local public goods that communes are obligated to provide, the central government transfers money to local governments for public service projects on a yearly basis. To date, the amount of these funds have been calculated based on formulaic criteria like population and poverty level. And the funds have systematically been spent with high levels of corruption by the elected mayors and commune councils.[5]

As one way to reduce misspending, the Government of Mali and the World Bank introduced a new performance-based financing scheme in which allocation amounts were additionally contingent on the quality of spending in prior years. This new policy required credible information about how funds are spent. In an information-poor environment and one where government officials might have incentives to collude, it is hard to get reliable information. One approach is working with local civil society

[5] Fawaz, Ahmad. 2010. External audit of local public investments, 1st annual report. SOCOTEC. Bamako, Mali.

organizations (CSOs) that might have both an interest in accountable spending by the local government and the capacity to collect and convey information to the central government.

But it would be naïve to think that all CSOs would be willing or able to monitor the government in this way. CSOs might instead have more to gain by colluding with the government and getting an informal payoff rather than a future promise of cleaner public spending. In advance of the new program's rollout, we fielded a survey of CSO leaders in which we asked whether they would be willing to participate in this formal monitoring mechanism. By asking about key characteristics of CSOs related to their autonomy from local government, hierarchical structure, and dependence on their members (as suggested by the above discussion), we sought to examine what might explain variation in their responses. We expected that the CSOs that had the most to gain from informal redistribution under the status quo would be the least willing to monitor the local government under the forthcoming performance-based funding program. The evidence I present next confirms this expectation.

Non-state organizations like the CSOs in our Mali survey are a common intermediary between citizens and the state. They can substitute for states, for example, by providing goods and services that weak states fail to deliver[6]; they can collaborate with states, for example, by collecting taxes on their behalf,[7] or they can challenge states, for example, by pushing them to be more accountable (Tsai 2007). In the Mali study, we are most interested in whether CSOs are willing to engage in this latter function. But we also recognize that because of the informational and coordination capacities that make them stable organizations, CSOs also serve as prime targets for clientelistic intermediation. In this role, a CSO could mobilize electoral or other political support for an incumbent in exchange for informal redistribution.

The trade-off that CSOs face in deciding whether to participate in a monitoring scheme provides an opportunity for us to examine which CSOs are willing to participate and which are not. A CSO's role as a clientelistic intermediary implicitly conflicts with its role in holding the

[6] Bodea and LeBas (2016), for instance, find that individuals with access to dense social capital and to non-state service providers report lower levels of tax morale and tax compliance than individuals who lack access to social institutions.

[7] States may recognize their relative weakness vis-à-vis non-state actors, and there is some evidence that weak states may attempt to "borrow" the capacity of these actors (Joshi and Ayee 2008; Goodfellow 2015; Balan et al. 2021).

state more accountable for the provision of public goods. If a CSO engages in a clientelistic bargain, providing political support in exchange for informal transfers, then its promise of support is only credible as long as it does not publicly denounce corrupt behaviors of the state. This choice resembles the choice outlined in the model in Chapter 2 in which a voter can either condition its vote on the receipt of particularistic transfers or on public goods. The model further suggests that individuals with relatively higher levels of k, or gifts obtained under the clientelistic status quo, would be more likely to resist transitions to a more programmatic or less discretionary state of the world.

In the Mali case, CSOs participating as monitors of state spending in the performance-based funding scheme represent one such transition to a less discretionary state of the world. We surveyed CSOs to understand variation in their willingness to serve as participants in such a scheme. We additionally measured perceived transitional losses. We did this by asking CSO leaders to estimate the amount that would be transferred directly to them if the government received the performance bonus (of about 9,000 USD), as described further below.

The sample for the study consists of 1,014 CSO leaders from a representative sample of urban and rural communes in Mali. An extensive mapping exercise to identify both formal and informal CSOs, for example, youth tea-drinking groups and women's savings clubs, generated the population from which we sampled. CSOs were asked to list their primary activity; the top three are public goods and service provision, economic activity, and savings or credit groups. About a quarter of groups are predominantly composed of youth, and another quarter are composed of women.

More Embedded CSOs Have More to Lose

If we consider a CSO's willingness to participate in formal monitoring as a sign of transitioning to a more programmatic or nondiscretionary equilibrium, then the theory would predict that the CSO leaders who perceive the most benefit from the clientelistic status quo will have the most to lose, and be the least willing to transition. To test this expectation, we use two key survey measures.

To measure perceived transitional losses (or benefits of remaining in the discretionary status quo), we ask participants the following question: "Sometimes the funds the mayor receives can benefit an officer or a citizen who is a member of a civil society group and sometimes not. How much of the 5,000,000 CFA bonus do you think the mayor would be likely

Usually, the transfers your local government gets from the national budget are based on things like population size and poverty level. However, there is **a new program being planned for your commune where your local government can get a bonus payment** of 5 million CFA, in addition to the standard transfer of about 30 million CFA, **if it spends its money well** in the previous year – that is, if it uses it for the intended purpose of providing services to citizens. The program will be piloted in your commune and several others for 5 years, and then brought to additional communes by the national government if successful. To determine how money is spent, bureaucratic agencies like the Ministry of Education and Ministry of Health will ask their local representatives to **measure how well the government has been spending its money** on infrastructure in these areas and whether services are actually being provided. However, **civil society groups like yours often also have additional insights** to contribute to such a process. Imagine that, **this year, your group will be given the opportunity to make a report evaluating the mayor's use of funds.** This report can be negative and indicate the mayor's misuse of funds, or positive and indicate no such misuse.

FIGURE 5.1 Vignette used in Mali survey to assess willingness to monitor government.

to spend in a way that benefits you or your CSO members personally?" Seventy-two percent of respondents answered that they would expect to receive nothing. Of the CSO leaders who said they expected to receive an informal transfer, about half thought it would be 10 percent or less of the total amount. Most of the remaining answers are between 20 percent and half of the total amount.

To measure willingness to participate in formal monitoring of the local government, participants first listen to a vignette read in their local language. (See Figure 5.1 for full text.) The enumerator then poses this question: "We know that there are a lot of considerations involved in whether you are reporting on performance of the mayor or not, as this could have both benefits and costs for you and your group. Taking all of this into account, on a scale of 0 to 10, how likely is it that you will submit a negative performance report?" The mean value of likelihood to report is 7.

As one way to test the theoretical expectation, we can simply look at whether CSOs that expect a nonzero transfer from the mayor are less willing to participate in formal monitoring. This is indeed the case. Those CSO leaders who expect no monetary transfers are 0.2 standard deviations more willing to participate in the formal monitoring program compared to those who expect some money. It is also the case that CSO leaders who expect higher amounts are less likely to say they would participate in the formal monitoring mechanism by issuing a negative performance report when merited.

Who are these CSO leaders who both expect informal transfers and are less willing to participate in formal sanctioning? The key characteristic that stands out on both counts is a construct we call "embeddedness", which captures the length of time a group has operated in a community and its connectedness to nonmembers in that community. It is comprised of constituent variables that measure how often members of the group meet with nonmember citizens to share their plans, how long ago the group was founded, the extent to which the group's goals are long-term as opposed to short-term, and the level of citizen awareness of the group's activities.

The embeddedness of a CSO and its leader is strongly positively correlated with the likelihood of expecting an informal monetary transfer and the amount of that transfer. Embeddedness is also strongly negatively correlated with willingness to formally sanction a corrupt leader. CSOs who cite their primary activity as religion or security are, by far, the most embedded. Groups comprised of older residents are also more embedded than groups comprised of youth.

These findings lend support to the idea that there is variation among intermediaries in the benefits they receive to remaining under the clientelistic status quo – benefits they might lose if there were a transition to a more programmatic (or nondiscretionary) equilibrium. They also show how this variation correlates with willingness to transition from one equilibrium to another. While the outcome of interest – formally monitoring the state's spending of public funds – is not a direct measure of programmatic politics or formalization, it is closely related. In this case, the act of monitoring was framed as an institutional shift. Local governments were going to benefit from a new performance-based monitoring program in which future local government transfers would be based on the performance of previous transfers. CSOs would play a role in monitoring local government expenditures. If CSOs monitor corrupt mayoral behavior, they would be participating in a new, impersonal governance regime in which citizens benefit from clean local spending rather than from ill-gotten personalistic transfers. These findings thus provide support for the idea that beneficiaries of the clientelistic status quo will be more resistant to supporting an institutional shift when it constitutes a greater threat to their preferential status.

5.3 INTERMEDIARIES RESIST CHANGES TO THE CLIENTELISTIC STATUS QUO

The previous section generates evidence of a negative relationship between the extent to which intermediaries benefit from the clientelistic status quo and their willingness to participate in a more formal institution that would undermine their informal status. One downside of this empirical exercise is that we do not observe actual behavior: We only observe the hypothetical willingness to participate in a new, more programmatic institution. In this section, I provide evidence of active resistance by intermediaries who feel threatened by an institutional change that privileges programmatism over discretionary politics.

The theory expects backlash by elites to be rare because it is off the equilibrium path: In a clientelistic equilibrium, we should not see large investments in state capacity or programmatic electoral competition because of weak voter demand. However, investments in state-building or programmatic policies may still occur as a result of economic crises, external pressure from international partners, or from schisms within the state. For an example of the latter, in a book with Adrienne LeBas (LeBas and Gottlieb 2025), we describe how clientelistic and technocratic forces are both at work in Lagos State, Nigeria, with technocratic visionaries planning state-building projects that directly connect citizens to the state alongside a political machine that continues to invest in intermediaries.

Senegal in the 1980s and 1990s provides an example of how state investments in the face of economic crises and internal schisms can be resisted by entrenched clientelistic actors. Diouf (1993) writes about the tentative move toward "technocracy" under the leadership of President Abdou Diouf when he was appointed Senghor's successor as former Prime Minister. We know now that this transition was fleeting as his successor, Wade, wielded more electoral power thanks to the clientelistic machine he took over from the Senghor years and then continued to grow over time.

President Diouf was able and motivated to restructure the state away from its patronage base for two reasons. First, a dire economic situation in the late 1970s required the state to seek help from the IMF to refinance the debt, thus obligating it to a set of austerity policies. Second, Diouf had been unable to assert his leadership within the party and faced many internal challenges when he took the reins as president. A technocratic approach allowed him to sideline the "old-style party bosses" and reshuffle the ruling elite (Diouf 1993). He did this by promoting technocrats who had risen to posts within the state and recruiting a new ruling class on the basis of expertise.

The problem with this approach was that it produced a constituency of discontented local partisans. As the new technocratic state placed protegés into party leadership positions at the local level, it created internal clashes and instigated migration to the main opposition party, the PDS. The PDS won handily in 2000 and President Wade consolidated his power through his two mandates by heavily investing in electoral targeting of responsive clienteles (Gottlieb et al. 2019).

To provide more systematic evidence of this sort of resistance to reform, I leverage a coordinated research project in which there were visible attempts to increase state capacity and institutional formality in several countries at the same time. Teams of academics and their policy partners sought to examine the effectiveness of attempts to formalize relationships between citizens and the state, coordinated by the research consortium Evidence in Governance and Politics (EGAP). This was EGAP's second such attempt at coordinating social science field experiments across multiple contexts, Metaketa II (De La O et al. 2020).[8] The individual country projects in the coordinated study were typically state-initiated policy interventions in collaboration with a research team tasked with evaluating the impact.

The research teams each sought to analyze the conditions under which citizens are willing to formalize their relationship to the state. I ask a different question here: Did these (sometimes successful) attempts to formalize citizen–state interactions result in resistance from actors that might have benefited from the often intermediated informal relationships citizens already had with the state? Because of the coordinated nature of the project, we have more than a single case to learn from; and, the interventions across cases have been purposefully harmonized to facilitate comparison. Much of the evidence I describe here comes from qualitative accounts in project documents and conversations with the authors.

What is common across all six country studies is a rapid, marked increase in (or attempt to increase) formal interactions between citizens and the state. These shocks to formalization or programmatic policymaking are usually rare. But this coordinated set of interventions and the research teams accompanying them offer a unique opportunity to study the response of political intermediaries and bureaucrats to these

[8] See also http://egap.org/metaketa/metaketa-ii-taxation.

policy changes. The fact that there were research teams on the ground makes it possible to uncover evidence of resistance that might normally go unnoticed.

In three of the country cases – the D.R. Congo, India, and Nigeria – study authors report explicit or implicit backlash by political elites consistent with the logic of transitional losses.[9] As citizens formalize their relationship to the state, the organizational infrastructure needed to facilitate targeted transfers is devalued, and well-connected bureaucrats and intermediaries lose their ability to seek rents. Below, I briefly review the evidence from each of these three cases.

In the D.R. Congo, the project sought to evaluate the impact of a randomized intervention reducing the price and transaction costs of formal land-titling. Study authors describe the existing land-titling system as complex, with a "convoluted process for obtaining new titles" and "byzantine administrative procedures and informal fees [that] discouraged citizens from obtaining a land title." At the start of the reform process, almost no property owner in customary areas had a land title. Because it stood to increase revenues, there was an appetite among some in the central and provincial governments to implement the land-titling reform that would reduce prices, simplify procedures, and increase access.

Halfway through the implementation of the policy, as new applications for land titles streamed in, however, the Provincial Government enacted stricter eligibility criteria to block a large proportion of the applications (Balan et al. 2021). One suspected reason for this was the fact that the process was more objective and rule-based, thereby eliminating discretion and the ability to favor certain insiders.[10] Indeed, most Congolese bureaucrats are either paid entirely through informal fees for service (when they do not have official status) or supplement their wages with fee income. "Because the titling campaign imposed a moratorium on all such fees, a number of agents refused to collaborate altogether, even when instructed to do so by their superiors." [11]

The project in India analyzed the impact of coordinated political pressure from citizens to increase access to Mumbai's public fee-based water services in slums that had previously relied on private, informal, or illegal

[9] In the other three country cases, authors did not observe or report such behavior. However, it is still possible that backlash occurred unobserved, so I will not speculate about how or why these two sets of countries are different.

[10] Email conversation with the authors, October 31, 2020.

[11] Draft of the team's Metaketa II book chapter, shared by the authors on October 7, 2022.

water connections. The advocacy intervention succeeded in promoting formal water connectivity only in places where the locally elected leaders were outside the dominant political coalition. Study authors explain this is partly a result of political resistance to formalization where dominant politicians "actively try to undercut bottom-up activism to secure water connectivity …, as such activism, when successful, may trigger backlash among the [dominant] electoral coalition which is resentful of other groups gaining a foothold in the city." This likely manifests as local politicians putting pressure on the bureaucracy "to find a pretext to deny connections" (Gaikwad, Nellis and Thomas 2020).

Finally, the project in Nigeria (conducted by me and Adrienne LeBas) sought to study the effect of appeals delivered to informal market vendors to register their business and pay formal taxes. The Lagos Internal Revenue Service (LIRS), our implementing partner, had long been searching for ways to expand the reach of the tax net to encompass the incredibly large population of informal sector workers and small firms, accounting for about 80 percent of the state's economic actors. In Lagos State, the current process of formalization involves registration for an electronic tax clearance card (e-TCC) for which the individual must also pay annual income tax liability (a low flat rate for small firms). Baseline rates of formal status among small firms are incredibly low – about 12 percent in the study sample. Historically, there were a variety of formal and informal ways in which vendors could comply with state income tax, including payment through marketplace associations. But LIRS sought to promote the e-TCC as the primary pathway to formalization.

Market vendors in Lagos are typically enmeshed in an informal institution – the historically Yoruba-dominant marketplace associations described earlier in the chapter. Individual markets have their own associations led by a "market mother" or *iyaloja* that are then united under a statewide umbrella association that meets weekly under the leadership of the Iyaloja General (who happens to be the daughter of the state's political godfather). Marketplace associations are active in solving conflicts between vendors, facilitating access to goods and services, and collecting fees, and they have historically played an intermediary role in both tax collection and service provision.

In partnership with the LIRS and the marketplace associations, our Metaketa study in Nigeria evaluated the relative effectiveness of deploying each agent – the state or an intermediary – as a messenger to encourage formalization among market vendors. The study found that, unlike the bureaucratic IRS messengers, non-state intermediaries were unable to induce increases in formal business registration (Gottlieb, Lebas and Magat 2025). In our book, we attribute this to the fact that the non-state messengers were also clientelistic brokers who benefited from the discretion they had under the informal status quo (LeBas and Gottlieb 2025). They were thus not credible messengers of appeals to formalize and exit the status quo, which would undermine their privileged position. We saw another pattern of behavior among vendors that is consistent with the theory. When approached by the formal IRS agents, Yoruba vendors – who are favored in clientelistic distribution under the status quo – were unmoved by the intervention. By contrast, members of the minority ethnic group who are disfavored under clientelism were induced to formally register by the campaign (Gottlieb, Lebas and Magat 2025).

Together, these examples provide plausible evidence of how the politically well-connected in a clientelistic system may respond when faced with a threat to their privileged status. A formal relationship between the citizen and the state is inherently impersonal and necessitates little mediation, whereas clientelistic relationships are inherently personal and often mediated. Thus, fearing transitional losses incurred by exiting the status quo, the actors that benefit from the political necessity of targeting personal benefits to citizens may respond to systematic attempts at formalization with active resistance.

5.4 SUMMING UP

This chapter has provided evidence to support one of the theory's main predictions of how embedded informality stymies one pathway out of the weak-state trap. Increasing state strength, which in turn makes programmatic linkages a more attractive electoral mobilization strategy, could push a polity out of the weak-state trap into a public goods equilibrium. However, embedded informality can impede that pathway out of the trap by creating demand for intermediaries who serve as a bridge between citizens in the informal sector and the state (in the absence of more regularized, legal relationships). I described one example from Lagos, Nigeria, showing how these same intermediaries who serve to connect the state to citizens in relationships of extraction and provision can also be exploited by political parties to increase the efficiency of clientelistic electoral exchange. Especially when intermediaries serve these dual purposes of linking the bureaucratic and political state to citizens and voters, they have bargaining power they can use to extract rents from the state.

I first tested one observable implication of the theory – that the ability to extract rents under a more clientelistic system discourages intermediaries from supporting transitions to a less discretionary or more programmatic institutional setup. I used within-country data from Mali, exploiting variation in the embeddedness of local leaders in clientelistic relationships with the local government. The evidence reveals that local actors who are more embedded in clientelistic networks both expect to receive greater rents from the state and are less willing to engage in a programmatic policy that could improve local governance but at the expense of privileged networks.

I then provided more direct evidence of resistance from intermediaries. Not only are some intermediaries not natural constituencies for programmatic policies, but they may even engage in backlash or obstruct programmatic or state-building policies upon implementation. Three cases – Nigeria, D.R. Congo, and India – provide illustrations of such backlash where intermediaries who benefit from the status quo actually resist the top-down implementation of policies that would result in a stronger, less discretionary state.

6

Is Increasing Competition a Way Out of the Trap?

If politics can help explain why informality has contributed to keeping the state weak, can politics also be a way out of the trap? The next two chapters interrogate this question by asking, first, whether political competitiveness can increase incentives of elected leaders to invest in the state (the short answer is no) and, second, whether waning clientelistic politics might change this outcome (the short answer is maybe).

Democratic competition can arguably have salutary effects for the welfare of the majority (Lake and Baum 2001; Deacon 2009). Indeed, democracy has been shown to improve health and education outcomes through the provision of public services (Stasavage 2005; Besley 2006).[1] If democracy can have these salutary effects, then should more democracy – in the form of greater political competitiveness – marginally improve these outcomes as well? If the electoral majority in weak states would benefit from increased public spending, then you might imagine that increasing political competition could be a way to induce pressure on the incumbent to invest in state-building and the provision of public goods.

This chapter provides evidence to the contrary: especially when electoral politics are not programmatic, political competition is unlikely to incentivize incumbents to invest in the state. It opens with a case comparison of two public bureaucracies charged with tax collection in contexts of widespread economic informality: Senegal and Lagos State, Nigeria. The case narratives, developed with the help of elite interviews

[1] Ross (2006), however, critiques cross-country analyses and shows that the benefits of additional public spending in democracies largely accrue to wealthier groups rather than the poor majority.

from each context, suggest that electoral competition can actually weaken incentives to regulate and tax the informal sector. A quantitative cross-country analysis, using existing data on overtime tax collection and political competition, then provides more general evidence for this claim. It shows that increasing electoral competition reduces tax revenue. The chapter concludes with a discussion of what we might learn from the Lagos case about incentives to invest in state-building and formalization.

So far, the book has focused largely on the demand side of state-building: whether and why actors in the informal sector remain there and whether and how they appeal to the state for change. We now turn our attention to state actors to paint a more complete picture of the two equilibria we have been describing. For embedded informality to survive alongside a clientelistic, weak state, we should expect limited attempts by the government to invest in increasing state capacity. The cases in the next section describe the incentive structure and choices made by two such governments with quite different outcomes.

6.1 A TALE OF TWO IRSS

In this section, I describe the approach of two government tax offices – in Senegal and Lagos State, Nigeria – to investing in the capacity to tax the informal sector, a sector of special interest to the book. The outcome in each is quite different: There is demonstrated political will to build capacity to tax in the second case, while politics appears to constrain fiscal investments in the first. The case comparison highlights several key features that distinguish the two the competitiveness of elections, the informal sector as a majority constituency, and the role of business interests in motivating the state to make programmatic investments.

Senegal

In Senegal, tax revenue from the informal sector is incredibly low relative to the extremely large size of the sector. It is estimated to make up about 40 percent of the total economy, and upwards of 95 percent of all economic units. Interviews with members of the national tax office in Dakar, the DGID (Direction Générale des Impôts et des Domaines), suggest that tax officials are well-aware of weak fiscal capacity in this sector but that there is limited political will to change it.

Relatedly, informational capacity with respect to taxation of the informal sector is also extremely weak. This became clear in doing research for the book: The tax office was unable to answer basic questions about the evolution of tax revenue in the informal sector over time because it does not aggregate or keep track of it. To see this, I first have to explain how tax works in the informal sector.

The state considers any economic unit to be informal if it makes less than 5 million CFA (~ 8,000 USD) in profit for selling goods, or less than 2 million CFA (~2,000 USD) in profit for selling services. The informal sector, and anyone who makes less than 50 million CFA, pay a simplified tax called the CGU (Contribution Globale Unique) that was instituted in 2004 to increase participation in tax payment and formalization by the informal sector. While declarations of the CGU are recorded and tracked for members of the formal sector (those making between 2/5 million CFA and 50 million CFA), they are not systematically recorded for members of the informal sector making less than that. This is due to the different way that tax payments are made in the informal sector; there is less paperwork, and payments are entered manually rather than into a digital system.

The amount of CGU declared (by the formal sector) has decreased over time; in 2021, it was about half of what it was in 2008. The only aggregate data I was able to get for tax revenue from the informal sector (due to the lack of records) was from 2021. The CGU revenue collected from the informal sector in 2021 was about 50 percent higher than the amount collected from the formal sector and reflects about 30,000 payors compared to only 6,500 in the formal sector.

The number of taxpayers in the informal sector is a very small proportion of the number of potential taxpayers. The DGID only has 50,000 members of the informal sector in their tax data, whereas the national statistics bureau (ANSD) estimates 450,000 economic units.

Consistent with these figures, the state has not taken an active role in persuading members of the informal sector to pay tax. In fact, only 6 percent of members of the informal sector that I surveyed in 2017 had ever heard of the CGU. A three-day state-sponsored information campaign followed the implementation of the CGU in 2004 (Fall 2004), but this was the only such information campaign on record. Similarly, while there were numerous articles written about the CGU in 2004 after its initial implementation, a comprehensive search of the local press yielded not a single article that mentioned the CGU since – including following a salutary rate decrease instituted by a 2013 fiscal policy that should have attracted public attention. When asked why this is the case, a long-time bureaucrat in the Tax Office offered that there is insufficient staff capacity to enforce this tax; most staff time is dedicated to the large firms.

So what explains the low informational and bureaucratic capacity dedicated to raising revenue from Senegal's incredibly large informal sector? The main reason cited in interviews with members of the state Tax Office is a lack of political will. Many of the larger informal firms are protected by government interests. And even though smaller firms do not boast such political connections, they are great in number. As such, there could be an electoral sanction for increasing tax capacity and enforcement on smaller firms.[2]

The lack of data and transparency around taxation is evidence of the political nature of investments in fiscal capacity. One interviewee said that when the administration does decide to collect data, it has very restrictive policies around it. This makes it difficult for agents inside the tax bureau to make evidence-based investments in raising fiscal revenue.[3]

In this case, we see how electoral politics can actually stymie investment in fiscal capacity. If elected leaders are thinking about newly enforcing fiscal policy or business regulations on a large number of firm owners who are also likely voters, they may think twice. This is consistent with existing evidence that shows politicians may fear electoral retribution for increasing enforcement. In a study from Brazil, term-limited mayors are much more likely than their counterparts facing reelection to invest in updating cadastral maps enabling greater property tax enforcement because the latter are more likely to worry about electoral retribution (Christensen and Garfias 2021). Historically, we have seen important increases in tax collection when the masses have been less well represented: Countries with lower enfranchisement were more likely to adopt the income tax (Mares and Queralt 2015).

Lagos State, Nigeria

I now turn to another context in which informality is widespread and the state is relatively weak: Lagos, Nigeria. There, fieldwork for another project afforded me the opportunity to witness its very different approach to taxing the informal sector. I focus on Lagos State rather than the country as a whole because Nigeria is a federal system in which the responsibility to tax income lies at the state level.

[2] Respondent 1. Interview with the author on July 14, 2022.
[3] Respondent 2. Interview with the author on July 14, 2022.

In the decades since Nigeria's return to democracy, tax revenues in Lagos State have increased exponentially – almost 30-fold – from N14.6 billion in 1999 to N419 billion (USD 1 billion) in 2020 (Onigbinde 2018, National Bureau of Statistics 2021) (Senegal's internally generated revenue increased about five-fold over the same period). While N278.89 billion comes from the Pay As You Earn (PAYE) taxes deducted directly from the paychecks of employees in formal companies, N17.07 billion (~ 22 million USD) is from direct assessment of self-employed individuals and small- and medium-sized firms, some of which operate in the informal sector.

To make this massive scale-up in fiscal revenue possible, Bola Tinubu, Lagos State's first elected governor since the 1999 return to democratic rule and Nigeria's current president, instituted key reforms to the Lagos Internal Revenue Service (LIRS). As a result, LIRS is now an agency characterized by both autonomy and professionalism. A former accountant, Tinubu was well aware of the unexploited fiscal potential in Lagos State. According to De Gramont (2015), "the turning point for Lagos tax institutions came in 2005, when the management of the existing internal revenue board was compulsorily retired and replaced with a new team led by Babatunde Fowler, a former bank executive." Fowler soon took LIRS out of the reporting line to the Ministry of Finance to make it autonomous. The resulting ability to hire and fire staff and increase their pay substantially curbed leakages, which were rampant when Tinubu and Fowler took the reins. Other reforms that helped increase efficiency included a move from cash transactions to electronic payments and an increase in the investigation capacity to better detect nonpayment or underpayment of taxes.[4]

But these initial investments largely affected the formal sector. The informal sector makes up an even larger proportion of Nigeria's economy than Senegal's – estimated between 50 and 60 percent, and about 80 percent or more of Lagos' labor force. As in Senegal, Lagos State collects only a small proportion of its revenue from this sector. However, unlike Senegal, Lagos State has demonstrated political will to change this. As evidence, the head of the Lagos Internal Revenue Service sought the help of a research team I was part of. The aim was to improve its strategies for appealing to informal market vendors to formally register and pay taxes.

4 Interview by the author with one of Fowler's Directors, March 11, 2022.

As in Senegal, the state recognizes that attempts to tax the large informal sector can come with electoral costs. A former director of the LIRS related this to Governor Tinubu's initial push to tax the formal sector. Tinubu knew that he could count on the political support of the informal sector thanks to his political machine. This made him less nervous about angering elites who would face greater tax burdens under the new system.[5]

It is thus somewhat surprising that Tinubu's successor, Governor Fashola who took power in 2007, made a concerted push into the informal sector. One reform to encourage compliance from the informal sector was the creation of a presumptive tax – a low, flat tax that is especially useful for businesses that do not do formal accounting. To better connect this cash-based sector to the tax bureaucracy, the LIRS established a network of more than 40 "mini tax stations" around Lagos, many of which are proximate to the large markets where a preponderance of informal sector vendors work. Unlike the lack of publicity campaigns in Senegal, the LIRS invested in billboards, TV and radio spots, and even in-person visits to markets to publicize the presumptive tax.

These investments paid off as revenue from direct assessments (mostly in the informal sector) has more than doubled in the decade following Fashola's initial innovations. While the levels and taxes are not directly comparable, the trends in the tax on small businesses across Lagos and Senegal are striking, with Lagos showing steady growth over time and Senegal showing stagnation (see Figure 6.1).

When asked what motivated the attempts to tax the informal sector in light of the political costs to doing so, an LIRS director from that period suggested that it was a signal to the formal sector that everyone was paying a fair share. In other words, the agency may have thought that continued compliance by the more lucrative formal sector depended on giving them the impression that they were not the only ones shouldering the tax burden.[6] If true, this is evidence that revenue goals are being weighted high by the Lagos State Government relative to political goals.

Why did the political costs of taxing the informal sector seem to affect incumbent governments differently in these two cases? One possibility is that electoral retribution was more worrisome in the Senegalese case relative to the Lagos one. This could be explained by the fact that political

[5] Interview with the author, Lagos, Nigeria, March 11, 2022.
[6] Interview with the author, Lagos, Nigeria, March 11, 2022.

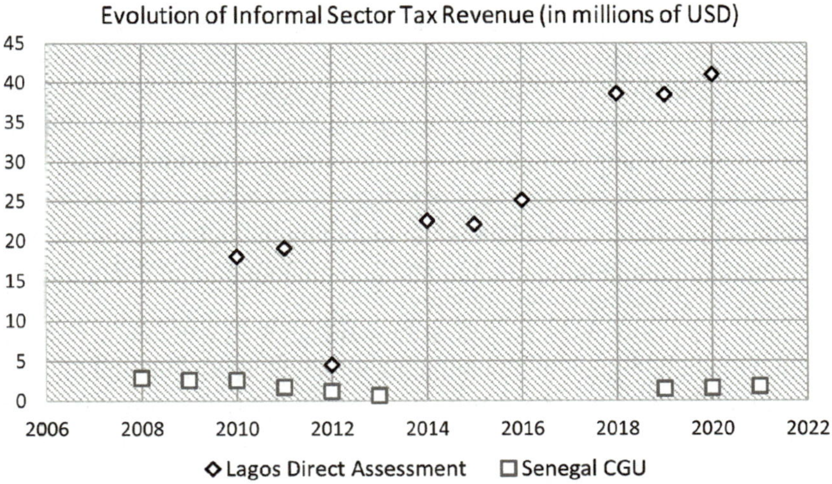

FIGURE 6.1 Taxing the informal sector in Senegal and Lagos.

uncertainty is relatively lower for the incumbent executive leader in Lagos State than in Senegal. The APC and Tinubu's hold on state power in Lagos was far more certain than for any incumbent party in Senegal since the rise of multiparty elections. In Senegal, a term-limited ruling party has never been reelected (since the transition to free and fair elections).

While Nigeria is a multiparty democracy, Lagos State has been dominated by a single party since its governor was elected in 1999. Bola Tinubu (now Nigeria's president) is frequently referred to as the state's "godfather," given his complete control of the party machine and the government. Since his original win with 73 percent of the vote, the vote share of his party in subsequent elections has varied between 55 and 81 percent. The legislature of Lagos State is even more strongly controlled by Tinubu's party (now called the APC), which has won between 80 and 100 percent of legislative seats in the last three elections. In the next section, I examine whether this insight from our two cases might be a more general phenomenon: that electoral competitiveness can reduce incentives to invest in the state.

6.2 POLITICAL COMPETITIVENESS AND STATE-BUILDING

The Senegal and Lagos cases illustrated that electoral considerations only sometimes seem to undermine the incentives of the state to invest in building fiscal capacity and increase tax enforcement. In the former case, they seem to have sapped the political will to tax the informal sector; in the latter case, there have instead been concerted government efforts to increase formalization rates. One explanation for the different outcomes is the level of political competition. Here, I examine whether this is a more general phenomenon by looking at the relationship between political competition and fiscal capacity across countries and over time. Specifically, I analyze a panel dataset of 31 countries from 1870 to 2010 to test whether increases in democratic competition incentivize state-building or increased fiscal capacity.

Ideally, I would want to measure the intensity of the reelection pressures that incumbents face as an indicator of the extent to which voters can hold politicians accountable. As a proxy, I use the Polity IV score which codes country years on a 21-point continuum from strongly autocratic to strongly democratic based on several institutional aspects of political competition: the competitiveness of executive recruitment, the openness of executive recruitment, constraints on the chief executive, and the competitiveness of political participation (Marshall, Gurr and Jaggers 2018).[7]

For the dependent variable, I sought a measure of investment in state-building that was available over many countries and years. I use the ratio of tax revenue to GDP from Rogers, Beramendi and Dincecco (2018).[8] The geographic scope of the sample is restricted to the 31 countries available in this dataset. While there are other existing measures of state capacity that span a larger range of countries, none have a similar temporal range. As the econometric analysis relies on within-country changes over time, I privileged temporal over geographic coverage in the data. That said, the sample usefully comprises countries that are relatively higher-income (e.g., Western Europe), middle-income (e.g., Eastern Europe), and lower-income (e.g., Uruguay, India) today, but also vary in their initial level of capacity at democratization. For instance, the US and Brazil democratized early and late, respectively, but both had relatively weak state capacity at democratization. Similarly, the UK and Japan have relatively higher initial capacity levels, also democratizing in different centuries.

7 The results are robust to using the executive competitiveness indicator *xrcomp* alone rather than the broader Polity IV score.

8 This measure was constructed by integrating "individual fiscal time series data from more than 30 secondary sources, including historical compilations, national statistical offices, and statistics from the IMF, OECD, World Bank, and other such organizations" (Rogers, Beramendi and Dincecco 2018).

The main empirical specification, Equation 6.1, is a panel regression with time and country fixed effects. The change in capacity between years t and $t-1$ is regressed on the prior change in political competition between years $t-1$ and $t-2$. This will tell us whether marginal increases in competitive pressures at a given level of initial capacity should prompt politicians to worry more about their electoral prospects and thus place greater weight on the political costs of such investment.

$$\Delta Tax/GDP_{i,t} = \beta_0 + \beta_1 \Delta Competition_{i,t-1} + \gamma_i + \alpha_t + \epsilon_{i,t} \qquad (6.1)$$

Levels of competition are likely endogenous to a host of other features of a polity that may correlate with its capacity. For instance, greater economic wealth is positively associated with both higher political competition and state capacity. However, marginal changes in competition are more likely due to idiosyncratic features of the polity in that year that are less likely to be generating omitted variable bias. A first differences estimator eliminates bias due to time-invariant omitted variables (Wooldridge 2002) and addresses the non-stationarity of the panel series. Furthermore, a test of serial correlation in the idiosyncratic errors of the linear panel data model reveals that a non-differenced model is serially autocorrelated, while the differenced model is not.

Results of the first differences model presented in Table 6.1 show the average relationship between competition and fiscal capacity across all country-years in the sample. The first column reports the results of Equation 6.1. Column two adds as a control variable, the change in logged GDP per capita, as prior changes in the size of the economy are the most likely omitted variable driving future changes in tax collection. Column three additionally controls for the lagged value of the dependent variable.[9]

The negative and significant relationship between prior changes in competition and changes in state capacity is not sensitive to model specification. In each case, the results predict that a one standard deviation

[9] Imbens and Wooldridge (2009) refer to this as the unconfoundedness-based approach, arguing that in the context of panel data and a first differences model, including a lagged dependent variable is a relatively attractive approach compared to a model that omits this control. The inclusion of the lagged dependent variable increases precision by making observations comparable on lagged outcomes and also flexibly allows countries to be on different trends according to initial levels of state capacity.

TABLE 6.1 *Effect of change in competitiveness on change in fiscal capacity*

	(1)	(2)	(3)
Δ Polity Score (lagged)	−0.012*	−0.011*	−0.013*
	(0.005)	(0.005)	(0.005)
Δ GDP per capita (lagged)		0.020	0.015
		(0.016)	(0.015)
Tax–GDP ratio (lagged)			−0.043+
			(0.022)
Constant	−0.004**	−0.000	0.001
	(0.001)	(0.002)	(0.002)
Observations	3,090	3,002	3,002

Includes country and year fixed effects. Standard errors clustered at the country level. Polity Score rescaled to range from 0 to 1.
$^{+}p < 0.10$, $^{*}p < 0.05$, $^{**}p < 0.01$,

change in the independent variable is responsible for a one-third standard deviation change in the dependent variable.[10]

A Conditional Relationship between Democracy and State-Building

The theory articulated in Chapter 2 posits that democratic competition should have differential implications for incentives to invest in state-building depending on the dominant linkage mechanism between parties and voters. In polities dominated by programmatic linkages, constituencies might reward politicians for investments in state-building that could lead to greater public goods provision, in spite of immediate costs to the individual voter. But in polities dominated by clientelistic linkages, democratic competition should instead disincentivize politicians from investing in the state because the costs will outweigh the expected benefits. In these latter cases, voters do not expect the incumbent to be able to provide large-scale public goods. And on the flip side, politicians with limited budgets are incentivized to invest in political machines rather than the state to maximize electoral support. So while the data depict an overall negative relationship between competitiveness and investments in fiscal capacity, this could be masking different patterns across states with more or less programmatic politics.

[10] The estimated within-country standard deviation of Δ Polity Score is 0.062, while the estimated within-country standard deviation of Δ Tax − GDP Ratio is 0.025. Multiplying 0.062 and the coefficient of 0.013 yields 0.0081, or one-third of 0.025.

To explore the nature of the conditional relationship between electoral competitiveness and fiscal capacity, we can examine whether places with lower levels of programmatic linkages are the ones driving this negative relationship. I use two cross-national measures of the programmatism of parties, as each has different advantages and disadvantages. The first is from the Democratic Accountability and Linkages Project (DALP) (Kitschelt 2009) and is only measured in one year (2008) using expert surveys to systematically rate the extent to which parties adopt programmatic, clientelistic, and charismatic linkage mechanisms.[11] If we assume that these characteristics of parties are relatively slow-moving, we can apply this 2008 measure to the data on political competition and fiscal capacity, going back in time. The second is from the *Varieties of Democracy* dataset (Coppedge et al. 2023) and is measured yearly, also by expert surveys.[12] The advantage of the V-Dem measure is that we can observe changes over time. The advantage of the DALP measure is that it is more informative. It combines several questions about linkage mechanisms for each party, which are then aggregated and weighted by party size, whereas the V-Dem indicator is based on an observation of the party system as a whole.

As before, the main empirical specification is a panel regression with time and country fixed effects, and it simply adds an interaction term for the lagged value of programmatic politics. For the V-Dem measure, I code an indicator variable that takes a 1 if the country-year value of the Party linkage variable was rated as "Programmatic," and a 0 if the country-year was rated as anything lower, including basing exchange relationships on clientelistic or collective goods. In all, 45 percent of the more than 3,000 country-year observations are coded as programmatic. For the DALP measure, I create a binary variable that indicates whether the

11 The measure I use here is *cosalpo_4nwe*, or an index of at least five questions about party linkages aggregated over parties weighted by party size. The specific questions ask about the parties' positions with respect to social spending on the disadvantaged, the state's role in governing the economy, public spending, national identity, and traditional authority. The indicator itself measures the cohesion of parties' appeals on an issue position, the salience of the issue position, and the degree of spatial distinctiveness or polarization of parties on issue positions.

12 The single measure used here, Party Linkages, is a 5-point scale where higher levels indicate greater programmatism: 0 indicates constituents are rewarded with goods, cash, and/or jobs; the midpoint, 2, indicates constituents are rewarded with local collective goods, for example, wells, toilets, markets, roads, bridges, and local development; while 4 indicates constituents respond to a party's positions on national policies, general party programs, and visions for society.

country scores above the median on the Programmatic Structure of parties measure, considering only the countries in the sample. When using the DALP data, the moderating variable, *Programmatic*, does not enter into the fixed effects equation by itself because it is constant within countries over time. The coefficient β_1 thus estimates the effect of competition in countries with below-median levels of party programmatism, and $\beta_1 + \beta_3$ estimates the effect of competition in countries with above-median levels of party programmatism.

$$\Delta\text{Tax/GDP}_{i,t} = \beta_0 + \beta_1 \Delta\text{Competition}_{i,t-1} + \beta_2 \text{Programmatic}_{i,t-1} + \beta_3 \Delta\text{Competition}_{i,t-1} \times \text{Programmatic}_i + \gamma_i + \alpha_t + \epsilon_{i,t}.$$

Results of the first differences model for each moderating variable are depicted graphically in Figure 6.2. Consistent with expectations, there is a differential relationship between political competitiveness and investment in state capacity, conditional on programmatic politics, irrespective of which measure is used as the moderating variable. Because the DALP data is only measured in 2008, I only plot data from the more recent years of 1990–2010 for which the 2008 observation is more likely to apply. This pattern holds, only weakening in magnitude, as we extend the data back in time.

In both tests, the less programmatic party systems exhibit a negative relationship between increasing political competition and the ability of the state to generate tax revenue. And in both cases, this relationship is statistically different in countries or country-years with different levels of programmatism. As for countries and country-years with higher levels of programmatism, the results differ by the measure used. In the V-Dem data, there is no relationship between political competitiveness and the tax–GDP ratio, while in the DALP data, the relationship is positive. This could reflect the fact that the extent of taxing and spending on public goods can vary considerably under programmatic parties; more conservative parties may prefer a more limited state mandate compared to larger welfare states preferred by more progressive parties. But both tests support the idea that the costs of investing in the state outweigh the benefits in contexts of non-programmatic linkage mechanisms.

This exercise illustrates that there may be differential incentives to invest in the state across democratic polities with more and less programmatic parties. Of course, there are other factors, correlated with the nature of linkage mechanisms, that might be responsible for this conditional relationship. So it is not necessarily the case that increasing programmatism

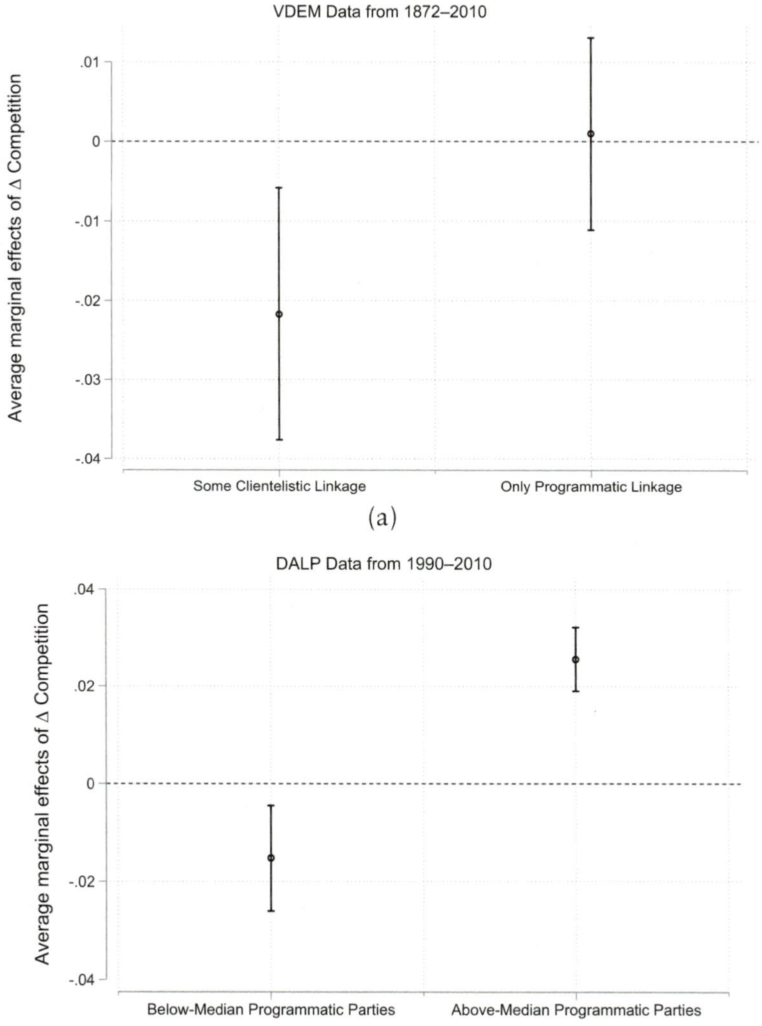

(b)

FIGURE 6.2 Differential incentives to invest in the state.

or decreasing clientelism will necessarily alter the relationship between political competition and fiscal capacity. In Chapter 7, I interrogate just this: whether declining clientelism induces greater programmatic claim-making and, with it, incentives to invest in the state.

6.3 INCENTIVES TO STATE-BUILD IN A WEAK STATE

So far, we have seen evidence that political competition can undermine incentives to invest in the state, especially when politics do not cleave along programmatic lines. In the Lagos case presented at the beginning of the chapter, we observed political will to invest in state-building and formalizing the informal sector. Because political competition is relatively lower there, one explanation for the state's behavior is that political disincentives to invest in the state are also relatively lower. But just because there are fewer obstacles to state investment does not necessarily imply that incumbents will choose to invest in the state. Indeed, investing in the state is costly for reasons other than political retribution as discussed below. So what is driving the decision to state-build there? In this section, I reflect on what might be learned from the Lagos case about when weak states with large informal sectors and clientelistic politics might actually buck the trend and invest in state-building.

Theories of State-Building

In addition to the aforementioned electoral costs of state-building, one financial cost to a politician's present investment in state capacity is the future increase in private tax payments he and his elite coalition will face as a result of increased fiscal extraction.[13] In addition to facing higher taxes, Martin (2023) argues that rent-maximizing political elites also face the cost of lower potential rents if they increase taxation, assuming a link between tax payment and demands for greater political accountability.

Historically, one of the main reasons states invested in the capacity to tax and provide services was the war motive. To be able to effectively fight interstate wars, states needed to train, arm, and conscript an army for which they needed resources (fiscal capacity) and the ability to provide public goods such as education and health (bureaucratic capacity) (Tilly 1990). Scheve and Stasavage (2016) describe an additional mechanism: that war-making can produce unequal sacrifice by the poor leading to increased motivation for state-building to provide compensatory redistribution from the rich to the poor.

[13] Hollenbach and Silva (2019) test one implication of this: the greater the wealth inequality between the political elite and citizens, the greater will be the burden incurred by redistribution. They find that more unequal localities in Brazil indeed have weaker fiscal capacity due to the greater disincentive to invest in state capacity.

During many periods in history, this motive was sufficiently important as to outweigh any future costs of building such capacity. But with the reduction in external threats following the peace accords of World War II, this incentive for governments to build state capacity declined in importance. And even when there is interstate war in these later periods, it has a weaker effect on state-building because global capital markets are more developed and loans become a plausible alternative to taxation in financing wars (Queralt 2018). Herbst (1990) and Bates (2001) have notably cited this absence of external threats as a key reason for the general weakness of states across sub-Saharan Africa.

Internal competition between elites has also been argued to prompt states to invest in increasing capacity. In particular, industrialization can create such competition, prompting new industrial elites to challenge the dominance and preferences of the old agricultural elite. Since industrial elites benefit from higher public goods provision than agricultural elites; such competition should result in the promotion or acceptance of more progressive tax regimes (Beramendi, Dincecco and Rogers 2019). But late-industrializers, like those in the developing world, experience less intra-elite competition and, as a result, less pressure to build fiscal states.

Even without these external or internal pressures, rulers themselves can have incentives to invest in state capacity if doing so increases their access to future rents (Olson 1993). If rulers can credibly commit not to expropriate too much, then investing in the capacity to extract tax revenue and provide public goods today increases future economic productivity and thus the possibility of future rents. But since it takes time for the ruler to convert investments in public goods into rents, time horizons matter. Only those rulers who have a sufficient expectation of being in power when subsequent rents accrue will invest in public goods today (Acemoglu 2005). Indeed, electoral competition in South Asia leads parties to have shorter time horizons, which they respond to by interfering in the day-to-day administration of the state to extract rents, thus undermining state capacity (Murtaza 2023).

Learning from the Lagos Case

Relatively low levels of political competition in Lagos have induced longer time horizons for Bola Tinubu and his party. This case provides an illustration of how investing in fiscal capacity and increasing revenue extraction can *directly* benefit a long-serving leader. In 2000, Lagos State hired

ALPHABETA Consulting (ABC), a private company, to manage its data and payment monitoring system in exchange for a commission on tax revenues. Basically, ABC monitored bank payments and reduced leakages by ensuring that tax payments at the bank actually reached state coffers. Its role, however, is limited to this payment monitoring; ABC does not engage in auditing companies or increasing tax compliance.

Tinubu has long been rumored to be a major shareholder in ABC, creating a direct personal benefit to increasing revenue collection through ABC's commission. More details of the arrangement came out in 2020 when a former Managing Director of ABC sued the company for his portion of the revenue he claims to still be owed. In that suit, it was claimed that Tinubu's proxies in the company held 70 percent of the shares and that the firm had received N150 billion through its 10 percent commission on all public revenues collected over the years (Ramon 2020). Tinubu and ABC denied claims of the controlling interest in the company as well as allegations of corruption. In another reported move linking Tinubu directly to ABC, the current governor of Lagos State, Sanwo-Olu, was said to have increased the commission ABC receives from N800 million to N2.5 billion per month to help finance Tinubu's campaign for the 2023 presidential elections (Olubajo 2020). This was reported by the People's Gazette, an internationally recognized source of investigative journalism founded by a journalist who had previously been arrested and detained for reporting undesirable stories about the Nigerian government. The newspaper's website was blocked and its offices raided by government officials.

Whether or not Tinubu has a controlling interest in the company, engaged in corrupt practices, or used proceeds from his stake in ABC to finance his presidential campaign, there is no doubt that Tinubu has some stake in the company. The example thus illustrates the very direct connection between the personal financial interests of the leader and the development of the fiscal state. In other words, tying the incentives of the leader to the long-term interests of the state may be one way to induce investments in fiscal capacity.

A less pessimistic lesson from the Lagos case is that it illustrates the importance of state executives with a technocratic vision. Tinubu and Fashola are commonly cited as technocratic leaders. They both came from the private sector, as did many in their cabinets. In an interview with Fashola, he reflected on his predecessor Tinubu saying, "if we do not get involved, people who did not have our skills would make laws for us and take decisions on our behalf by which we would have to be bound."

Not only did private sector experience give them skills and standards of operational efficiency, but it also made them more responsive to that sector. Fashola said, "The public sector as a government exists only for one reason, for the private sector ... from the unemployed chap to the biggest corporation. Who better to write the manual of operation, to write the process of implementation for the public sector, than the private sector on whose behalf they exist. If they continue to speak different languages, they won't function" (Fashola 2009).

Stefan Dercon echoes the importance of technocratic leaders for successful economic development in his recent book (Dercon 2022). As the Chief Economist for the UK international aid agency, he worked first-hand with some of these leaders and credits them with working within political constraints to realize growth-enhancing economic policies. To do this, they had to be aware of influential groups and coordinate with business interests at home and abroad. Notably, many of the success stories are from relatively less competitive regimes, for example, Ethiopia, Uganda, and Botswana. Perhaps there, the elite bargains necessary to secure development-friendly policies were less politically risky because of lower electoral uncertainty.

Dercon talks about these "development bargains" among the country's elite as a gamble. From the above discussion, it appears that such gambles are more likely under conditions of lower political uncertainty and where there are politically relevant business interests available to participate in the bargain. The Lagos experience is more the exception than the rule in Nigeria. Lagos State is leaps and bounds beyond other states in Nigeria in terms of tax revenue generation. Bloomberg called Lagos the "tax capital of West Africa" because of the intensity and effectiveness of taxation (Monye and Abang 2020). Instead, most African democracies look more like Senegal than Lagos in their approach to state-building with relatively limited investment in the statistical and administrative capacities that would be needed to significantly improve internally generated revenue and service provision. In the concluding chapter, I discuss some of the contemporary politicians and business interests in Senegal who might be more willing to enter into one of these development bargains.

7

Is Declining Clientelism a Way Out of the Trap?

The previous chapter was pessimistic about the prospect of electoral competition inducing democratic leaders to invest in state-building. We saw that the negative relationship between electoral competition and fiscal capacity manifested in contexts of high clientelistic linkages between parties and voters; not so in contexts of programmatic competition. So what if the use of clientelism as an electoral mobilization strategy were to decline in a weak state? Could that, on its own, lead to more programmatic competition as a way out of the weak-state trap? In other words, I have already argued that increasing programmatism on its own is a promising pathway out of the weak-state trap. But declining clientelism would only lead to the same outcome if it were a substitute for programmatism.

This question is important because mobilizing programmatic constituencies is hard and rare in weak states with large informal sectors. But the waning utility of clientelism is more common. Clientelism works less well to mobilize support in urban compared to rural areas (Harding 2020) and urban areas are more often the site of opposition to clientelistic incumbents (Resnick 2012). Africa is urbanizing faster than any other region, with urban populations expected to triple by 2050. Urban voting populations may soon outpace rural ones, potentially threatening the viability of old clientelistic machines. What will this imply for the development of programmatic linkages between parties and, especially, urban voters?

In this chapter, we return to the Senegal case as an opportunity to explore this question. In the first part of the chapter, I describe how the power of clientelistic intermediaries has seen a decline in recent decades, especially in urban Dakar, even though levels of economic informality remain high. This highlights the importance of the urban formal sector as the potential locus of an emergent constituency for programmatism. In the second section, I describe the types of linkage mechanisms that have replaced collective clientelism in the city; they are largely not programmatic in nature. While a transition to programmatic politics has not yet happened in Senegal, there are potential openings of note that I describe in the concluding chapter.

7.1 THE DECLINE OF CLIENTELISM IN URBAN SENEGAL

In this section, I provide evidence that clientelism has been declining in urban Senegal in recent decades. I study temporal trends using a mixed-methods approach. I first show that collective clientelism – the exchange of club goods for blocs of votes – is a prominent phenomenon in rural Senegal. I then employ historical geographic data to show that this used to be a viable electoral strategy in urban Dakar, but its use by parties has declined over time. Interview data suggests two main reasons for this change: the decline in demand for locally excludable goods like water standpipes and the decline in reliance on social networks and local leaders. These trends make clientelistic offerings less valuable at the same time that they make clientelistic brokers less effective.

These factors are consistent with changes in the push and pull factors that other scholars have identified as opening space for programmatic politics. The supply of clientelism declines when voters become wealthier and better informed, increasing costs and reducing the effectiveness of targeted exchange (Weitz-Shapiro 2012; Kramon 2016, 2017). The demand for clientelism declines as incomes rise and, with them, programmatic or universalistic preferences (Reid Jr. and Kurth 1992).

The Senegalese Context

Though Senegal's elections have been described as clientelistic with a strong presence of brokers or political intermediaries, this depiction generally refers to rural areas where the preponderance of local elites – often of ethnic or religious significance – with strong ties to their communities makes clientelism via local brokers an attractive electoral mobilization strategy (O'Brien 1975; Beck 2008; Koter 2013). Less has been written about clientelistic brokerage in urban settings.

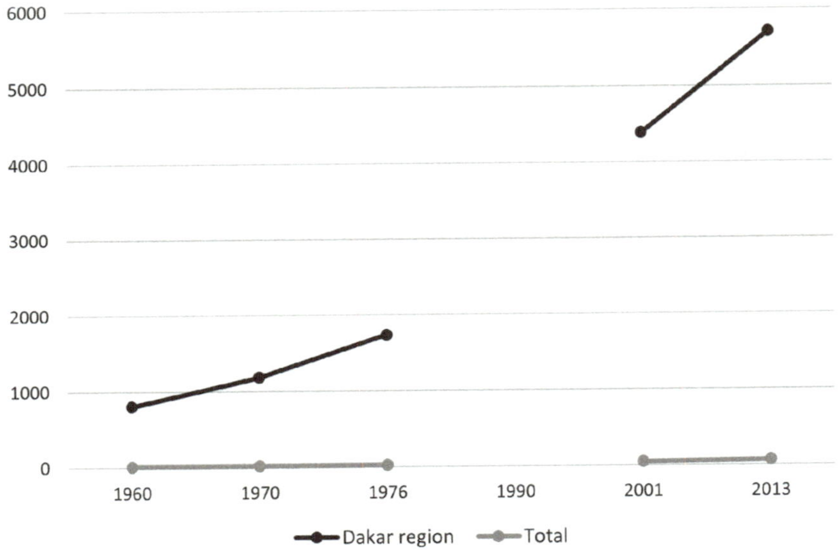

FIGURE 7.1 Population density over time (pp/km²).

Neighborhood chiefs (the urban equivalent of village chiefs) are a natural focal point for urban political entrepreneurs, but their usefulness in electoral mobilization remains an open question. At their founding, urban neighborhoods were led by chiefs or *chefs de quartier*. In 1996, the position legally changed to the *delegué de quartier*, or the neighborhood representative, with a more circumscribed and regulated set of administrative duties. The early neighborhood chiefs were closely affiliated with the ruling PS party, and as described below, played an important role in politics. By contrast, modern neighborhood representatives are, by law, supposed to be apolitical. However, this is not always the case in reality, as illustrated by a recent pledge by 400 representatives in the Pikine district to vote with the president in a 2016 referendum (Aziz 2016).

Urban voters have been growing in number and in wealth level at a faster rate than those in rural areas – making urban constituencies increasingly more important to politicians. As one stark illustration of the population dynamics in rural and urban settings in Senegal, Figure 7.1 shows how rapidly population density has increased over time in the mostly urban region of Dakar relative to the rest of the country. Gross domestic product (GDP) has also grown quickly and steadily since the early 2000s, after the economic crises of the 1990s, with 65 percent of Senegal's GDP produced in urban centers.

In this analysis, I focus strictly on the urban districts surrounding the country's capital, henceforth Greater Urban Dakar, as these dense urban spaces are distinct from some of the smaller urban centers in the periphery. Urban growth has been mainly driven by Dakar. It produces 55 percent of GDP, is home to more than 80 percent of registered firms, and boasts more than 52 percent of jobs created. The Dakar region is also home to half of the country's total urban population and approximately one quarter of all registered voters. I first illustrate the existence of collective clientelism in rural Senegal, affirming observations from the existing literature.

Collective Clientelism as an Electoral Strategy in Rural Senegal

Measuring collective clientelism requires demonstrating the targeting of locally excludable goods to reciprocal voters (or voting blocs). In both this and the next section, I will evaluate whether the targeting of water standpipes, a locally excludable and publicly provided good, follows such a pattern. In 2000 and 2009, the Senegalese National Statistics Agency produced a survey of local infrastructure in all rural villages of Senegal. Electoral precinct-level data are available for the presidential elections immediately before and after this period – in 2000 and 2012.

Matching the 3,725 rural polling stations to rural villages, we can first assess whether a village having a water standpipe by 2000 is associated with voting at a higher rate for the incumbent party in the 2000 presidential election. Such an analysis assumes that standpipes built by 2000 would be attributed to the incumbent *Parti Socialiste* (PS) running in the 2000 elections. To isolate the relationship between water access and voting, the electoral and infrastructure data are merged with village-level census data. Controls are flexibly added for logged population, logged ethnic and religious group size, availability of private goods in 2000, and logged assets. In addition, fixed effects are entered at the commune or municipality level to reflect the fact that most clientelistic targeting occurs within, rather than across, municipalities due to the greater information that local party agents hold and the seeming adherence to formulaic intergovernmental transfers, which evens out spending across (though not within) municipalities.

Indeed, we see in Column 1 of Table 7.1 that having access to water in 2000 is positively and significantly correlated with voting for the incumbent PS.[1] Specifically, a village with access to water has a incumbent vote share that is, on average, 1.4 percentage points higher than villages in the municipality without water access. We can also test whether a *change* in access to water over the period from 2000 to 2009 is associated with greater support for the PDS party's Abdoulaye Wade in the 2012 presidential elections. Such a change would be attributed to Wade, who was in power during that entire period. In the second column of Table 7.1, we indeed see a strong and significant correlation between receiving greater access to water over Wade's mandate and voting for his party in 2012. A village gaining access to water is associated with a 1 percentage point increase in the incumbent party's vote share in that village in 2012.

These voting patterns could either be evidence of clientelistic targeting or simply retrospective performance voting. In other words, parties could be discretionarily targeting goods to loyal voters, or they could be targeting based on some other logic, and voters could be rewarding an incumbent's good performance at the ballot box. As one way of adjudicating between the two possible interpretations of the data, we can examine whether Wade's PDS engaged in differential targeting of goods based on voter behavior in the 2000 election. If Wade was more likely to provide goods to villages that bloc voted for his party in the past, this evidence would favor the interpretation of discretionary or clientelistic targeting over retrospective voting.

The third column of Table 7.1 reports results of regressing the change in water access over the available 2000 to 2009 period on the vote share for Wade in the 2000 presidential elections. The analysis controls for baseline levels of water access since, by construction, places that already have access to water in 2000 cannot get more access (although they can lose access). We see a significant positive relationship between voting for the PDS in 2000 and getting access to water in the subsequent decade. In other words, this evidence favors the explanation of a strategy of clientelistic targeting by the incumbent. Another observable implication of clientelistic targeting is that incumbents should target more goods to places with polling stations than to places without because the former are easier to

[1] I code a vote for the incumbent party as a vote for either the incumbent president, Abdou Diouf, or Moustapha Niasse, who split off from the ruling party, the PS, shortly before the election to create his own party, thus splitting the votes of PS loyalists.

TABLE 7.1 *Relationship between water access and voting in rural Senegal*

	(1) '00 Voteshare PS	(2) '12 Voteshare PDS	(3) Δ Water access ('00–'09)
Access to water ('00)	0.014^{+}		-0.873^{***}
	(0.008)		(0.019)
Δ Water ('00–'09)		0.010^{+}	
		(0.006)	
PDS vote share in ('00)			0.107^{**}
			(0.035)
Observations	3,725	4,177	3,725

Notes: Robust standard errors are in parentheses, clustered at the commune level. Included controls are logged population (flexible), logged ethnic and religious group size (linear, quadratic, cubic), availability of private goods in 2000, and logged assets (linear, quadratic, cubic). Fixed effects are entered at the commune level. $^{+}$ $p < 0.10$, ** $p < 0.01$, *** $p < 0.001$.

monitor. Gottlieb and Larreguy (2016) show that Wade's PDS indeed targeted more goods to villages with polling stations than those without.

A History of Collective Clientelism in the City

The practice of collective clientelism in rural Senegal is not surprising. Others have documented the availability of local brokers that make this strategy efficient (O'Brien 1975; Beck 2008) and have even attributed the pervasiveness of clientelism in Senegal to this rural phenomenon (Koter 2013). But the extent of collective clientelism has not been similarly interrogated in urban areas. At least in the Senegalese case, a key constraint to such an analysis is that data on locally excludable goods only exists in a systematic way for rural areas. But data collected by a geographer in the 1990's changes this.

Gérard Salem, writing in 1992, noticed that the placement of standpipes in a peripheral area of Greater Dakar (Pikine district)[2] was not consistent with what an urban planner might prescribe: spaced according

[2] The département of Pikine is one of four in the region of Dakar as of 2002. It is the second largest after Dakar but the fastest growing in terms of population. Guediawaye has a higher population density than Pikine, but was not created until 2002, when it was carved out of the existing département of Pikine. Because the below analysis uses maps from prior to the split, Guediawaye is included in the analysis of the Pikine district.

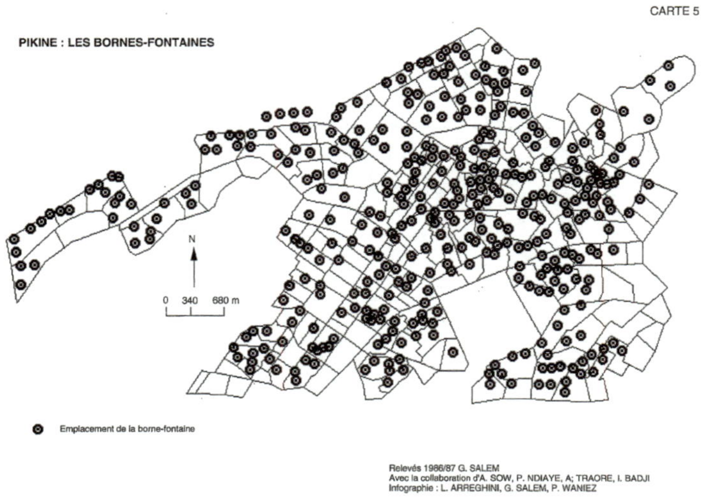

FIGURE 7.2 Map of neighborhood boundaries and standpipes in Pikine.

to population density and need. Instead, the placement of water access across space was more reflective of the uneven distribution of political power across the city (Salem 1992). He noted that "this clientelism relied on an exchange of services … the authority of the State on the one hand, and a survival strategy on the other." More specifically, those political agents with the most status and support in the party are best situated to provide payment compensation to neighborhood chiefs along with goods and services. In return, the targeted neighborhood representatives sell party memberships, assure favorable behavior on election day, and mobilize popular showings of support for the party. According to Salem, this exchange is most evidently manifest in the distribution of standpipes or shared taps, given that access to water is the primary demand that the neighborhood representatives make of local elected officials.

In 1986, Salem not only recorded the outlines of neighborhoods in the largest peri-urban district of Pikine, but also the geographic placement of standpipes and other features of neighborhoods (see Figure 7.2). To more systematically test whether Salem's observations of clientelism are indeed borne out in subsequent electoral behavior, I digitized and spatially matched his maps of standpipes in Pikine in 1986 with polling stations in the 2000 election (see Figure 7.3). There are 52 polling stations in the area mapped by Salem, and a total of 241 standpipes. The modal neighborhood has one standpipe, but many have two or three.

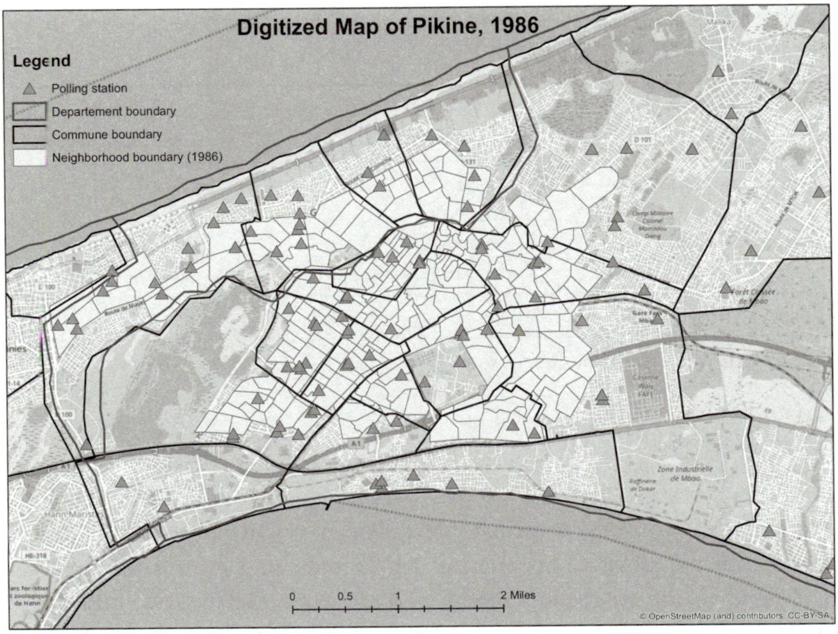

FIGURE 7.3 Polling stations in Pikine.

Polling stations are not allocated on the basis of neighborhoods; as seen in Figure 7.3, there are many more neighborhoods than polling stations. Because we do not have data on how individual voters in each neighborhood were assigned to which polling station, the most conservative mapping of registered voters to assigned polling stations would assume that individuals residing in the neighborhood that houses a polling station are assigned to vote in that polling station. Using this assumption, I then test whether residents of neighborhoods that received more standpipes in 1986 are more likely to vote for the incumbent party in 2000. According to Salem, getting a standpipe in 1986 is a sign of a strong local political intermediary or neighborhood chief. Assuming relatively high durability of these PS intermediaries, we might expect to see them influencing the voting behavior of local residents even years later.

Table 7.2 presents the results of regressing the vote share for the incumbent party in 2000 on the number of standpipes in 1986.[3] Because several neighborhoods contain multiple polling stations, I cluster standard errors

3 As before, I code a vote for the incumbent party as a vote for either the incumbent president Abdou Diouf or for Moustapha Niasse.

TABLE 7.2 *Relationship between local good and voting in 2000 in urban Senegal*

	(1) Incumbent party	(2) Opposition party
Standpipes (1986)	0.007*	−0.006+
	(0.003)	(0.003)
Constant	0.368***	0.529***
	(0.011)	(0.012)
Observations	52	52

OLS models with robust standard errors. $^{+}p < 0.10$, $^{*}p < 0.05$, $^{***}p < 0.001$.

at the neighborhood level. Even with only 43 clusters, and a thus relatively low-powered analysis, we see statistically significant relationships. There is a significant positive correlation between having more standpipes in 1986 and voting for the incumbent party in 2000. Getting two additional standpipes is associated with a one-quarter standard deviation increase in the vote share for the incumbent party. Conversely, there is a negative correlation between having standpipes and voting for the largest opposition party, the PDS, which ultimately won the election.

The Decline of Collective Clientelism in the City

To investigate whether the type of collective clientelism described by Salem in 1986 and evidenced by data in 2000 is still in practice in Pikine today, I conducted interviews in 2018 with contemporary delegués de quartier or neighborhood representatives – the modern version of the neighborhood chiefs described by Salem as brokers in the political exchange between party operatives and urbanites. I asked questions that could shed light on whether there still exists an exchange relationship between local neighborhoods and political parties that is mediated either by the neighborhood representatives themselves or other political intermediaries. In total, I spoke with seven neighborhood representatives in four different neighborhoods of Pikine, chosen to maximize variation in the competitiveness of elections and the level of development of the neighborhood. I also recruited representatives who had been in their position for varying lengths of time to better understand how things may have changed over time.

One representative who had been in his position for two decades confirmed the existence of the type of clientelism that Salem described early in his career. He said that in the early years, the state needed him as much as he needed the state; party militants came to him for votes, and he got two standpipes in his community in return.[4] Today, however, he said everyone has access to water, so this would no longer be a feasible strategy.

Other interviews supported the idea that water standpipes are no longer a good way to measure locally excludable goods in urban areas, because almost everyone has access to piped water (see Figure 7.4 for a map of piped water in 2000). Even "branchements sociaux" or hookups for poorer families, where the usage rate was lower, have not been used for over ten years; nearly everyone now has faucets in their homes. Instead, the interviewees suggested that the most valued local goods were working street lights, remediation after flooding, paved roads, and sewage. Some of these goods are less locally excludable than standpipes, and others are more valuable in areas where you work rather than where you reside and vote.

Interviewees provided insight into why collective voting and their roles as intermediaries have changed over the past two decades. Several neighborhood representatives said that there has been an increase in autonomy of vote choice: "You can no longer tell your children how to vote," which would make collective clientelism harder. One gave a poignant example of how his grandfather used to unite the family and instruct them on how to vote.[5] Similarly, others said that dependency relationships between brokers and voters have declined, so brokers are no longer able to trust voters to follow through on an exchange.

However, this has not stopped the practice of vote buying, which almost everyone explicitly said is still used. While several neighborhood representatives concurred that "all candidates buy votes before elections," others said that personal donations also happen at other times of the year or mandate.[6] One said that it can happen through the *imam* or other local influencers and that parties have cells in most neighborhoods that inform the party of the identity of the influencers, who are then targeted with money to distribute to get voters.[7] I met with the leader of a women's savings group who acted as such an intermediary and would organize her

4 Neighborhood chief interviews, Respondent 1.
5 Neighborhood chief interviews, Respondent 2.
6 Neighborhood chief interviews, Respondents 3, 4.
7 Neighborhood chief interviews, Respondent 3.

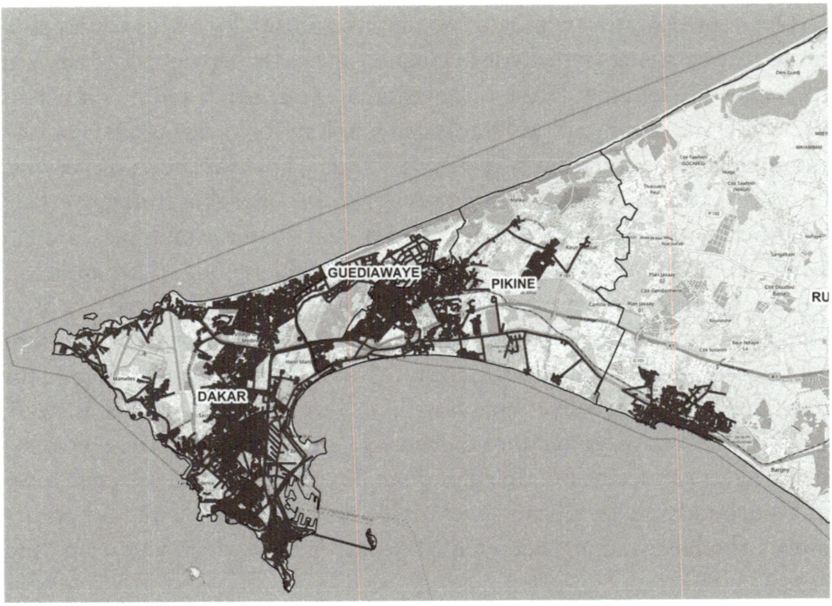

FIGURE 7.4 Piped water in 2000 in Dakar, Senegal.
Source: Agence Nationale de la Statistique et de la Démographie, Sénégal, 2000.

members to attend rallies or deliver votes in exchange for contributions to their savings pool. But rather than developing sustained reciprocal relationships with a particular party as was common in the past, their votes were for sale to the highest bidder. She bemoaned the fact that attending multiple campaign rallies for cash is no longer feasible since parties have started placing spies at the rallies of other politicians to prevent such behavior.

Some representatives also described the origin story of their neighborhoods, illustrating the rapid rural to urban migration that has occurred over the past several decades, especially in peri-urban areas. As migrants came from different parts of the country and for different reasons, the population of their neighborhoods expanded quickly, and agricultural areas were transformed for residential and commercial use. What were once tight-knit communities settled by a single family or kin group are now dense and diversely populated neighborhoods with much looser social ties.

This deeper look at a quickly developing peri-urban district that went from rural backwater to urban sprawl in a few short decades gives us insight into the changes that may have led to the decline in the effectiveness of collective clientelism. First, infrastructural development made widespread access to amenities more feasible and thus weakened the demand for targeted provision of excludable goods. Second, economic growth made some people less vulnerable and thus less reliant on informal networks, and the brokers within them, for survival. And third, the increased interaction with people from other identity groups weakened ties to members of one's own group in ways that can be useful for more cross-cutting political mobilization. Together, these conversations illustrate and confirm existing arguments about how economic and demographic changes reduce the effectiveness of clientelism (see Hicken 2011 for a review of the long literature on this relationship). One distinct contribution of this case study is that it applies the intuition more specifically to collective clientelism, which has been a dominant electoral strategy in Senegal.

The Differential Fate of Collective Clientelism across Space

To more systematically assess the decline in collective clientelism reported by today's neighborhood representatives, I now turn to rich disaggregated electoral data. Specifically, I use overtime data from several elections to examine whether there are differences in voting patterns across rural and urban areas. One way to measure the extent of collective clientelism as an electoral strategy is to observe patterns of local vote coordination. Collective clientelism requires that communities or groups vote in a coordinated manner for a single party to demonstrate they are holding up their end of the clientelistic exchange.

When voting results are reported at the precinct level, as they are in Senegal, a proxy for the extent of coordinated voting is the observed plurality vote share for any party within a precinct. Such a phenomenon is more informative to party agents where precincts map onto distinct groups of voters, such as villages (Kitschelt and Wilkinson 2007). We thus expect, and see, that rural areas exhibit higher levels of coordinated voting. But more importantly for our purposes here, observing changes in plurality voting within precincts over time can serve as an indication of the change in the capacity of voters to coordinate.[8]

[8] Such an analysis assumes that the informativeness of election outcomes is not changing differentially across space such that differential trends could be attributed to changing party tactics rather than changing voter behavior.

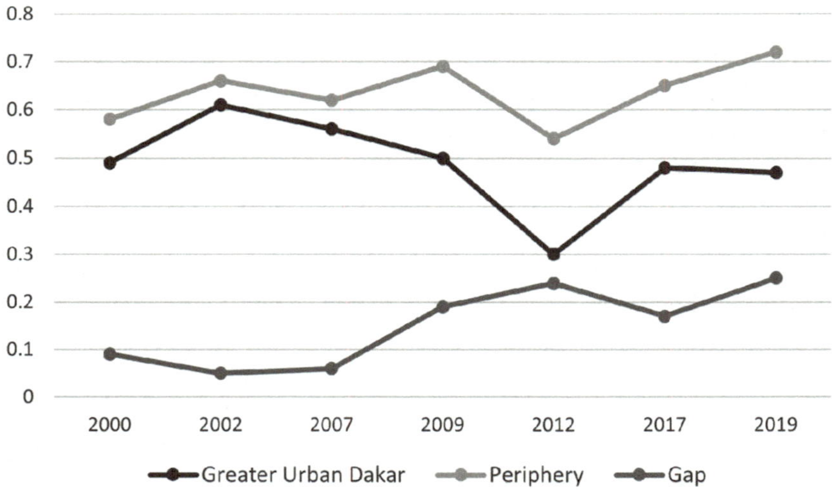

FIGURE 7.5 Average precinct-level plurality vote share in Senegal's elections since 2000.

If collective clientelism is declining in cities relative to rural areas, we should see a growing gap in the rate of coordinated voting over time. Figure 7.5 plots the average vote share of each precinct's winning party in every election since 2000.[9] The sample is divided into Greater Urban Dakar, or precincts in the capital of Dakar and its peri-urban districts of Pikine and Guediawaye; all other precincts are coded as "Periphery." The figure shows that the urban–rural gap in the extent of coordinated voting has indeed been increasing over time, with urban voters becoming increasingly less coordinated relative to rural voters.

A second observable implication we can leverage to study collective clientelism is that places that are good at it in one election should stay good at it in subsequent elections due, in part, to successful intermediaries who remain in their constituencies over multiple elections. If both supply of and demand for collective clientelism persist over time in rural areas and decline in urban ones, then coordinated voting in 2000 should predict coordinated voting in later elections for rural areas more than urban ones. Merging precinct-level data over multiple elections, we can evaluate these trends. Table 7.3 illustrates that plurality vote share in 2000 is differentially predictive of plurality vote share in later years across urban

9 The first round is recorded when presidential elections have two rounds to reflect initial coordinating capacity.

TABLE 7.3 *Relationship between coordinated voting in 2000 and that in later elections*

	Periphery			Greater Urban Dakar		
	2007	2012	2019	2007	2012	2019
Plurality share 2000	0.098***	0.171***	0.191***	0.688***	0.129+	−0.143*
	(0.016)	(0.015)	(0.017)	(0.089)	(0.066)	(0.056)
Constant	0.556***	0.438***	0.601***	0.219***	0.244***	0.551***
	(0.010)	(0.009)	(0.010)	(0.044)	(0.033)	(0.027)
Observations	4,400	4,382	4,382	148	148	148

OLS models with robust standard errors. $^{+}p < 0.10$, $^{*}p < 0.05$, $^{***}p < 0.001$.

and rural areas. The correlation between vote coordination in 2000 and later elections goes down over time in urban areas while it goes up in rural ones.

A threat to this interpretation of the data is the possibility that local election results are becoming more or less informative of voting behavior at differential rates across urban and rural areas. One way in which a local election outcome could become diluted or less informative is if the number of registered voters in a precinct increases. A greater number of registrants could make targeting goods to them more difficult or less valuable. Indeed, an increase in registered voters over time makes coordinated voting in 2019 less likely (see Table 7.4). But importantly, controlling for the change in registered voters over time actually strengthens the conclusion that

TABLE 7.4 *Relationship between coordinated voting in 2000 and 2019 accounting for informativeness*

	(1)	(2)
Plurality share 2000	0.189***	0.170***
	(0.016)	(0.016)
Greater Urban Dakar	−0.051	0.040
	(0.109)	(0.109)
Greater Urban Dakar × plurality share 2000	−0.332	−0.392+
	(0.222)	(0.221)
Δ Registered voters in 1000's (2000–2019)		−0.003***
		(0.000)
Constant	0.602***	0.622***
	(0.010)	(0.010)
Observations	4,571	4,571

OLS models with robust standard errors. $^{+}p < 0.10$, $^{***}p < 0.001$.

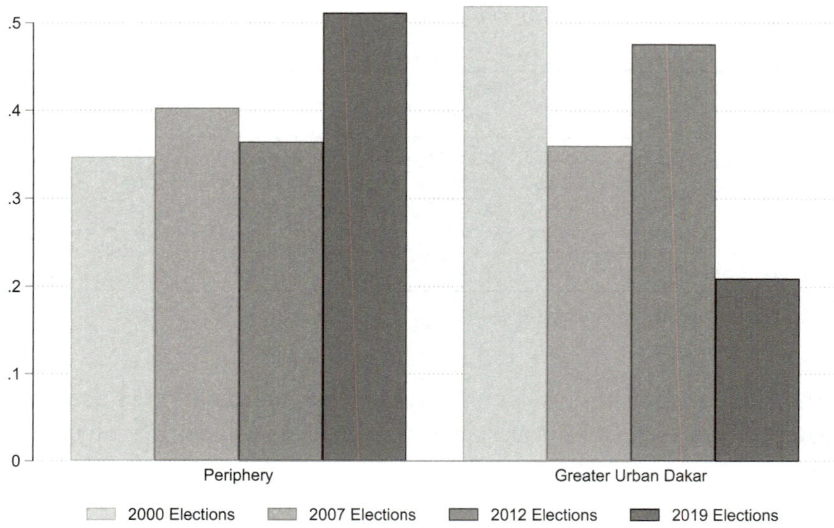

FIGURE 7.6 Margin of victory in Senegal's presidential elections since 2000. *Note:* The second round is reported when presidential elections have two rounds.

trends in coordinated voting over time are different across rural and urban Senegal.

A third observable implication of a decline in coordinated voting in urban relative to rural areas is that electoral competition should increase more in urban relative to rural areas over time. Charting the precinct-level margin of victory between the top two parties over time in rural and urban precincts in Figure 7.6, we indeed see that competition has actually been mostly decreasing across elections in rural precincts while it has been mostly increasing in urban ones.

Finally, if collective clientelism is more successful in rural areas relative to urban areas, we should see the incumbent gaining more loyal voters who self-identify as copartisans over time. Afrobarometer surveys from Senegal allow us to examine changes in self-reported copartisanship between elections. While partisanship is asked in all six rounds of Senegal's Afrobarometer surveys, distance to an election affects self-reporting of copartisanship (Michelitch and Utych 2018). Thus, I compare Afrobarometer rounds conducted at similar distances from elections: two and three years into Abdoulaye Wade's and Macky Sall's first terms, repectively, and two and one year before their first reelection opportunity. In Figure 7.7, we see that incumbents in both cases gained copartisans over time in rural areas, while they lost copartisans over time in urban Dakar.

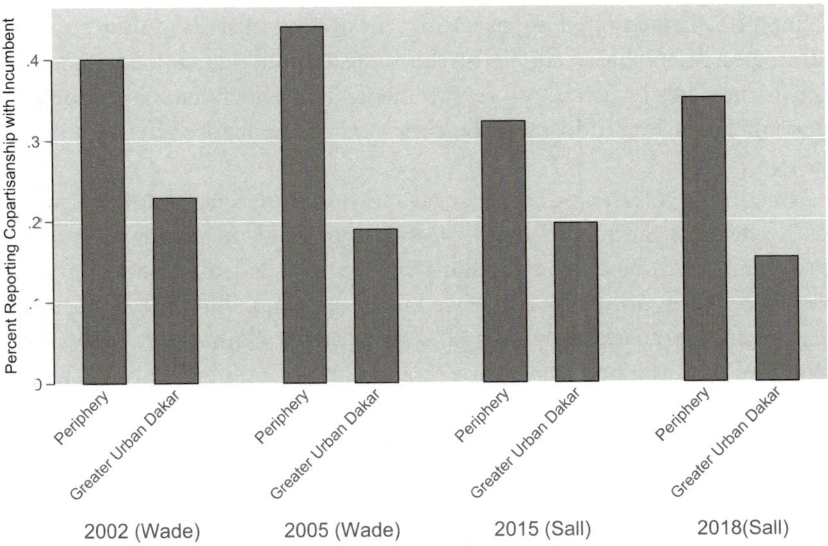

FIGURE 7.7 Incumbents gain in rural, lose in urban.

7.2 OTHER ELECTORAL LINKAGE MECHANISMS IN CONTEMPORARY SENEGAL

The qualitative and quantitative evidence presented above suggest that collective clientelism is in decline in urban Senegal, which begs the question of what strategies parties will use in its place. Will programmatic politics emerge as a substitute for clientelistic politics? Kitschelt (2000) discusses why these two citizen–party linkage mechanisms may be incompatible:[10] the competing principles of universalism and particularism, and a limited budget of resources and effort forcing a choice of one over the other. So it is possible that the decline of one could facilitate the emergence of the other. But Kitschelt also asserts the existence of another key linkage mechanism – charisma.

Indeed, in the case of urban Dakar, declining clientelism has not (until perhaps the 2024 elections) implied increasing programmatic linkages. Instead, politicians have largely relied on charismatic linkages that require less costly investments in state capacity. This has taken the form of populist rhetoric and vote-buying to mobilize urban voters, with the exception of one more programmatic candidate and party that we will discuss in

[10] That said, Kitschelt and others (see, e.g., Weghorst and Lindberg (2013)) stress that these party linkages are not mutually exclusive.

Chapter 8. Unmediated appeals differentiate populist from non-populist strategies. As mediated clientelism becomes less tenable, unmediated populism may be an attractive replacement. The effectiveness of populist appeals has a lot to do with the charisma of the leader (Resnick 2017, p. 109).[11]

According to Osei (2012), Senegal's former president Abdoulaye Wade used clientelist and charismatic strategies to hold on to power, but not programmatic ones. Even though the PDS is called the liberal party, it violated liberal norms by engaging in corruption, stifling the opposition, and trying to create a dynasty. Resnick (2014) claims that Abdoulaye Wade re-won the presidency in 2007 in spite of failing to appeal to the urban poor during his first mandate. Opposition parties in that election were "reliant on purely personalistic linkages that espouse vague, indistinguishable platforms." While Resnick cites a smaller set of programmatic opposition parties with appeals around workers' rights and economic nationalism, these messages were only attractive to "a small segment of unionized urbanites and salaried professionals rather than the mass of the urban poor." Wade's subsequent policies were also populist in nature. Writing about his reaction to the 2007/8 food crisis, Resnick (2013*b*, 24) says "the government forfeited the opportunity to devise a well-targeted social protection programme ... [and] instead ... were reactionary, myopic, and resulted in significant policy volatility, including the retraction of unpopular salary taxes."

In the 2012 presidential elections, programmatic policies were similarly absent from campaigns. Notably, Macky Sall, the eventual winner, focused much of his effort on rural rather than urban areas. When candidates did campaign on policies, they did not do so in a way that distinguished themselves from others. For instance, Sall's response to high food prices of consumer subsidies and agricultural investments "were not very dissimilar from Wade's responses to the 2008 food price crisis" (Resnick 2013*a*). But perhaps the clearest example of the absence of programmatic policies from the 2012 elections is the refusal by Wade and Sall to "elaborate on their policy proposals through a televised debate that the national audiovisual regulatory agency had offered to organize" (Resnick 2013*a*).

11 Kitschelt (2000, p. 858) discusses how charismatic, pro-poor parties in India competed successfully with clientelistic ones.

In the 2019 presidential elections, the incumbent again shied away from discrete programmatic promises and instead touted the major infrastructural achievements he made during his mandate – for example, a bridge across the Gambia and a rapid train to the new airport – and promised more of the same, "More roads will be built. Electricity will be provided to many households as well as 50,000 streetlights" (AFP 2019). Sall's record on programmatic issues was weak. He also failed to reduce his own first term to five years as promised in 2012, and he jailed his two primary opposition candidates on corruption charges. Perhaps for this reason, Sall again did not agree to participate in a public debate held in the capital – due to "constraints of agenda" (Nsongon 2019), but a debate was still held (though not televised) among some opposition candidates.

So how did Wade and Sall mobilize voters in urban Senegal if not through programmatic appeals or collective clientelism? Resnick (2014) points to the success of populist appeals among the urban poor. For example, Wade attempted to address urban economic problems after his 2007 reelection by granting land to potential migrants if they returned to farming. Other populist programs were implemented to respond to food price hikes. While initially attractive to urbanites, these policies were poorly conceived and implemented, offering little concrete or long-term benefit. Similarly, some of Macky Sall's most popular social policies included lowering urban rents, increasing subsidies for poor families, and lowering the price of utilities. While these more populist initiatives have had differential rates of success, most have been criticized for their irregular implementation and short-sightedness, as was the case with Wade.

As mentioned in interviews with neighborhood representatives, vote-buying is also a strategy used by parties in urban Senegal. Though difficult to get reliable measures, Afrobarometer surveys offer some insights. In 2005 (round 3), 7 percent of respondents said they were offered a gift in exchange for their vote during the 2000 elections. In 2013 (round 5), 12 percent of respondents said they were offered a gift in exchange for their vote during the 2012 elections. There is no difference between responses in rural and urban areas. In round 6 (2015), 85 percent of respondents said voters are bribed during elections. Controlling for education, voters in Dakar are about five percent more likely to report this. We cannot assess temporal patterns in vote-buying with these data since the round 6 question asks about a general phenomenon, while rounds 3 and 5 ask about personal experience. We can, however, say that recent vote-buying appears more common in urban than rural areas, which is consistent with the idea that collective clientelism has become a less feasible strategy there.

7.3 SUMMING UP

In this chapter, I interrogated one alternative pathway out of the weak-state trap: reducing clientelistic linkages which have been said to naturally decline as urbanization increases (Reid Jr. and Kurth 1992; Kitschelt and Wilkinson 2007; Stokes et al. 2013; Weitz-Shapiro 2014). I showed in this chapter that the case of Senegal is no exception. Not only do we see less clientelism in urban spaces, we also see clientelism declining over time in urban Dakar while persisting elsewhere. This begs the question of whether parties would adopt programmatic strategies to attract urban voters, replacing weakening clientelistic ties. This has not happened to a measurable extent in Senegal, due perhaps to the lack of demand from informal sector actors who comprise a majority of voters in Dakar. Instead, candidates and parties have largely used charismatic and populist appeals to attract the urban poor. This suggests that attempting to reduce clientelist party linkages is not, on its own, a promising lever to push polities out of the weak-state trap. However, it may be the case that reducing the attractiveness of clientelism is necessary, if not sufficient. In the next, and final, chapter, I discuss potential signs of a rise in programmatic politics in Senegal. It is possible that these openings would not have occurred were it not for the weakening of clientelistic linkages among urban voters.

8

Conclusion

This concluding chapter has three aims: to speculate about openings or promising pathways out of the trap, to probe how cases that do not fit the theory might help us understand more about the cases that do, and to provide some guidance from the book's theory and evidence about a way forward. First, I describe some promising developments from inside Senegal and lessons from related transitions elsewhere that offer alternative insights about escaping the weak-state trap. Second, I consider how my theory's implications might extend beyond the continent of Africa that has been the main focus of this book, and in particular how cases in Latin America might offer additional insight into how constituencies for programmatism might develop on the African continent. Finally, I conclude with a discussion of the book's academic contributions and policy implications.

8.1 SEEDS OF A CONSTITUENCY FOR PROGRAMMATISM

The reason I initially chose Senegal as the primary country case for this book project is that it seemed to be a most-likely case for transitioning to programmatism despite its large informal sector. Namely, the Senegalese economy has experienced relatively stable growth – increasing the likelihood of a constituency for programmatism in the business sector, and electoral politics have been highly competitive and largely free and fair. Since beginning my work on this project, there have been signs that programmatic demands are growing and, perhaps relatedly, a programmatic party emerging. In this section, I first describe a Senegalese leader in the formal economy, Serigne Mboup, who has demonstrated preferences consistent with those of a constituency for programmatism. His conflicts with big informal business and even established members of the formal sector signal the beginnings of a potential break with the older generation of a more state-dependent bourgeoisie. Then, I return to a discussion of Ousmane Sonko, the bureaucrat-cum-politician who rose to prominence after being fired from the Tax Office when he blew the whistle on corruption (as described in Chapter 4). His profile makes his programmatic policy promises more credible, and he and his party PASTEF won local and legislative elections, and more recently, the presidential election.

Only time will tell whether these openings will be sufficient to result in a transition to a new equilibrium. I describe them here as potential alternative pathways out of the clientelistic weak-state trap.

The Rise of an Independent Bourgeoisie?

First, I tell the story of Serigne Mboup, who is notable for being the first Senegalese billionaire and the richest man in Senegal (Razafindrafito 2023). His recent conflicts with other economic leaders in the country signal a possible break with the past and the emergence of programmatic preferences, at least for one key member of the bourgeoisie. Contrary to the rich businessmen in the informal sector who historically have united (often unsuccessfully) under the banner of UNACOIS, as discussed in Chapter 4, Mboup's wealth is derived from formal business activities and, consequently, his associational activities have been conducted through the formal Chamber of Commerce.

Part of the reason Mboup's story is so notable is that his economic success in the formal sector is rare. He is the exception that proves the rule. Mboup and his company are one of the very rare cases of an informal firm that succeeded in profitably entering the formal sector (Fédération Internationale Des Experts comptables Francophones 2014). It is also a rare case of a successful firm that was not started with foreign capital – to the point that Mboup said in an interview that people are always asking him if his company has international partners. Instead, Mboup asserts that it is up to local capital to develop the country because that capital and those individuals are going to stay in the country, and because they will be willing to take more risk as the stakes for them are greater (Kaly and Ka 2010).[1]

[1] That said, CCBM has lots of connections with foreign firms as it is the key distributor for Samsung and works with Volkswagen and other car manufacturers to locally build automobiles.

Mboup's economic group, Comptoir Commercial Barra Mboup (CCBM) created in 1992, is the extension of his father's company "Ètablissement Bara Mboup," which itself was created in the region of Kaolack in 1960. Mboup started working with his father in 1989 in Dakar's famous Sandaga market, the largest informal market in the capital, selling food, clothes, and cosmetics. When Serigne took over in 1992 following his father's death, he created a family company in the informal sector. But even at the time, he didn't think of the company in those terms because he had ambitions that extended beyond the informal sector, which he eventually realized. Today, the company specializes in six key markets such as food, electronics, and cars and has built textile and peanut-processing factories in his home region of Kaolack. It has evolved from a wholesaler to a producer with its own brand (Kaly and Ka 2010) and now employs over 800 people.

In important ways, Mboup bridges the gap between the formal and informal sectors. His upbringing is more common among those in the informal sector. He went to an Arabic (rather than French) primary school and then continued at a *daara* where he learned to memorize the Koran. He attributes this as key to his success: "Those who have succeeded in this country don't have French diplomas" (Faye 2022). Perhaps this legitimacy and ability to connect with average Senegalese have contributed to his political success. In early 2022, he was elected mayor of Kaolack.

The rare combination of having economic power and operating a formal business has often put Mboup at odds with existing powerful constituencies: informal businessmen and political elites. This is best illustrated by recent conflicts within the Chamber of Commerce. Mboup has long been the president of the Chamber of Commerce in his home region of Kaolack. Historically, the powerful Dakar Chamber of Commerce and all other regional Chambers held the same administrative status under the supervision of the Ministry of Commerce. But in 2016, a group of employers' organizations, including UNACOIS (alongside the CNP, CNES, and the GES), proposed a reform that would create a national Chamber of Commerce, bringing all regional chambers underneath it. This would effectively reduce the autonomy of any regional chamber, while raising the profile of the powerholders in the Dakar chamber. Mboup spoke out against this proposal, saying that the employers' organizations were not legitimate spokesmen for the entire private sector (Diallo 2016). The proposal to create a national chamber of commerce was written into law in 2017. However, the old regional chambers continue to function as the new institutions are put into place (Fédération Atlantique des Agences de Presse Africaines 2020).

In addition to the dispute over the reorganization, there was also an electoral clash within the Chamber of Commerce between Mboup and the representatives of the employers' organizations. When the president of the Dakar Chamber of Commerce, who had served since 1991, died in 2016, new elections were held. Mboup lost to a representative of the employers' union, Abdoulaye Sow. In his role since 2015 as the president of the national union of chambers of commerce (UNCCIAS), Mboup has made his dissatisfaction with the leadership of the Dakar Chamber of Commerce known. In response, the Dakar Chamber rescinded its membership in the UNCCIAS in 2020, followed by the St-Louis Chamber of Commerce in 2021 (Sow 2021).

These clashes are certainly driven, in part, by Mboup's personal interest in increasing his own influence and access to power. However, there also appear to be real ideological differences at the heart of these divisions. For one, Mboup represents a different background and leadership style than the more established profiles of the employers' organizations as described above. And Mboup purports to hold a different vision of the economic policies that are best for the country.

Mboup's policy preferences resemble those of the corporate interests Kuo (2018) describes as pushing for less discretion and more public goods provision in the US and UK. He decries the inability of the state to raise fiscal revenue that it could then spend on necessary public goods and infrastructure. In a recent interview, Mboup gave the example of the national shipping council (COSEC), a public agency created in 1972 to define and promote policy concerning the import-export business. He stated that the 0.2 percent of declared merchandise that merchants owe to COSEC should raise between 30 and 60 million USD annually, which could be spent on improvements to the ports. He attributed the lack of any such spending to the close ties between the employers' organizations and the state, and the rents derived from this relationship. He claims that the same dynamic is apparent in the public agencies responsible for retirement and social security, pointing out that spending of these public resources is neither voted on by the National Assembly nor managed with any transparency (Gueye 2022).

There is a clear alignment between Mboup's anti-corruption views and the policy platform of Ousmane Sonko. While Mboup did not choose sides in the 2022 legislative elections (Touré 2022) and has claimed not to belong to a political party (Gueye 2022), he finally supported Sonko's

PASTEF party in the 2024 legislative elections.[2] When Sonko came to visit him at his region's Chamber of Commerce during the campaign period, he said, "You always dissuaded me from engaging in politics. But when you became a politician, I decided to follow you. Today, it is only natural that I am at your side. Our vision for Senegal is aligned, and from today on, you have our support for advancing the country" (Gueye 2024).[3]

Had we not seen the extinction of the local bourgeoisie in 1900, this gives us a picture of what might have been. History gives us another example in the life of Ngalandou Diouf. He is known for being the first African elected to a formal political position during the colonial period – the General Assembly in Saint-Louis, Senegal's then capital. But he is also described as one of the last Senegalese businessmen to lose his autonomy during the economic crisis in the 1930s (Amin 1969). While Diouf was not born into wealth, he established a trade house in the peanut basin after clerking in some of the top French merchant houses and building up a network of economic ties there (Topouzis 1989). In fact, Diouf started off as a teacher and then a civil servant, but turned to the private sector when he became disenchanted by the salary gap between indigenous and French workers.

Similar to Mboup, Ngalandou Diouf's economic autonomy influenced his political views. In his early political career, he publicly denounced abuse by the colonial administration and fought for more equality between African and French salaries (Topouzis 1989). He was initially mentored by Justin Devès from one of the wealthy Franco-Senegalese merchant families. In fact, Devès' autonomy also allowed him to pursue policies that were in opposition to the colonial metropole. "The extensive investments of the Devès and their intricate network of kin, clients, employees, and business associates afforded it greater independence in political affairs than other families in the Saint Louis community" (Jones 2013, p. 10). They advocated for the rights of indigenous Senegalese and organized a coalition that went against that of the other French settlers.

Also foreshadowing Serigne Mboup's pride in his non-assimilation, Diouf was only moderately assimilated into French culture. Though he received a Catholic education, he was raised a Muslim and spent time in

[2] Mboup has had his own brief political career. He was elected as mayor of Kaolack in 2022 but recently in 2025 declared he would not run for reelection. He also ran as an independent in the 2024 presidential election but got a minuscule percentage of the vote.

[3] Translated by the author from the original French.

the private sector. Like Mboup, Diouf is proud of this, saying "For the moment, Senegal has no need for a learned representative in parliament … It needs a cultivator to help the administration vanquish this crisis" (Topouzis 1989, p. 71).[4]

Diouf was elected to the French parliament in 1934, becoming Senegal's second Black African deputy after Blaise Diagne. It was at this moment that he changed his tune from one of opposition to the colonial government to one of cooperation with it (Topouzis 1989). Perhaps this was due to finally being in a position of real power. Or perhaps it was due to his own declining economic prospects – liquidated by the economic crisis of the 1930s.

The Rise of a Programmatic Candidate?

A programmatic constituency like the one that Mboup represents requires a programmatic party to respond to their new claims. This raises the question of how transitions to programmatism actually materialize in the party system. Are existing parties with clientelistic linkages slowly pushed to respond to programmatic demands, or are opposition parties with programmatic linkages more likely to beat out clientelistic incumbents? Shefter's (1977) review of cases from the Global North suggests the latter.

Chapter 4 described how Ousmane Sonko rose to prominence as a former tax inspector, turned whistleblower. Survey data illustrated how Senegalese voters perceive him and his party as offering a more programmatic platform than the incumbent coalition, and also how that platform was more attractive to members of the formal sector than members of the informal sector. Since that survey was fielded in early 2022, Sonko suffered a series of setbacks that eliminated him from candidacy in the 2024 presidential election. However, Sonko's successor as head of his new party PASTEF, Bassirou Diomaye Faye, campaigned instead and won the office of president in March 2024 in a landslide victory, beating Macky Sall's incumbent party by almost 20 points.

If incumbent parties with clientelistic linkages cannot compete effectively against opposition parties that offer a programmatic platform to meet new demands, they may be incentivized to undermine the opposition.[5] We see evidence of this with the rise and then fall of Ousmane

4 Translated from the French by the author.

5 This would be an alternative strategy to the one cited by Fergusson, Larreguy and Riaño (2022) wherein incumbents abstain from increasing local bureaucratic capacity so as not

Sonko. Sonko and members of his coalition were consistently targeted by Macky Sall's government in efforts to stymie their ability to gain political power. These acts could be interpreted as the incumbent government feeling threatened by an opposition coalition that offered a more programmatic platform, which was harder to effectively compete against.

First, Sonko was arrested in 2021 on charges of rape that he denied and said were politically motivated; he was acquitted of those charges in 2023.[6] Second, although Sonko was able to stand in the January 2022 local elections that made him mayor of Ziguinchor, he was prohibited from standing in the legislative elections later that year. The candidate list put forth by his party, which included Sonko, was rejected by the government's Constitutional Council on technical grounds. Subsequently, another opposition member of parliament received a suspended sentence for his role in organizing a protest, partly around the rejection of the candidate list. Third, Sonko was charged in June 2023 with "corrupting youth." Its two-year sentence disqualified him from running in the 2024 presidential elections. The charge stems from the original rape allegation, finding that he acted immorally toward an individual younger than 21. Sonko again attributed this conviction to political motivations.

Each of these attempts to prevent Sonko's participation in politics was met with active protest by his supporters, and many of these protests were violently put down by Sall's security forces. Fourteen people were killed and 590 were injured in the countrywide protests following Sonko's 2021 arrest. Three people were killed and about 200 were arrested in the 2022 protests in Dakar. And protests following his June 23 conviction "led to 16 deaths according to the government, 24 according to Amnesty International and 30 according to Sonko's party" (*Al-Jazeera* 2023). Sonko was arrested a month later in July 2023, accused of calling for an insurrection, criminal conspiracy to commit terrorism, compromising public security, and theft. According to the Associated Press, "it is unclear what led to the charges [as] Sonko has mostly stayed in his house since being sentenced to prison" on the previous charges (Irwin and Dione 2023). The government

to increase the opportunity cost to engaging in clientelism, giving opponents a competitive edge.

6 In a related event, a journalist, Pape Alé Niang was arrested on charges of publishing anti-state information – itself a new law enacted by Sall in 2021 that Freedom House describes as reducing freedom of expression (Freedom House 2023) – for his reporting on a leaked government document that allegedly exonerates Sonko of the rape charge.

subsequently dissolved Sonko's party, PASTEF. National protests again followed, along with Sonko's hunger strike from prison to protest his arrest.

There is no way to know with certainty the role that Sonko's more programmatic policy agenda played in his being targeted by the incumbent government. However, it is notable that no other opposition coalition was singled out in this way. In fact, two opposition candidates who had previously been barred from running in the 2019 elections, also due to legal issues, Karim Wade and Khalifa Sall, were cleared to run in the 2024 presidential elections. But their electoral appeals were not distinctly programmatic in any way.

It was only after an attempt by incumbent president Macky Sall in February 2024 to postpone the elections, and the resulting widespread protests, that Sall expressed his willingness to release Sonko, Faye, and their supporters from prison. Because of uncertainty over Sonko's eligibility for candidacy, PASTEF had endorsed Faye in November 2023 as its presidential candidate for the 2024 election. Despite being in detention at the time, Faye's candidacy was validated because he was never convicted of a crime. Sonko immediately supported Faye, who even ran under the slogan, *Diomaye mooy Ousmane*, or "Diomaye is Ousmane" in Wolof.

At this writing, it is too soon to tell whether Sonko and Faye's programmatic electoral promises will translate into real policies with real impact.[7] Like Sall in 2019, PASTEF campaigned on job creation, creating more equitable partnerships with foreign business interests, and against corruption. And like Sall (and Wade before him), President Faye implemented easy populist policies such as reducing the price of basic commodities like oil and sugar, only to change course when it became unsustainable (Badiane 2025). But as one indication of whether the new ruling party will uphold promises regarding anti-corruption, Faye publicly declared his assets during the campaign, calling upon others to do the same. In the name of transparency, the state also conducted an audit of public finances in its first year. While a political win, it also revealed the dire economic situation of the country – and the difficulty of implementing sound economic policies, especially in the short term. It remains to be seen whether Faye and Sonko will follow through on other efforts to increase transparency and reduce corruption or if they will fall prey to the temptations of power like others before them.

7 According to the director of Senegal's Center for Applied Economic Research, the results of the first year in office are mixed (Brouck 2025)

8.2 ALTERNATIVE PATHWAYS OUT OF THE WEAK-STATE TRAP

Developing constituencies for programmatic politics is one way out of the weak-state trap. There may be openings like those we saw in the previous section: business leaders in the formal sector who are interested in reform or parties who capitalize on mass disaffection with the status quo. But I have argued that the inescapable reality – of a majority of the population operating in the informal sector – will make bottom-up demand for programmatic politics less likely. In this section, I explore lessons from other programmatic transitions that may be applicable for state leaders with some political will to escape the weak-state trap, and perhaps circumvent the constraints posed by economic informality.

Mixing Campaign Strategies

In my proposed definition of a weak-state trap, parties find it in their interest to campaign strictly on particularistic appeals. A transition to programmatic politics is unlikely to occur in one fell swoop, where all parties simultaneously change their campaign tactics from particularistic to programmatic. Instead, there will more likely be a transition period where we see a mixing of both strategies either within or across parties. As illustrated in Figure 8.1, programmatic and clientelistic appeals are highly negatively correlated at the country level – countries that score high on programmatism score low on clientelism, and at the party level – parties that use one campaign tactic are much less likely to use the other.[8] However, there are some country cases that score relatively high on both measures, mostly in Eastern Europe. These are useful comparison cases because, like the countries of interest to the book, they are relatively young democracies. However, unlike the cases of interest in the book, they have relatively high levels of initial state capacity alongside relatively low levels of informality.

Scholars of the programmatic transition in post-Communist countries attribute variable success in adopting programmatic appeals to several factors. Among communist successor parties, those that were the most successful in adopting credible programmatic linkages with voters were those that had organizational advantages, such as skilled elites who could

[8] The correlation coefficient for clientelistic and programmatic appeals across parties is -0.51. The intraclass correlation coefficient for the party-level variation in use of programmatism and clientelism within countries is very high, 0.76 and 0.62, respectively, according to DALP data (Kitschelt 2013).

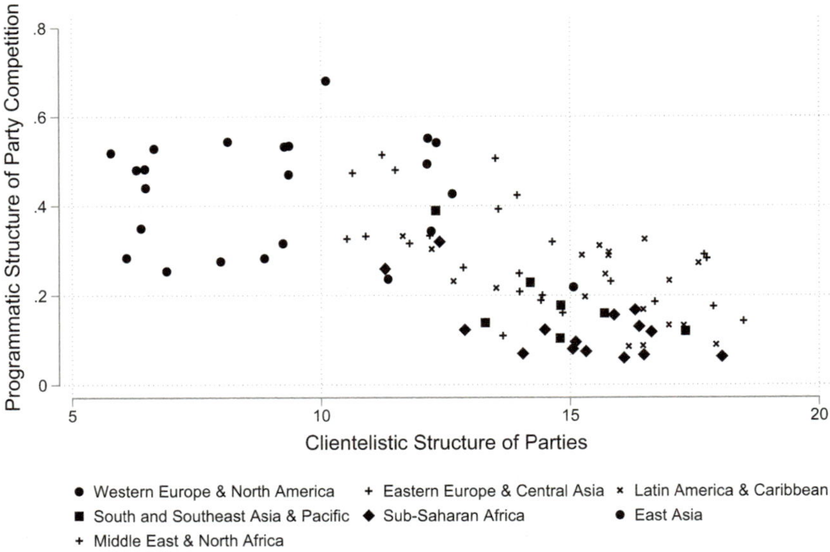

FIGURE 8.1 Cross-national comparison of primary modes of party linkages.
Note: Measures of party linkages are from the DALP dataset compiled in 2009 (Kitschelt 2013); party-level measures are weighted by party size and aggregated to the country level. The clientelistic structure of party competition is measured by an index of questions about the extent to which parties use exchange mechanisms in which promises of material goods, preferential access, or influence are used as inducements to secure votes. The programmatic structure of party competition is an index of questions asked about the parties' positions with respect to social spending on the disadvantaged, the state's role in governing the economy, public spending, tolerance of minority groups, and freedom from state interference into privacy. The indicator itself measures the cohesion of parties' appeals on an issue position, the salience of the issue position, and the degree of spatial distinctiveness or polarization of parties on issue positions. The economic issue structure measure is a subset of the larger programmatic measure, focusing only on economic issues.

create responsive programs that signaled a true break from the past and effectively centralize the party organization (as happened in Hungary and Poland) (Grzymala-Busse 2002). More generally, countries that have been more successful in adopting programmatic appeals are more likely to have a history of political mobilization and party structures with connections to the grassroots, along with a more professionalized civil service that will limit the potential for clientelism (Kitschelt and Smyth 2002).

These lessons are somewhat discouraging in terms of their application to other contemporary young democracies. First, communist successor parties were motivated to campaign on programmatic policies when access to patronage resources of the state was abruptly cut off during the post-Communist transition. A similar seismic shock to strong incumbent party structures in low-income democracies is unlikely. Second, the frequency of weak party institutionalization (Riedl 2014) and political uncertainty (Lupu and Riedl 2013) in low-income democracies, along with relatively weak and unprofessional bureaucracies, does not bode well for the emergence of credible programmatic party restructuring.

Reducing Backlash

A successful programmatic transition will not only need parties to translate programmatic demands into state investments through electoral politics but will also require that the state overcome potential backlash from intermediaries and others who might benefit from the status quo. One strategy the state might use to tamp down such backlash is directly compensating intermediaries for the costs borne by the transition away from the status quo. In a historical example from China, Chen, Wang and Zhang (2025) explain how the state softened resistance by local intermediaries to state-building by compensating them with a bureaucratic government office offering monetary remuneration, power, and prestige. The challenge in making such an exchange effective for state-building is ensuring local powerholders realign their interests with the state and away from interests they derived from autonomy, for example, through senior posts in central or regional governments away from local constituencies. Such a scheme requires the existence of a reasonably impersonal and capable bureaucracy, which is uncommon in the weak states of interest to this book.

Another reason intermediary compensation is challenging in the context of the informal economy is that many intermediaries have assets or advantages that are not easily capitalized. Often, the source of an intermediary's informational advantage is their social authority rather than their economic clout. Finding a way to incorporate such intermediaries into the bureaucracy or a rational-legal procedure for otherwise compensating them is thus a challenge. Pardelli (2024) finds that, in Brazil, places with higher levels of landholding concentration were associated with higher levels of fiscal and administrative capacity. Here, the state was successful in inducing local powerholders to align with the state because they benefited from investments in the state in ways that were proportional to their capital endowments – rather than idiosyncratic and based on personal relationships. This logic of compensation is harder to implement where intermediary authority is not based on capital accumulation or land concentration but rather social authority.

In addition to compensating intermediaries, there are other strategies the state might take to reduce backlash. The political economy literature on the transition from socialism to capitalism offers relevant insights as, in the case of informal intermediaries, there are elites under the status quo who lose out as economies liberalize. First, as evidenced in several Eastern European cases, leaders can sequence reforms such that they undertake initial policies that could benefit or at least not be as costly to transitional losers; more costly reforms undertaken later then seem less objectionable (Roland 2002, p. 43). Under liberalization, more successful initial reforms have included privatizing profitable firms – as in Hungary (Gatsios 1992) and the Czech Republic (Gupta, Ham and Svejnar 2008) – and supporting a private industrial and service sector, leaving the more unpopular shuttering of inefficient enterprises for later. This tracks with the very successful approach of technocratic leaders in Lagos, Nigeria, in their efforts to reform the corrupt and inefficient tax system. They first went after larger private firms in the formal sector that were easier to identify and potentially had more to gain from compliance with the state. The later, harder task of formalizing and collecting revenue from informal firms has proved more difficult, however (LeBas and Gottlieb 2025).

Second, as an example from China, reforms can be undertaken along a dual-track system wherein some sectors or policy areas are preserved under the status quo (with their attendant benefits to the intermediary class) while reforms are simultaneously undertaken in other sectors (Roland 2002, p. 40). This helps to preserve some status quo rents while creating new opportunities elsewhere. Applying this logic to the case of the informal sector, we might imagine the state choosing to develop a formalistic relationship with a specific set of informal firms, perhaps certain markets or certain economic sectors. Below, I discuss how first approaching certain ethnic or identity groups could be a promising strategy.

Appealing to Outgroups

In Chapter 6.1, we learned about the relatively successful technocratic investments by Lagos State, Nigeria, in tax collection in both the formal and informal sectors. I speculated that the political will to make these investments may be attributable to a relatively low level of democratic competition and consequent longer time horizon of ruling party elites.

However, as the state approached the hard problem of bringing informal sector members into the tax net, they met typical obstacles of low information about these unregulated entities and low levels of willingness to formalize. The state's internal revenue service thought one way of overcoming these obstacles might be to work directly with locally legitimate social authorities, marketplace associations. Not only had these associations been used before by the state to mobilize taxes in the informal sector, but they also had relatively high levels of information and mobilization capacity among vendors in their markets.

In our Lagos market field experiment, LeBas and I find that marketplace associations are not good partners in mobilizing formal fiscal exchange among informal market vendors (Gottlieb, Lebas and Magat 2025). As described in Chapter 5, we attribute this failure, in part, to the fact that marketplace associations benefit from their intermediary status under clientelistic exchange and would suffer future losses if the state developed a more formalized fiscal relationship with their market vendors. However, the resistance to formalization was not ubiquitous. Members of ethnic-minority groups within markets governed by ethnic-majority-led marketplace associations were the most willing to formalize their business and tax status with the state. We argue that this is because they are the least likely to benefit from (and may even suffer discrimination as a result of) the clientelistic status quo (LeBas and Gottlieb 2025). While members of the ethnic majority may benefit from the marketplace association's privileged position and ability to bargain with the state, similar benefits would not accrue to members of the ethnic minority, who not only lack relational ties but may also pose a political threat as more likely supporters of the opposition.

This case suggests that one possible way out of the trap – conditional on there being sufficient political will from the state – is to mobilize members of an ethnic or other identity-based minority group who experience discrimination or exclusion or are otherwise losers under the clientelistic status quo. While by virtue of being in the minority, they will not form a sufficient constituency for programmatism, they could represent a leading-edge constituency – one that could be mobilized more easily than others.

That said, this pathway is not easy or straightforward. Even though these minority group members in Lagos form a potentially viable constituency for programmatism, they did not organize on their own. It took a campaign by the state tax agency to move them to formalize, and we only know of the differential effect of compliance by ethnic group status because of the research partnership. This finding was entirely unexpected by the state. Instead, in meetings with the leaders of the tax office, minority vendors were described as recalcitrant and unlikely compliers. So the existence of such a potential constituency for programmatism with a latent willingness to comply with the state is not sufficient. The state or some external actor would need to activate this group with direct appeals. And the willingness of state agents – who are more likely to hail from ethnic-majority groups – to explicitly target ethnic-minority groups for inclusion state outreach may be an uphill climb.

In sum, the very nature of informality and the inherent discretion it implies may contain the seeds of a pathway out of the trap. Just as there are intermediaries and their constituencies who benefit from preferential access to rents under the status quo, there are also large numbers of informal sector members who suffer from lack of access or are vulnerable to mistreatment under the status quo. The argument in the book suggests that these marginalized groups may not be sufficiently disgruntled to initiate a change to their status because they have low expectations that the state could do better for them. However, there may be a latent willingness among these outgroups to comply with state regulation that could be leveraged by a technocratic leader or programmatic party.

8.3 APPLICATION OUTSIDE AFRICA

If informality is indeed a constraint to a transition to programmatic politics and investment in state capacity, then the lessons from the African cases in this book should extend to other democracies with large informal sectors and initially weak states outside Africa. Of the other postcolonial regions, much has been written on informality in Latin America. There, we also see evidence that members of the informal economy have low expectations of receiving government assistance – and thereby, evidence of a weak social contract. Holland (2018) describes a "truncated welfare state" in Latin America where "heavy spending on contributory social insurance for formal-sector workers, flat or regressive subsidies, and informal access barriers mean that social spending does far less for the poor in Latin America than it does in advanced industrial economies." As in Senegal, the poor have low expectations of state service provision and express weak support for redistributive social policy.

By contrast, Garay (2023) finds evidence from several Latin American countries that informal sector workers, in coalition with formal sector labor unions, have successfully demanded and received state investments in social welfare programs. In fact, Garay (2016) claims that electoral competition even helped to induce these increases in programmatic social policy.

So what might explain the conditions under which informality will constrain the rise of programmatic politics and thereby investment in the state? A simple one is the sheer size of the informal sector. If the median voter is not a member of that sector, then the role of informality will play a less important role in shaping electoral accountability. However, the rate of informal employment has exceeded 50 percent in two of Garay's cases in Latin America – Argentina and Mexico – where we have seen important improvements in programmatic policies.

So what else might explain the different outcomes in Latin American countries with large informal sectors? Recall the importance of the Senegal case of low expectations of informal sector members with respect to state capacity. States vary in the extent to which they support the informal sector (Portes and Schauffler 1993), so it is possible that informal sector members in Latin America receive more state support leading to higher expectations of its capacity. State support might come in the form of "provision of institutional resources such as training programmes, credit facilities and marketing assistance" (Yusuff 2011, p. 634). This type of state support is rare in sub-Saharan Africa, even though this was the advice of the ILO and the World Bank to developing country governments in the 1970s. But such redistribution toward the urban poor never happened due largely to "the predictable reluctance of those in government in developing countries to give up the economic power they hold" (Gerry 1987, p. 116).

Relatedly, informal sector members may adopt the expectations and preferences of formal sector members as the sectors become more integrated. Formal firms, for example, often outsource to the informal economy where labor is cheaper, creating opportunities for growth in that sector. But Yusuff (2011, p. 629) highlights regional disparities in this respect: "While industrial subcontracting is a central feature of informal activity in Latin America cities, it is a comparatively insignificant feature of informal activity in developing countries. The common feature in African informality is … the 'subsistence' informal economy in which economic actors are occupied on informal means of income generation."

Scholars who point to the growth-enhancing potential of the informal sector, especially in more developed country cases, describe the utility of the informal sector as a safety valve or source of labor. This implies that workers are moving fluidly across these boundaries. It also assumes there are low barriers to entry into the formal sector. That may be true to a varying extent across contexts. For example, successful entrepreneurs may owe some of their success to preferential access to resources because of their membership in a particular ascriptive group, or they have access to resources through connections with formal sector employment and education (Aboagye 1988). As a result of such financial, educational, and ethnic barriers, "entrepreneurs in many of the more lucrative activities are often found to belong disproportionately to certain ethnic groups or regions" (Yusuff 2011, p. 631). Such barriers make the informal sector less likely to be as dynamic and productive, as they restrict upward mobility.

Barriers to Entry

This discussion highlights the importance of the origins of the informal sector. Some informal sectors grow out of economic resourcefulness – providing goods or services more cheaply or efficiently without government regulation. Other informal sectors originate from the exclusion of certain groups from the formal market. This was the case in colonial sub-Saharan Africa. We might expect such exclusion of indigenous groups from the formal market to be less apparent in Latin America, where colonization preceded the industrial revolution, and there were other mechanisms of controlling indigenous groups and their economic productivity.

That said, De Soto (1989) writes about urban elites in Latin America as blocking access to the formal sector as one of the key reasons for the rise of informality in the region. He conceptualized the informal economy as a response, not to rapid urbanization and a formal sector that could not accommodate the excess labor, but rather to increased competition among urban elites who doubled down on legal barriers to participation in the mainstream economy. Urban elites were hostile to urban migrants because "each person who migrates to the capital is in some way a potential competitor and it is a natural inclination to try to avoid competition" (De Soto 1989, 11). So while exclusion here was not strictly based on indigeneity, it certainly has roots in colonialism with urban settler elites being concentrated in the capital cities.

This manifestation of informality is similar to the dualism that arose out of colonization, where a well-defined elite created an informal sector through deliberate exclusion of access to the formal one. Uzzell (1974) describes two types of people and institutions in Peru that overlap in many ways with the economic dualism that arose from colonization. He distinguishes the population into two groups: *creoles* and *cholos*. The former he defines as "that set of the population who consider it possible for themselves to participate in the activities controlled by those institutions on terms favorable to themselves," for example, banking, commercial housing, and large industry. The latter comprise the remaining population, who tend to occupy the bottom "class" in urban spaces but are not necessarily in low social positions; they may also be wealthy and have lucrative occupations. This is similar to the observation that members of the informal sector in sub-Saharan Africa can also be very wealthy and in high social positions.

To conclude, we might expect informality to breed low expectations of the state, especially where barriers to entry to the formal sector are high. When there are high barriers to entry, the experiences of the state among members of the informal sector will be more distinct. When other social identities map onto those sectoral boundaries, they aid in policing the barriers that exist and reinforcing differences in preferences and demands.

8.4 CONTRIBUTIONS AND IMPLICATIONS

This book has grappled with a confounding question facing students of African politics: why have states remained persistently weak, especially in light of increasing democratic consolidation? As Africans in many states are now able to select their own leaders, shouldn't we expect to see them choosing people who will invest in state capacities to provide the types of basic public goods desired by the majority? I argue that part of the answer to this question lies in the pervasiveness of the informal economy. Embedded informality – where states and citizens accept a certain level of unavoidable interactions that are necessarily irregular – reduces expectations of state capacity and the likelihood of coordinated economic interest groups demanding programmatic policies. The rational choice of parties to rely on particularistic voter appeals then removes incentives for elected leaders to make costly investments in the state.

With this idea, I join a recent chorus of scholars arguing that the roots of state capacity lie not only in exogenous or historical factors like the threat of international war or technological progress, but also in endogenous factors like political institutions and social cleavages in the polity (Suryanarayan 2024). This increased attention to the role of political actors and citizens in determining state capacity outcomes has highlighted the role of features relevant to my argument, such as clientelism

(Fergusson, Larreguy and Riaño 2022), capitalist elites (Beramendi, Dincecco and Rogers 2019), and kinship networks (Wang 2022). But my book does two novel things.

First, it highlights the importance of programmatic party competition for creating the necessary incentive structure for democratic elections to translate into political will to invest in state-building. Olson (1993) was thus only partly right when he argued that democratic leaders should be motivated to invest in state-provided public goods because the majority will have an "encompassing" interest in the consequent benefits to market productivity. When elections cleave around particularistic rather than programmatic lines, this salutary consequence of democratic competition will not necessarily materialize.

Second, the book connects a common feature of weak states – pervasive economic informality – to the political economy of state-building in young democracies. Whereas programmatic party competition could indeed induce elected leaders to invest in state capacity, the median voter with largely informal and irregular contact with the state will expect programmatic promises not to be credible. Parties will instead do better to appeal to her with more credible particularistic promises. Furthermore, the networks of intermediaries that rise up to facilitate personalistic relationships between states and citizens become bulwarks against transitions to programmatic politics, making the clientelistic weak-state trap even more difficult to escape.

In this way, the book highlights the Janus-faced nature of competitive elections when it comes to state-building. While a certain type of party competition can indeed induce leaders to make costly but welfare-enhancing investments in the state, another type of party competition can actually contribute to keeping the state weak. It also points to the nature of the constituencies that are necessary to motivate change from one type of party competition to another. Constituencies for programmatism are those that have an economic interest in the stable, predictable, and public goods providing regulatory and fiscal environment that only a strong state can offer. Successful constituencies for programmatism will additionally need to be able to coordinate around these shared interests to translate them into real political demand.

While a small group of scholars has begun to extend thinking about the economic consequences of informality to also consider its political consequences (see, e.g., Holland 2017; Hummel 2021), this book is the first to directly consider the effects of informality on state capacity. While economic informality has always been considered an obvious consequence of state weakness, I show how it can also be a determinant. Widespread economic informality impedes the formation of a politically relevant constituency for programmatism. By exploring the different ways in which it does this, I open the door for future research on how some of those constraints might be overcome.

Policy Recommendations

If a goal of international donors and even some technocratic leaders of weak states is to hasten the programmatic transition or contribute to state-building, then this book offers some advice. First, it offers a cautionary tale about the promise of formalization or other state-building projects that are driven by outside actors. Without internal political will, these programs are likely to be weakly implemented, as was the case with structural adjustment programs in the 1990s. And without a constituency to defend the programs, they might be actively dismantled or resisted by bureaucrats or intermediaries who perceive personal losses in their successful implementation. As such, actors seeking to support state-building and formalization programs in weak states should identify and support political champions who will defend and promote these policies – perhaps like the excluded ethnic-minority group in the Lagos case.

Is there a way to increase formalization without meeting resistance from intermediaries or elites? States or even outside actors could aim to increase the regularity with which citizens interact with the state without necessarily subjecting them to a formal regime. In the case of taxation of the informal sector in Senegal, this could be achieved with a more systematic and transparent taxation process. The current approach of relying on local officials (police, agents of the mayor, etc.) means there is a lot of variation across places and over time in how many members of the sector get taxed, who gets visited by tax agents, how much is asked of them, and whether they receive a receipt. Making this process more systematic would not officially formalize the taxpayers, but could still increase their perceptions of state capacity. Similarly, states could provide more economic support to informal sector actors, something that has been more common in Latin America than in Africa, as discussed earlier.

The state could also co-opt or partner with informal actors.[9] One example of this in Senegal and some of its neighboring Muslim-majority

[9] However, in our book on Lagos markets, Adrienne LeBas and I caution that informal intermediaries may not be credible partners in formal state-building (LeBas and Gottlieb 2025).

countries is an attempt by the state to assimilate parallel systems of religious education into the public system. These reforms acknowledge the success of these informal religious schools in providing education to populations that have been ill-served by the public system, and to the potential benefits of formalizing them. As might be expected, there has been some resistance among leaders and supporters of the existing religious schools, but incorporating them and their input has helped. The precarious economic situation of many of these schools has also made leaders more willing to accept changes (Villalón and Bodian 2012).

This example reflects a more bottom-up approach to state-building, in which public systems are constructed on the basis of existing social organization rather than conceived of by elites and grafted onto citizens. A similar dynamic can be seen in the example of Serigne Mboup, whom we discussed in Chapter 7 as a wealthy formal business owner whose origins were in the informal sector. Socially or culturally, he more closely resembles members of the informal sector, having attended religious schooling rather than francophone public schools. But seeing the limitations of remaining in the informal sector, he leveraged the economic benefits of formalization to build upon his father's initial success in the informal sector.

More generally, the book cautions against overinvestment in standard formalization interventions that simply change the legal status of a firm. The book underscores the role of an individual's experience of and relationship with the state in setting expectations and creating focal points for coordination. A regulatory status change on paper will do little to affect those experiences, beliefs, and expectations. Rather, the theory implies the need to change firms' relationships to the state in ways that lead them to better coordinate policy demands and to cut out intermediaries. On the coordination side, such interventions might consist of information dissemination about grievances among small businesses, abuses by government, or challenges they face to expansion. This could help a fractionalized set of small businesses see common challenges as the basis for future organization and mobilization. On the articulation of impersonal, programmatic preferences, one tactic could be identifying and connecting businesses that are typically on the losing end of discretionary politics or that do not have access to well-connected intermediaries, for example, political minorities or outgroups.

References

Aboagye, AA. 1988. *The informal sector in Mogadishu: An analysis of a survey.* Addis Ababa: Jobs and Skills Programme for Africa.

Acemoglu, Daron. 2005. "Politics and economics in weak and strong states." *Journal of Monetary Economics* 52(7):1199–1226.

Acemoglu, Daron, Jacob Moscona and James A. Robinson. 2016. "State capacity and American technology: Evidence from the nineteenth century." *American Economic Review* 106(5):61–67.

Acemoglu, Daron and James A. Robinson. 2006. *Economic origins of dictatorship and democracy.* Cambridge: Cambridge University Press.

Acemoglu, Daron, Simon Johnson and James A. Robinson. 2001. "The colonial origins of comparative development: An empirical investigation." *American Economic Review* 91(5):1369–1401.

Adida, Claire, Jessica Gottlieb, Eric Kramon and Gwyneth McClendon. 2020. "When does information influence voters? The joint importance of salience and coordination." *Comparative Political Studies* 53(6):851–891.

AFP. 2019. "Senegal president touts achievements at Dakar rally." *Africanews.* URL: *www.africanews.com/2019/02/20/senegal-president-macky-sall-touts-achievements-to-supporters-at-dakar-rally/*

Agarwala, Rina. 2013. *Informal labor, formal politics, and dignified discontent in India.* Cambridge: Cambridge University Press.

Aidt, Toke S., Facundo Albornoz and Martin Gassebner. 2018. "The golden hello and political transitions." *Journal of Comparative Economics* 46(1):157–173.

Al-Jazeera. 2023. "Senegal's Ousmane Sonko hospitalised after one week on hunger strike."
URL: *www.aljazeera.com/news/2023/8/7/senegals-ousmane-sonko-hospitalised-after-one-week-on-hunger-strike*

Albers, Thilo N.H., Morten Jerven and Marvin Suesse. 2023. "The fiscal state in Africa: Evidence from a century of growth." *International Organization* 77(1):65–101.

Aldrich, John H. 1995. *Why parties?: The origin and transformation of political parties in America*. Chicago: University of Chicago Press.

Alfani, Guido and Federico Tadei. 2019. "Income inequality in French West Africa: Building social tables for pre-independence Senegal and Ivory Coast." *UB Economics – Working Papers, 2019, E19/396*.

Amin, Samir. 1969. "La bourgeoisie d'affaires sénégalaise." *L'Homme et la société* 12(1):29–41.

André, Pierre and Jean-Luc Demonsant. 2009. "Koranic Schools in Senegal: An actual barrier to formal education?" *Paris School of Economics Working Papers*.

ANSD. 2002. *Recensement général de la population et de l'habitat*. Dakar: Agence Nationale de la Statistique et de la Démographie (ANSD), Ministère de l'Economie et des Finances, République du Sénégal.

ANSD. 2016. *Synthèse des resultats du projet de renovation des comptes nationaux*. Dakar: Agence Nationale de la Statistique et de la Démographie (ANSD), Ministère de l'Economie des Finances, et du Plan, République du Sénégal.

Ansell, Ben W. and David J. Samuels. 2014. *Inequality and democratization: An elite-competition approach*. Cambridge: Cambridge University Press.

Ansolabehere, Stephen, Jaclyn Kaslovsky, Michael P. Olson et al. 2022. "Franchise expansion and legislative representation in the early United States." *Journal of Political Institutions and Political Economy* 3(2):243–271.

Anyidoho, Nana Akua, Max Gallien, Michael Rogan and Vanessa van den Boogaard. 2025. "The taxed informal economy: Fiscal burdens and inequality in Accra." *World Development* 187:106879.

Asunka, Joseph. 2017. "Non-discretionary resource allocation as political investment: Evidence from Ghana." *The Journal of Modern African Studies* 55(1):29–53.

Auerbach, Adam Michael. 2017. "Neighborhood associations and the urban poor: India's slum development committees." *World Development* 96:119–135.

Auerbach, Adam Michael. 2019. *Demanding development: The politics of public goods provision in India's urban slums*. Cambridge: Cambridge University Press.

Auerbach, Adam M., Adrienne LeBas, Alison E. Post and Rebecca Weitz-Shapiro. 2018. "State, society, and informality in cities of the Global South." *Studies in Comparative International Development* 53(3):261–280.

Austin, Gareth. 2010. *African economic development and colonial legacies*. Vol. 1. Institut de hautes études internationales et du développement.

Auyero, Javier. 2000. "The logic of clientelism in Argentina: An ethnographic account." *Latin American Research Review* 35(3):55–81.

Awuah, Emmanuel. 1997. "Mobilizing for change: A case study of market trader activism in Ghana." *Canadian Journal of African Studies/La revue canadienne des études africaines* 31(3):401–423.

Aziz, Abdul. 2016. "Pikine: Plus de 400 délégués de quartier promettent de faire triompher le OUI." *SENEGO*.

URL: *https://senego.com/pikine-plus-de-400-delegues-de-quartier-promett-ent-de-faire-triompher-le-oui_304679.html*

Baack, Bennett D. and Edward John Ray. 1985. "Special interests and the adoption of the income tax in the United States." *The Journal of Economic History* 45(3):607–625.

Baba, Abdoul. 2018. "Importation du sucre : l'Unacois/yessal prend le contre-pied de l'Unacois Jappo." *La vie senegalaise.*
URL: *https://laviesenegalaise.com/importation-du-sucre-lunacois-yessal-prend-le-contre-pied-de-lunacois-jappo/*

Badiane, Ousmane. 2025. "An 1 de Bassirou Diomaye Faye au pouvoir au Sénégal: Quel bilan retenir?" *BBC News Afrique.*
URL: *www.bbc.com/afrique/articles/ckg1nzjr1dko*

Bak, Ane Karoline. 2024. "Brokered fiscal contracts." In *The Politics of Revenue Bargaining in Africa: Triggers, Processes, and Outcomes*, ed. Anne Mette Kjær, Marianne S. Ulriksen and Ane Karoline Bak. Oxford: Oxford University Press.

Baker, Andy and Vania Ximena Velasco-Guachalla. 2018. "Is the informal sector politically different? (Null) answers from Latin America." *World Development* 102:170–182.

Balan, Pablo, Augustin Bergeron, Gabriel Tourek and Jonathan Weigel. 2020. "Metaketa II DRC book chapter draft."

Balan, Pablo, Augustin Bergeron, Gabriel Tourek and Jonathan Weigel. 2021. "Property rights and social dependence: How informal institutions shape land formalization in weak states."
URL: *www.dropbox.com/s/8johppgap8mccso/bbtw_titling_202104.pdf?dl=0*

Barnes, Sandra T. 1986. *Patrons and power: Creating a political community in metropolitan Lagos*. London: Routledge.

Barro, Robert J. 1973. "The control of politicians: An economic model." *Public Choice* 14(1):19–42.

Bates, Robert H. 1981. *Markets and states in tropical Africa: The political basis of agricultural policies*. University of California Press.

Bates, Robert H. 2001. *Prosperity and violence*. New York: W. W. Norton.

Bayart, Jean-François. 1993. *The State in Africa: The politics of the belly*. London: Longman.

Beck, Linda J. 2002. "Le clientélisme au Sénégal: Un adieu sans regrets?" In *Le Sénégal contemporain*, ed. Momar Coumba Diop. Paris: Karthala. pp. 529–549.

Beck, Linda J. 2008. *Brokering democracy in Africa: The rise of clientelist democracy in Senegal*. Palgrave Macmillan.

Benhassine, Najy, David McKenzie, Victor Pouliquen and Massimiliano Santini. 2018. "Does inducing informal firms to formalize make sense? Experimental evidence from Benin." *Journal of Public Economics* 157:1–14.

Beramendi, Pablo, Mark Dincecco and Melissa Rogers. 2019. "Intra-elite competition and long-run fiscal development." *The Journal of Politics* 81(1):49-65000–000.

Berwick, Elissa and Fotini Christia. 2018. "State capacity redux: Integrating classical and experimental contributions to an enduring debate." *Annual Review of Political Science* 21:71–91.

Besley, Timothy. 2006. *Principled agents?: The political economy of good government*. New York: Oxford University Press.

Besley, Timothy and Masayuki Kudamatsu. 2006. "Health and democracy." *American Economic Review* 96(2):313–318.

Besley, Timothy and Torsten Persson. 2009. "The origins of state capacity: Property rights, taxation and politics." *American Economic Review* 99(4):1218–1244.

Besley, Timothy and Torsten Persson. 2010. "State capacity, conflict, and development." *Econometrica* 78(1):1–34.

Bhandari, Abhit. 2023. "Social, formal, and political determinants of trade under weak rule of law: Experimental evidence from Senegalese firms." *Comparative Political Studies* 56(2):163–192.

Blackburn, Keith, Niloy Bose and Salvatore Capasso. 2012. "Tax evasion, the underground economy and financial development." *Journal of Economic Behavior & Organization* 83(2):243–253.

Bleck, Jaimie, Jessica Gottlieb and Katrina Kosec. 2023. "When will civil society sanction the state? Evidence from Mali." *IFPRI Discussion Paper* 02169. URL: *https://ebrary.ifpri.org/digital/collection/p15738coll2/id/136571/*

Bodea, Cristina and Adrienne LeBas. 2016. "The origins of voluntary compliance: Attitudes toward taxation in urban Nigeria." *British Journal of Political Science* 46(1):215–238.

Boone, Catherine. 1992. *Merchant capital and the roots of state power in Senegal, 1930–1985*. Cambridge: Cambridge University Press.

Boone, Catherine. 1994. "Trade, taxes, and tribute: Market liberalizations and the new importers in West Africa." *World Development* 22(3):453–467.

Boone, Catherine. 1998. "State building in the African countryside: Structure and politics at the grassroots." *The Journal of Development Studies* 34(4):1–31.

Boone, Catherine. 2003. *Political topographies of the African state: Territorial authority and institutional choice*. Cambridge: Cambridge University Press.

Boone, Catherine. 2014. *Property and political order in Africa: Land rights and the structure of politics*. Cambridge: Cambridge University Press.

Boulay, Harvey and Alan DiGaetano. 1985. "Why did political machines disappear?" *Journal of Urban History* 12(1):25–49.

Breman, Jan. 2023. "A short history of the informal economy." *Global Labour Journal* 14(1): 21–39.

Brouck, Thaïs. 2025. "Sénégal : 'Le bilan économique de Bassirou Diomaye Faye est pour le moins mitigé'" *Jeune Afrique*. URL: *www.jeuneafrique.com/1671991/economie-entreprises/senegal-le-bilan-economique-de-bassirou-diomaye-faye-est-pour-le-moins-mitige/*

Brown, Alison, Colman Msoka and Ibrahima Dankoco. 2015. "A refugee in my own country: Evictions or property rights in the urban informal economy?" *Urban Studies* 52(12):2234–2249.

Cammett, Melani and Lauren M. MacLean. 2014. *The politics of non-state social welfare*. Ithaca, NY: Cornell University Press.

Chandra, Kanchan. 2007. *Why ethnic parties succeed: Patronage and ethnic head counts in India*. Cambridge University Press.

Charmes, Jacques. 2000. "The contribution of informal sector to GDP in developing countries: Assessment, estimates, methods, orientations for the future." Paper presented at the Fourth Meeting of the Expert Group on Informal Sector Statistics (Delhi Group), Geneva, 28-30 August 2000.

Chatterjee, Partha. 2004. *The politics of the governed: Reflections on popular politics in most of the world*. New York: Columbia University Press.

Chen, Joy, Erik H. Wang and Xiaoming Zhang. 2025. "From powerholders to stakeholders: State-building with elite compensation in early medieval China." *American Journal of Political Science* 69(2):607–623.

Christensen, Darin and Francisco Garfias. 2021. "The politics of property taxation: Fiscal infrastructure and electoral incentives in Brazil." *The Journal of Politics* 83(4):1399–1416.

Chwe, Michael Suk-Young. 2001. *Rational ritual: Culture, coordination, and common knowledge*. Princeton, NJ: Princeton University Press.

Cogneau, Denis. 2023. *Un empire bon marché: Histoire et économie politique de la colonisation française, XIXe–XXIe siècle*. Paris: Éditions du Seuil.

Cohen, Michael A. 1973. "The myth of the expanding centre – Politics in the Ivory Coast." *The Journal of Modern African Studies* 11(2):227–246.

Collier, Ruth Berins. 1999. *Paths toward democracy: The working class and elites in Western Europe and South America*. Cambridge: Cambridge University Press.

Copans, Jean. 1980. *Les Marabouts de l'Arachide: La Xonfrérie Mouride et les Paysans du Sénégal*. Paris: Le Sycomore.

Coppedge, Michael, John Gerring, Carl Henrik Knutsen, Staffan I. Lindberg, Jan Teorell, David Altman, Michael Bernhard, Agnes Cornell, M. Steven Fish, Lisa Gastaldi, Haakon Gjerløw, Adam Glynn, Ana Good God, Sandra Grahn, Allen Hicken, Katrin Kinzelbach, Joshua Krusell, Kyle L. Marquardt, Kelly McMann, Valeriya Mechkova, Juraj Medzihorsky, Natalia Natsika, Anja Neundorf, Pamela Paxton, Daniel Pemstein, Josefine Pernes, Oskar Rydén, Johannes von Römer, Brigitte Seim, Rachel Sigman, Svend-Erik Skaaning, Jeffrey Staton, Aksel Sundström, Eitan Tzelgov, Yi ting Wang, Tore Wig, Steven Wilson and Daniel Ziblatt. 2023. "V-Dem Country-Year Dataset v13." *Varieties of Democracy (V-Dem) Project*.
URL: *https://doi.org/10.23696/vdemds23*

Cross, John Christopher. 1998. *Informal politics: Street vendors and the state in Mexico City*. Stanford: Stanford University Press.

Dabo, Bacary. 2018. "L'UNACOIS, voix des commerçants." *Center for International Private Enterprise*.
URL: *www.cipe.org/resources/lunacois-voix-des-commercants/*

De Gramont, Diane. 2015. *Governing Lagos: Unlocking the politics of reform*. Vol. 12, Carnegie Endowment for International Peace.

De La O, Ana. 2024. "How clientelism undermines state capacity: Evidence from Mexican municipalities." *World Development* 173:106344.

De La O, Ana L., Don Green, Peter John et al. 2020. "Transaction costs, collective benefits, and selective incentives: A six-country randomized trial design to encourage formalization."

De Mel, Suresh, David McKenzie and Christopher Woodruff. 2013. "The demand for, and consequences of, formalization among informal firms in Sri Lanka." *American Economic Journal: Applied Economics* 5(2):122–150.

De Soto, Hernando. 1989. *The other path: The invisible revolution in the third world*. London: I.B. Tauris.

De Weerdt, Joachim and Marcel Fafchamps. 2011. "Social identity and the formation of health insurance networks." *Journal of Development Studies* 47(8):1152–1177.

Deacon, Robert T. 2009. "Public good provision under dictatorship and democracy." *Public Choice* 139:241–262.

Demirguc-Kunt, Asli, Luc Laeven and Ross Levine. 2003. "Regulations, market structure, institutions, and the cost of financial intermediation." NBER Working Paper 9890. National Bureau of Economic Research

Dercon, Stefan. 2022. *Gambling on development*. London: Hurst publishers.

Dercon, Stefan, Joachim De Weerdt, Tessa Bold and Alula Pankhurst. 2006. "Group-based funeral insurance in Ethiopia and Tanzania." *World Development* 34(4):685–703.

Diallo, Amadou Oury. 2016. "Institutions: Guerre des patrons à Dakar." *Jeune Afrique*. URL: *www.jeuneafrique.com/mag/354157/economie/institutions-guerre-patrons-a-dakar/*

Diaz-Cayeros, Alberto, Federico Estévez and Beatriz Magaloni. 2016. *The political logic of poverty relief: Electoral strategies and social policy in Mexico*. Cambridge: Cambridge University Press.

Dincecco, Mark and Gabriel Katz. 2016. "State capacity and long-run economic performance." *The Economic Journal* 126(590):189–218.

Diop, Boubacar Boris and Moussa Sene Absa. 2021. "Senegal: Impunity for Macky Sall's regime must end." *Al-Jazeera*. URL: *www.aljazeera.com/opinions/2021/3/10/senegal-impunity-for-macky-salls-regime-must-end*

Diop, El Hadji Omar. 2011. *Partis politiques: Démocratie et réalitès sociales au Sénégal: Essai critique pour une étude réaliste du multipartisme*. CREDILA.

Diop, Momar Coumba. 1993. *Senegal: Essays in statecraft*. Dakar: CODESRIA.

Diouf, Mamadou. 1993. Beyond Patronage and Technocracy? In *Senegal: Essays in statecraft*, ed. Momar Coumba Diop. Dakar: CODESRIA, pp. 221–268.

Djité, Paulin G. 2020. Economy and language in Africa. In *Bridging linguistics and economics*, ed. Cécile B. Vigouroux and Salikoko S. Mufwene. Cambridge: Cambridge University Press, pp. 182–202.

Downing, Brian M. 1992. *The military revolution and political change: Origins of democracy and autocracy in early modern Europe*. Princeton, NJ: Princeton University Press.

Dube, Godwin and Daniela Casale. 2016. "The implementation of informal sector taxation: Evidence from selected African countries." *eJTR* 14(3):601–623.

Easterly, William. 2001. "The middle class consensus and economic development." *Journal of Economic Growth* 6(4):317–335.

Easterly, William and Ross Levine. 2016. "The European origins of economic development." *Journal of Economic Growth* 21:225–257.

Ekeh, Peter P. 1975. "Colonialism and the two publics in Africa: A theoretical statement." *Comparative Studies in Society and History* 17(1):91–112.

Englebert, Pierre. 2009. *Africa: Unity, sovereignty, sorrow*. Boulder: Lynne Rienner Publishers.

Ertman, Thomas. 1997. *Birth of the Leviathan: Building states and regimes in medieval and early modern Europe*. Cambridge: Cambridge University Press.

Evans, Peter B. 1995. *Embedded autonomy: States and industrial transformation*. Princeton, NJ: Princeton University Press.

Fall, Mounirou. 2004. "Sénégal: Réforme de la fiscalité: la contribution globale unique comme solution." *Sud Quotidien*. 20 February 2004. Available: URL: *http://fr.allafrica.com/stories/200402200374.html* [Last accessed: 2 January 2018].

Fashola, Babatunde. 2009. "Oral History Program. Interview by Graeme Blair." *Innovations for Successful Societies* D12. URL: *https://successfulsocieties.princeton.edu/sites/g/files/toruqf5601/files/interviews/transcripts/3348/Babatunde_Fashola.pdf*

Fatton, Robert. 1987. *The making of a liberal democracy: Senegal's passive revolution, 1975–1985*. Boulder: Lynne Rienner.

Faye, M. Junior. 2022. "Serigne Mboup Maire de Kaolack: La leçon d'un soldat de l'économie aux hommes politiques." *SeptAfrique.com*. URL: *www.septafrique.com/2022/01/serigne-mboup-maire-de-kaolack-la-lecon-dun-soldat-de-leconomie-aux-hommes-politiques/*

Fearon, James. 1999. Electoral accountability and the control of politicians: Selecting good types versus sanctioning poor performance. In *Democracy, accountability, and representation*, ed. Adam Przeworski, Susan C. Stokes and Bernard Manin. Cambridge: Cambridge University Press pp. 55–97.

Fédération Atlantique des Agences de Presse Africaines. 2020. "Le Président de la CCIAD veut privilégier le dialogue pour une chambre consulaire 'forte'." URL: *www.faapa.info/en/2020/09/02/le-president-de-la-cciad-veut-privilegier-le-dialogue-pour-une-chambre-consulaire-forte/*

Fédération Internationale des experts comptables francophones. 2014. Economie informelle, économie émergente, la profession comptable francophone s'engage. Technical Report, XVèmes Assises de la FIDEF. URL: *https://idl-bnc-idrc.dspacedirect.org/bitstream/handle/10625/54413/IDL-54413.pdf*

Feierherd, Germán. 2022. "Courting informal workers: Exclusion, forbearance, and the left." *American Journal of Political Science* 66(2):418–433.

Ferejohn, John. 1986. "Incumbent performance and electoral control." *Public Choice* 50(1):5–25.

Fergusson, Leopoldo, Carlos A. Molina and James A. Robinson. 2022. "The weak state trap." *Economica* 89(354):293–331.

Fergusson, Leopoldo, Horacio Larreguy and Juan Felipe Riaño. 2022. "Political competition and state capacity: Evidence from a land allocation program in Mexico." *The Economic Journal* 132(648):2815–2834.

Freedom House. 2023. "Freedom in the World Report: Senegal." URL: *https://freedomhouse.org/country/senegal/freedom-world/2023*

Gaikwad, Nikhar, Gareth Nellis and Anjali Thomas. 2020. "Bureaucratic hurdles, political resistance, and public service access: Evidence from a field experiment in India." *Presented at the Annual meeting of the American Political Science Association, August 2020*

Gallien, Max and Vanessa van den Boogaard. 2023. "Formalization and its discontents: Conceptual fallacies and ways forward." *Development and Change* 54(3):490–513.

Garay, Candelaria. 2016. *Social policy expansion in Latin America*. Cambridge University Press.

Garay, Candelaria. 2023. *Labor coalitions in unequal societies*. Manuscript.

Garfias, Francisco. 2018. "Elite competition and state capacity development: Theory and evidence from post-revolutionary Mexico." *American Political Science Review* 112(2):339–357.

Garfias, Francisco and Emily A Sellars. 2022. "When state building backfires: Elite coordination and popular grievance in rebellion." *American Journal of Political Science* 66(4):977–992.

Gatsios, Konstantine. 1992. Privatization in Hungary: Past, present and future. Technical Report CEPR Discussion Papers.

Geddes, Barbara. 1996. *Politician's dilemma: Building state capacity in Latin America*. Berkeley and Los Angeles: University of California Press.

Gellar, Sheldon. 2005. *Democracy in Senegal: Tocquevillian analytics in Africa*. Springer.

Gerry, Chris. 1987. "Developing economies and the informal sector in historical perspective." *The Annals of the American Academy of Political and Social Science* 493(1):100–119.

Golub, Stephen S. and Jamie Hansen-Lewis. 2012. Informal trading networks in West Africa: The Mourides of Senegal/The Gambia and the Yoruba of Benin/Nigeria. In *The informal sector in francophone Africa: Firm size, productivity, and institutions*, ed. Nancy Benjamin and Ahmadou Aly Mbaye. World Bank.

Good, Kenneth. 1992. "Interpreting the exceptionality of Botswana." *The Journal of Modern African Studies* 30(1):69–95.

Goodfellow, Tom. 2015. "Taming the "rogue" sector: Studying state effectiveness in Africa through informal transport politics." *Comparative Politics* 47(2):127–147.

Gottlieb, Jessica. 2016. "Greater expectations: A field experiment to improve accountability in Mali." *American Journal of Political Science* 60(1):143–157.

Gottlieb, Jessica. 2017. "Explaining variation in broker strategies: A lab-in-the-field experiment in Senegal." *Comparative Political Studies* 50(11):1556–1592.

Gottlieb, Jessica. 2024. "How economic informality constrains demand for programmatic policy." *American Journal of Political Science* 68(1):271–288.

Gottlieb, Jessica and Adrienne LeBas. 2022. Taxing the informal sector: Market vendors and tax appeals in Lagos State. Technical Report, Hobby School of Public Affairs, University of Houston.
URL: *www.dropbox.com/scl/fi/xsxckqx7qnphrf59scojv/UH_AU%20Report%20to%20LIRS_12_03_2022.pdf?rlkey=keie2f64e0g94ybgie10qikx6&dl=0*

LeBas, Adrienne and Jessica Gottlieb. 2025. *Can social intermediaries build the state? Taxation and state-building in Lagos, Nigeria.* Unpublished manuscript.

Gottlieb, Jessica, Adrienne Lebas and Janica Magat. 2025. "Can social intermediaries build the state? Evidence from an experiment in Lagos, Nigeria." *British Journal of Political Science* 55:e99.

Gottlieb, Jessica, Guy Grossman, Horacio Larreguy and Benjamin Marx. 2019. "A signaling theory of distributive policy choice: Evidence from Senegal." *The Journal of Politics* 81(2):631–647.

Gottlieb, Jessica and Horacio Larreguy. 2016. "An informational theory of electoral targeting in young clientelistic democracies: Evidence from Senegal." *Berkeley Center on the Politics of Development Working Paper 2016-15.*
URL: *www.dropbox.com/s/7zwr9io5lcpghuf/GL_SenegalElectoralBehavior_Website.pdf?dl=0*

Gottlieb, Jessica and Horacio Larreguy. 2020. "An informational theory of electoral targeting in young clientelistic democracies: Evidence from Senegal." *Quarterly Journal of Political Science* 15(1):73–104.

Greif, Avner. 1993. "Contract enforceability and economic institutions in early trade: The Maghribi traders' coalition." *The American Economic Review* 83(3):525–548.

Greven, Thomas. 2017. Organizing the informal economy in Senegal. In *Work, Institutions and Sustainable Livelihood* ed. Virginius Xava, Debdulal Saha and Rajdeep Singha. Singapore: Palgrave Macmillan, pp. 303–322.

Grossman, Shelby. 2020. "The politics of order in informal markets: Evidence from Lagos." *World Politics* 72(1):47–79.

Grzymala-Busse, Anna. 2002. "The programmatic turnaround of communist successor parties in East Central Europe, 1989–1998." *Communist and Post-Communist Studies* 35(1):51–66.

Gueye, Mohamed. 2022. "ITW – Serigne Mboup, maire de Kaolack, président de l'Unccias: 'Personne ne va m'embarquer dans la politique politicienne'." *Le Quotidien.*
URL: *https://lequotidien.sn/itw-serigne-mboup-maire-de-kaolack-president-de-lunccias-personne-ne-va-membarquer-dans-la-politique-politicienne/*

Gueye, Thierno. 2024. "Législatives 2024 : A Kaolack, Ousmane Sonko s'allie aussi avec Serigne Mboup." *Sene.News.*
URL: *www.senenews.com/actualites/legislatives-2024-a-kaolack-ousmane-sonko-sallie-aussi-avec-serigne-mboup_514874.html*

Gupta, Nandini, Jhon C Ham and Jan Svejnar. 2008. "Priorities and sequencing in privatization: Evidence from Czech firm panel data." *European Economic Review* 52(2):183–208.

Haavik, Viljar and Abdoul Wahab Cissé. 2024. "Taxing the informal sector: Coping with coercion in Bamako, Mali." *Development Policy Review* 42(4):e12775.

Habyarimana, James, Youdi Schipper et al. 2022. "The cyclical electoral impacts of programmatic policies: Evidence from education reforms in Tanzania." URL: *https://portal.sds.ox.ac.uk/articles/preprint/The_Cyclical_Electoral_Impacts_of_Programmatic_Policies_Evidence_From_Education_Reforms_in_ Tanzania/21107932*

Handley, Antoinette. 2015. "Varieties of capitalists? The middle-class, private sector and economic outcomes in Africa." *Journal of International Development* 27(5):609–627.

Hanson, Jonathan K. and Rachel Sigman. 2021. "Leviathan's latent dimensions: Measuring state capacity for comparative political research." *The Journal of Politics* 83(4):1495–1510.

Harding, Robin. 2020. *Rural democracy: Elections and development in Africa.* Oxford University Press.

Hart, Keith. 1973. "Informal income opportunities and urban employment in Ghana." *The Journal of Modern African Studies* 11(1):61–89.

Henn, Soeren J. 2023. "Complements or substitutes? How institutional arrangements bind traditional authorities and the state in Africa." *American Political Science Review* 117(3):871–890.

Herbst, Jeffrey. 1990. "War and the state in Africa." *International Security* 14(4):117–139.

Herbst, Jeffrey. 2014. *States and power in Africa: Comparative lessons in authority and control.* Vol. 149, Princeton, NJ: Princeton University Press.

Hicken, Allen. 2011. "Clientelism." *Annual Review of Political Science* 14:289–310.

Hicken, Allen and Noah L Nathan. 2020. "Clientelism's red herrings: Dead ends and new directions in the study of nonprogrammatic politics." *Annual Review of Political Science* 23(1):277–294.

Hill, Polly. 1997. *The migrant cocoa-farmers of southern Ghana: A study in rural capitalism.* Hamburg: LIT Verlag Münster.

Holland, Alisha C. 2016. "Forbearance." *American Political Science Review* 110(2):232–246.

Holland, Alisha C. 2017. *Forbearance as redistribution: The politics of informal welfare in Latin America.* Cambridge University Press.

Holland, Alisha C. 2018. "Diminished expectations: Redistributive preferences in truncated welfare states." *World Politics* 70(4):555–594.

Holland, Alisha C and Brian Palmer-Rubin. 2015. "Beyond the machine clientelist brokers and interest organizations in Latin America." *Comparative Political Studies* 48(9):1186–1223.

Hollenbach, Florian M. and Thiago N. Silva. 2019. "Fiscal capacity and inequality: Evidence from Brazilian municipalities." *The Journal of Politics* 81(4):1434–1445.

Honig, Lauren. 2022. *Land Politics: How customary institutions shape state building in Zambia and Senegal.* Cambridge: Cambridge University Press.

Huber, Evelyne and John D. Stephens. 2001. *Development and crisis of the welfare state: Parties and policies in global markets.* Chicago: University of Chicago Press.

Hummel, Calla. 2017. "Disobedient markets: Street vendors, enforcement, and state intervention in collective action." *Comparative Political Studies* 50(11):1524–1555.

Hummel, Calla. 2021. *Why informal workers organize: Contentious politics, enforcement, and the state.* Oxford: Oxford University Press.

Imbens, Guido W. and Jeffrey M. Wooldridge. 2009. "Recent developments in the econometrics of program evaluation." *Journal of Economic Literature* 47(1):5–86.

International Labour Organization. 2015. *Recommendation concerning the transition from the informal to the formal economy.* ILO Recommendation no. 204.
URL: *www.ilo.org/dyn/normlex/en/f?p=NORMLEXPUB:12100:0::NO::P12100_ILO_CODE:R204*

International Labour Office. 2018. "Women and men in the informal economy: A statistical picture (third edition)." Geneva: ILO.

Irwin, Zane and Babacar Dione. 2023. "Senegal's opposition leader charged with conspiracy against the state and calls for insurrection." *Associate Press.*
URL: *https://apnews.com/article/senegal-ousmane-sonko-opposition-politician-charged-insurrection-1f8e99a3a706b865c72c13c60049c63d*

Jones, Hilary. 2013. *The Metis of Senegal: Urban life and politics in French West Africa.* Indiana University Press.

Joshi, Anuradha and Joseph Ayee. 2008. Associational taxation: A pathway into the informal sector? In *Taxation and state building in developing countries: Capacity and consent*, ed. Deborah Brautigam, Odd-Helge Fjeldstad and Mick Moore. Cambridge: Cambridge University Press. pp. 183–211.

Kaly, Eugène and Seydou Ka. 2010. "SERIGNE MBOUP, PDG DE CCBM ET PRESIDENT DE LA CHAMBRE DE COMMERCE DE KAOLACK." *Seneweb.*
URL: *www.seneweb.com/news/Economie/serigne-mboup-pdg-de-ccbm-et-president-de-la-chambre-de-commerce-de-kaolack-laquo-bientot-nous-allons-mettre-en-place-une-ligne-de-montage-de-vehicules-raquo_n_37725.html*

Kamm, Emily. 2016. "Price control, profiteering, and public cooperation: The Lagos Market Women's Association and the limits of colonial control." PhD Thesis, Portland State University.

Keefer, Philip. 2007. "Clientelism, credibility, and the policy choices of young democracies." *American Journal of Political Science* 51(4):804–821.

Keefer, Philip and Razvan Vlaicu. 2008. "Democracy, credibility, and clientelism." *The Journal of Law, Economics, & Organization* 24(2):371–406.

Khemani, Stuti. 2015. "Buying votes versus supplying public services: Political incentives to under-invest in pro-poor policies." *Journal of Development Economics* 117:84–93.

King, Desmond and David Rueda. 2008. "Cheap labor: The new politics of 'bread and roses' in industrial democracies." *Perspectives on Politics* 6(2):279–297.

Kitschelt, Herbert. 2000. "Linkages between citizens and politicians in democratic polities." *Comparative Political Studies* 33(6–7):845–879.

Kitschelt, Herbert. 2009. "Political accountability in democratic party competition and economic governance."
URL: *https://sites.duke.edu/democracylinkage/data/*

Kitschelt, Herbert. 2013. *Dataset of the democratic accountability and linkages project (DALP)*. Durham, NC: Duke University.
URL: *https://sites.duke.edu/democracylinkage*

Kitschelt, Herbert and Regina Smyth. 2002. "Programmatic party cohesion in emerging postcommunist democracies: Russia in comparative context." *Comparative Political Studies* 35(10):1228–1256.

Kitschelt, Herbert and Steven I. Wilkinson. 2007. *Patrons, clients and policies: Patterns of democratic accountability and political competition*. Cambridge: Cambridge University Press.

Klaus, Kathleen, Jeffrey W. Paller and Martha Wilfahrt. 2023. "Demanding recognition: A new framework for the study of political clientelism." *African Affairs* 122(487):185–203.

Knebelmann, Justine. 2022. Digitalisation of property taxation in developing countries: Recent advances and remaining challenges. Technical Report ODI Report.
URL: *https://cdn.odi.org/media/documents/Digitalisation_of_property_taxation_in_developing_countries.pdf*

Knebelmann, Justine, Victor Pouliquen and Bassirou Sarr. 2023. "Discretion versus algorithms: Bureaucrats and tax equity in senegal." *Working Paper*.
URL: *https://drive.google.com/file/d/1EAPqRR7GWkP8PrOVV-uUItsB09NGx7uq/view*

Koehler-Derrick, Gabriel and Melissa M. Lee. 2023. "War and welfare in colonial Algeria." *International Organization* 77(2):263–293.

Koter, Dominika. 2013. "King makers: Local leaders and ethnic politics in Africa." *World Politics* 65(2):187–232.

Kramon, Eric. 2016. "Where is vote buying effective? Evidence from a list experiment in Kenya." *Electoral Studies* 44:397–408.

Kramon, Eric. 2017. *Money for votes: The causes and consequences of electoral clientelism in Africa*. Cambridge: Cambridge University Press.

Krishna, Anirudh. 2011. "Gaining access to public services and the democratic state in India: Institutions in the middle." *Studies in Comparative International Development* 46(1):98–117.

Kruks-Wisner, Gabrielle. 2022. "Social brokerage: Accountability and the social life of information." *Comparative Political Studies* 55(14):2382–2415.

Kuo, Didi. 2018. *Clientelism, capitalism, and democracy: The rise of programmatic politics in the United States and Britain*. Cambridge: Cambridge University Press.

La Porta, Rafael and Andrei Shleifer. 2014. "Informality and development." *Journal of Economic Perspectives* 28(3):109–126.

Lake, David A. and Matthew A. Baum. 2001. "The invisible hand of democracy: Political control and the provision of public services." *Comparative Political Studies* 34(6):587–621.

Lankina, Tomila V. and Alexander Libman. 2021. "The two-pronged middle class: The old bourgeoisie, new state-engineered middle class, and democratic development." *American Political Science Review* 115(3):948–966.

Larreguy, Horacio, Cesar E. Montiel Olea and Pablo Querubin. 2017. "Political brokers: Partisans or agents? Evidence from the Mexican teachers' union." *American Journal of Political Science* 61(4):877–891.

Levi, Margaret. 1989. *Of rule and revenue*. Berkeley, CA: University of California Press.

Levtzion, Nehemia and Randall L. Pouwels. 2000. *The history of Islam in Africa*. Ohio University Press.

Leys, Colin. 1973. "Interpreting African underdevelopment: Reflections on the ILO report on employment, incomes and equality in Kenya." *African Affairs* 72(289):419–429.

Lipset, Seymour Martin. 1959. "Some social requisites of democracy: Economic development and political legitimacy." *American Political Science Review* 53(1):69–105.

Lipset, Seymour Martin and Stein Rokkan. 1967. *Party systems and voter alignments: Cross-national perspectives*. New York: The Free Press.

Lizzeri, Alessandro and Nicola Persico. 2001. "The provision of public goods under alternative electoral incentives." *American Economic Review* 91(1):225–239.

Loayza, Norman V. 1996. The economics of the informal sector: A simple model and some empirical evidence from Latin America. *Carnegie-Rochester Conference Series on Public Policy* 45: 129–162. DOI: https://doi.org/10.1016/S0167-2231(96)00021-8

Lupu, Noam and Rachel Beatty Riedl. 2013. "Political parties and uncertainty in developing democracies." *Comparative Political Studies* 46(11):1339–1365.

Lust, Ellen and Lise Rakner. 2018. "The other side of taxation: Extraction and social institutions in the developing world." *Annual Review of Political Science* 21:277–294.

Mamdani, Mahmood. 1996. *Citizen and subject: Contemporary Africa and the legacy of late colonialism*. Princeton University Press.

Mampilly, Zachariah. 2025. "What 'the Global South' Really Means." *Foreign Affairs*.
URL: *www.foreignaffairs.com/world/what-global-south-really-means*

Mann, Michael. 1984. "The autonomous power of the state: Its origins, mechanisms and results." *European Journal of Sociology* 25(2):185–213.

Mares, Isabela and Didac Queralt. 2015. "The non-democratic origins of income taxation." *Comparative Political Studies* 48(14):1974–2009.

Mares, Isabela and Lauren E Young. 2019. *Conditionality & coercion: Electoral clientelism in Eastern Europe*. Oxford: Oxford University Press.

Marfaing, Laurence and Alena Thiel. 2013. "The impact of Chinese business on market entry in Ghana and Senegal." *Africa* 83(4):646–669.

Marshall, Monty G., Ted Robert Gurr and Keith Jaggers. 2018. "Political regime characteristics and transitions, 1800–2017." *Polity IV Project*. URL: *www.systemicpeace.org/inscrdata.html*

Martin, Lucy E.S. 2023. *Strategic taxation: Fiscal capacity and accountability in African states*. New York: Oxford University Press.

Mazzuca, Sebastián L. 2010. "Access to power versus exercise of power reconceptualizing the quality of democracy in Latin America." *Studies in Comparative International Development* 45:334–357.

Mbaye, Ahmadou A., Stephen S. Golub and P. English. 2018. "Policies, prices, and poverty: The sugar, vegetable oil, and flour industries in Senegal." In *Race to the next income frontier: How Senegal and other low-income countries can reach the finish line*, ed. Ali Mansoor, Salifou Issoufou and Daouda Sembene. International Monetary Fund, p. 373.

McLane, Margaret O. 1986. "Commercial rivalries and French policy on the Senegal River, 1831–1858." *African Economic History* 15:39–67.

Meagher, Kate. 2011. "Informal economies and urban governance in Nigeria: Popular empowerment or political exclusion?" *African Studies Review* 54(2):47–72.

Meagher, Kate. 2014. "Disempowerment from below: Informal enterprise networks and the limits of political voice in Nigeria." *Oxford Development Studies* 42(3):419–438.

Medina, Leandro and Friedrich Schneider. 2018. "Shadow economies around the world: What did we learn over the last 20 years?" *IMF Working Paper WP/18/17*. URL: *https://papers.ssrn.com/sol3/papers.cfm?abstract_id=3124402#*

Melber, Henning. 2017. "The African middle class(es) – In the middle of what?" *Review of African Political Economy* 44(151):142–154.

Merton, Robert King. 1949. *Social theory and social structure*. Glencoe, IL: Free Press.

Michelitch, Kristin and Stephen Utych. 2018. "Electoral cycle fluctuations in partisanship: Global evidence from eighty-six countries." *The Journal of Politics* 80(2):412–427.

Mkandawire, Thandika. 2010. "On tax efforts and colonial heritage in Africa." *The Journal of Development Studies* 46(10):1647–1669.

Monks, Kieron. 2019. "Senegal voters head to polls as presidential challenger hopes to cause upset." *CNN*. URL: *www.cnn.com/2019/02/22/africa/senegal-election-sonko/index.html*

Monye, Judith and Oyintare Abang. 2020. "Taxing the informal sector – Nigeria's missing goldmine." *Bloomberg Daily Tax Report*. URL: *https://news.bloombergtax.com/daily-tax-report-international/taxing-the-informal-sector-nigerias-missing-goldmine*

Moore, Barrington. 1966. *Social origins of dictatorship and democracy: Lord and peasant in the making of the modern world*. Boston: Beacon Press.

Moore, Mick. 2008. "Between coercion and contract: Competing narratives on taxation and governance." In *Taxation and state building in developing countries: Capacity and Consent*, ed. Deborah Brautigam, Odd-Helge Fjeldstad and Mick Moore. Cambridge: Cambridge University Press, 34–63.

Moore, Mick. 2023. "Tax obsessions: Taxpayer registration and the 'informal sector' in sub-Saharan Africa." *Development Policy Review* 41(1):e12649.

Murtaza, Natasha. 2023. "Governing the state: The erosion of bureaucratic capacity under party competition in India." URL: *https://scholar.harvard.edu/sites/scholar.harvard.edu/files/nmurtaza/files/governing_the_state.pdf*

Mwaniki, Munene. 2016. "Indigenous languages and the informal economy in Africa: A qualitative analysis of the economics of language dynamics in rural Kenya." *Southern African Linguistics and Applied Language Studies* 34(4):265–277.

Nathan, Noah L. 2016*a*. "Does participation reinforce patronage? Policy preferences, turnout and class in urban Ghana." *British Journal of Political Science* 49(1):229–255.

Nathan, Noah L. 2016*b*. "Local ethnic geography, expectations of favoritism, and voting in urban Ghana." *Comparative Political Studies* 49(14):1896–1929.

Nathan, Noah L. 2019. *Electoral politics and Africa's Urban transition: Class and ethnicity in Ghana*. Cambridge: Cambridge University Press.

Nathan, Noah L. 2023. *The scarce state: Inequality and political power in the Hinterland*. Cambridge: Cambridge University Press.

National Bureau of Statistics. 2021. Internally Generated Revenue At State Level. Abuja, Nigeria.

Nsongon, Philemon Mbale. 2019. "Senegal opposition aspirants face citizens at a public debate." *Africanews*. URL: *www.africanews.com/2019/02/22/senegal-elections-see-two-candidates-face-citizens-at-a-public-debate/*

O'Brien, Donald B. Cruise. 1971. *The Mourides of Senegal*. Oxford: Oxford University Press.

O'Brien, Donald B. Cruise. 1975. *Saints and politicians: Essays in the organisation of a Senegalese peasant society*. Cambridge: Cambridge University Press.

Olken, Benjamin A. and Monica Singhal. 2011. "Informal taxation." *American Economic Journal: Applied Economics* 3(4):1–28.

Olson, Mancur. 1993. "Dictatorship, democracy, and development." *American Political Science Review* 87(3):567–576.

Olubajo, Ayindamola. 2020. "EXCLUSIVE: Sanwo-Olu increases Alpha Beta's monthly payment to N2.5 billion to fund Tinubu's presidential election." *People's Gazette*. URL: *https://gazettengr.com/exclusive-sanwo-olu-increases-alpha-betas-monthly-payment-to-n2-5-billion-to-fund-tinubus-presidential-election/*

Olukoju, Ayodeji. 2005. "Actors and institutions in urban politics in Nigeria: Agege Lagos since the 1950s." *Afrika Zamani (Codesria)* 13–14:153–178.

Onigbinde, Oluseun. 2018. "What we know about Lagos state finances." *BudgIT*. URL: *https://yourbudgit.com/wp-content/uploads/2018/05/LAGOS-STATE-DATA-BOOK.pdf*

Onoma, Ato Kwamena. 2009. *The politics of property rights institutions in Africa*. Cambridge University Press.

Opalo, Ken Ochieng'. 2019. *Legislative development in Africa: Politics and postcolonial legacies*. Cambridge: Cambridge University Press.

Osei, Anja. 2012. *Party–voter linkage in Africa: Ghana and Senegal in comparative perspective*. Springer Science & Business Media.

Pardelli, Giuliana. 2024. "Agrarian elites, wealth inequality, and state capacity: Evidence from early twentieth-century Brazil." *World Politics* 76(4):735–776.

Pardelli, Giuliana and Julieta Peveri. 2025. "State capacity, informality and clientelism." *NICEP Working Paper 2025-05*.

Peattie, Lisa Redfield. 1975. *Living poor: A view from the bottom*. Vol. 4 School of Architecture and Urban Planning, University of California.

Pellicer, Miquel, Eva Wegner et al. 2013. "Electoral rules and clientelistic parties: A regression discontinuity approach." *Quarterly Journal of Political Science* 8(4):339–371.

Portes, Alejandro and Richard Schauffler. 1993. "Competing perspectives on the Latin American informal sector." *Population and Development Review* 19(1):33–60.

Potts, Deborah. 2008. "The urban informal sector in sub-Saharan Africa: From bad to good (and back again?)." *Development Southern Africa* 25(2):151–167.

Power, Joey. 1992. "'Individualism is the antithesis of indirect rule': Cooperative development and indirect rule in colonial Malawi." *Journal of Southern African Studies* 18(2):317–347.

Prichard, Wilson. 2018. "Electoral competitiveness, tax bargaining and political incentives in developing countries: Evidence from political budget cycles affecting taxation." *British Journal of Political Science* 48(2):427–457.

Przeworski, Adam. 2009. "Conquered or granted? A history of suffrage extensions." *British Journal of Political Science* 39(2):291–321.

Queralt, Didac. 2018. "The legacy of war on fiscal capacity." *Working Paper*.
URL: *https://rppe.princeton.edu/sites/rppe/files/queralt_war_legacy_jan18_20.pdf*

Queralt, Didac. 2019. "War, international finance, and fiscal capacity in the long run." *International Organization* 73(4):713–753.

Rains, Emily and Erik Wibbels. 2023. "Informal work, risk, and clientelism: Evidence from 223 slums across India." *British Journal of Political Science* 53(1):1–24.

Ramon, Oladimeji. 2020. "Alpha-Beta got over N150bn commission on Lagos revenue – Ex-MD." *Punch Nigeria*.
URL: *https://punchng.com/alpha-beta-got-over-n150bn-commission-on-lagos-revenue-ex-md/*

Razafindrafito, Volanirina. 2023. "Les 10 personnes les plus riches du Sénégal." *L'Echo du Sud*.
URL: *www.lechodusud.com/post/les-10-personnes-les-plus-riches-du-sénégal*

Reid Jr., Joseph D. and Michael M. Kurth. 1992. The rise and fall of urban political patronage machines. In *Strategic factors in nineteenth century American economic history: A volume to honor Robert W. Fogel*, ed. Claudia Goldin and Hugh Rockoff. Chicago: University of Chicago Press, pp. 427–445.

Resnick, Danielle. 2012. "Opposition parties and the urban poor in African democracies." *Comparative Political Studies* 45(11):1351–1378.

Resnick, Danielle. 2013*a*. "Continuity and change in Senegalese party politics: Lessons from the 2012 elections." *African Affairs* 112(449):623–645.

Resnick, Danielle. 2013*b*. "Personalistic policy-making in a vibrant democracy: Senegal's fragmented response to the 2007/08 food price crisis". *Vol. 2013/015 WIDER Working Paper.*

Resnick, Danielle. 2014. *Urban poverty and party populism in African democracies*. Cambridge University Press.

Resnick, Danielle E. 2017. Populism in Africa. In *The Oxford handbook of populism*, ed. Cristóbal Rovira Kaltwasser, Paul Taggart, Paulina Ochoa Espejo, and Pierre Ostiguy. Oxford: Oxford University Press, pp. 101–120.

Riedl, Rachel Beatty. 2014. *Authoritarian origins of democratic party systems in Africa*. Cambridge University Press.

Roberts, Kenneth M. 2002. "Social inequalities without class cleavages in Latin America's neoliberal era." *Studies in Comparative International Development* 36(4):3–33.

Robinson, James A., Daron Acemoglu and Simon Johnson. 2003. An African success story: Botswana. In *In Search of Prosperity: Analytic Narratives on Economic Growth*, ed. Dani Rodrik. Princeton, NJ: Princeton University Press pp. 80–119.

Robinson, James A. and Thierry Verdier. 2013. "The political economy of clientelism." *Scandinavian Journal of Economics* 115(2):260–291.

Rogers, Melissa, Pablo Beramendi and Mark Dincecco. 2018. "Replication data for: Intra-elite competition and long-run fiscal development. V1." *Harvard Dataverse* .
URL: *https://doi.org/10.7910/DVN/TTK06U*

Roland, Gerard. 2002. "The political economy of transition." *Journal of Economic Perspectives* 16(1):29–50.

Rosenfeld, Bryn. 2021. "State dependency and the limits of middle class support for democracy." *Comparative Political Studies* 54(3–4):411–444.

Ross, Michael. 2006. "Is democracy good for the poor?" *American Journal of Political Science* 50(4):860–874.

Roubaud, Émile. 1918. "L'état actuel et l'avenir du commerce des arachides au Sénégal." *Annales de géographie* 27(148/149):357–371.

Rueschemeyer, Dietrich, Evelyne Huber Stephens, John D. Stephens et al. 1992. *Capitalist development and democracy*, Vol. 22. Cambridge Polity.

Salem, Gérard. 1992. "Crise urbaine et contrôle social à Pikine: Bornes-fontaines et clientélisme." *Politique africaine* 45:21–38.

Santos, Milton. 1979. *The shared space: The two circuits of the urban economy in underdeveloped countries*. New York: Meuthen.

Saylor, Ryan. 2014. *State building in boom times: Commodities and coalitions in Latin America and Africa*. New York: Oxford University Press.

Scheve, Kenneth and David Stasavage. 2016. *Taxing the rich: A history of fiscal fairness in the United States and Europe*. Princeton, NJ: Princeton University Press.

Schuster, Christian. 2016. "When the victor cannot claim the spoils: Institutional incentives for professionalizing patronage states." *Inter-American Development Bank, Department of Research and Chief Economist Working Paper Series IDB-WP-667*.

Scott, James C. 1972. "Patron–client politics and political change in Southeast Asia." *American Political Science Review* 66(1):91–113.

Seawright, Jason and John Gerring. 2008. "Case selection techniques in case study research: A menu of qualitative and quantitative options." *Political Research Quarterly* 61(2):294–308.

Shefter, Martin. 1977. "Party and patronage: Germany, England, and Italy." *Politics & Society* 7(4):403–451.

Skowronek, Stephen 1982. *Building a new American state: The expansion of national administrative capacities, 1877–1920*. Cambridge: Cambridge University Press.

Smith, Alastair and Bruce Bueno De Mesquita. 2012. "Contingent prize allocation and pivotal voting." *British Journal of Political Science* 42(2):371–392.

Sokoloff, Kenneth L and Stanley L Engerman. 2000. "History lessons: Institutions, factor endowments, and paths of development in the new world." *Journal of Economic Perspectives* 14(3):217–232.

Sow, El Hadj. 2021. "Le Malaise continue à L'Union des Chambres de Commerce de Serigne Mboup." *Seneplus Economie*.
URL: *www.seneplus.com/economie/le-malaise-continue-lunion-des-chambres-de-commerce-de-serigne*

Stasavage, David. 2005. "Democracy and education spending in Africa." *American Journal of Political Science* 49(2):343–358.

Stokes, Susan C., Thad Dunning, Marcelo Nazareno and Valeria Brusco. 2013. *Brokers, voters, and clientelism: The puzzle of distributive politics*. Cambridge: Cambridge University Press.

Suryanarayan, Pavithra. 2021. "Status politics hollows out the state: Evidence from Colonial India." *Baltimore: Johns Hopkins University*.
URL: *https://pavisuridotcom.files.wordpress.com/2021/02/suryanarayan-2021_hollowing_out_the_state.pdf*

Suryanarayan, Pavithra. 2024. "Endogenous state capacity." *Annual Review of Political Science* 27.

Suryanarayan, Pavithra and Steven White. 2021. "Slavery, reconstruction, and bureaucratic capacity in the American South." *American Political Science Review* 115:568–584.

Sy-Sahande, Sanata. 2017. Taxing clients: The effects of clientelism on citizen tax attitudes. Technical Report.

Tall, Serigne Mansour. 2004. "Senegalese émigrés: New information & communication technologies." *Review of African Political Economy* 31(99):31–48.

Tendler, Judith. 2002. "Small firms, the informal sector, and the devil's deal." *IDS Bulletin* 33(3):1–15.

Thioub, Ibrahima, Momar-Coumba Diop and Catherine Boone. 1998. "Economic liberalization in Senegal: Shifting politics of indigenous business interests." *African Studies Review* 41(2):63–90.

Tilly, Charles. 1990. *Coercion, capital, and European states, AD 990–1990*. Oxford: Blackwell.

Tilly, Charles. 2005. *Trust and rule*. Cambridge: Cambridge University Press.

Topcuzis, Daphne N. 1989. "Popular front, war and fourth republic politics in Senegal: From Galandou Diouf to L.S. Senghor". PhD Thesis, School of Oriental and African Studies London University.

Touré, Babacar. 2022. "Kaolack / Législatives 2022: Serigne MBOUP a pris sa décision." *Senenews* .
URL: *www.senenews.com/actualites/regions/kaolack/kaolack-elections-legislatives-serigne-mboup-a-pris-sa-decision_410301.html*

Tsai, Lily L. 2007. "Solidary groups, informal accountability, and local public goods provision in rural China." *American Political Science Review* 101(2):355–372.

Tullock, Gordon. 1975. "The transitional gains trap." *The Bell Journal of Economics* 6(2):671–678.

Ulyssea, Gabriel. 2018. "Firms, informality, and development: Theory and evidence from Brazil." *American Economic Review* 108(8):2015–2047.

Ulyssea, Gabriel. 2020. "Informality: Causes and consequences for development." *Annual Review of Economics* 12(1):525–546.

Uzzell, Douglas. 1974. "A strategic analysis of social structure in Lima, Peru, using the concept of 'Plays'." *Urban Anthropology* 3(1):034–046.

Vigouroux, Cécile B. and Salikoko S. Mufwene. 2020. Do linguists need economics and economists linguistics? In *Bridging Linguistics and Economics*, ed. Cécile B. Vigouroux and Salikoko S. Mufwene. Cambridge: Cambridge University Press, pp. 1–55.

Villalón, Leonardo A. 1999. "Generational changes, political stagnation, and the evolving dynamics of religion and politics in Senegal." *Africa Today* 46 (3/4): 129–147.

Villalón, Leonardo A and Mamadou Bodian. 2012. "Religion, demande sociale, et réformes éducatives au Sénégal: Quand l'Etat introduit l'éducation arabo-islamique dans l'enseignement publique pour concurrencer l'école franco-arabe et capturer les daara." *African Politics and Power Programme Research* 5, pp. 1–54.
URL: *https://sahelresearch.africa.ufl.edu/wp-content/uploads/sites/170/rr05.pdf*

Villalón, Leonardo Alfonso. 1995. *Islamic society and state power in Senegal: Disciples and citizens in Fatick*. Cambridge: Cambridge University Press.

Vorisek, Dana, Gene Kindberg-Hanlon, Wee Chian Koh, Yoki Okawa, Temel Taskin, Ekaterine Vashakmadze and Lei Sandy Ye. 2022. Informality in emerging market and developing economies: Regional dimensions. In *The long shadow of informality: Challenges and policies*, ed. Franziska Ohnsorge and Shu Yu. World Bank Publications.

Wahman, Michael and Catherine Boone. 2018. "Captured countryside? Stability and change in sub-national support for African incumbent parties." *Comparative Politics* 50(2):189–216.

Wang, Yuhua. 2022. "Blood is thicker than water: Elite kinship networks and state building in imperial China." *American Political Science Review* 116(3):896–910.

Weber, Max. 1946. Bureaucracy. In *From Max Weber: Essays in sociology*, ed. H. H. Gerth and C. Wright Mills. New York: Oxford University Press, pp. 196–244.

Weber, Max. 1978. *Economy and society: An outline of interpretive sociology*, Vol. 1. Berkeley, CA: University of California Press.

Weghorst, Keith R and Staffan I Lindberg. 2013. "What drives the swing voter in Africa?" *American Journal of Political Science* 57(3):717–734.

Weitz-Shapiro, Rebecca. 2012. "What wins votes: Why some politicians opt out of clientelism." *American Journal of Political Science* 56(3):568–583.

Weitz-Shapiro, Rebecca. 2014. *Curbing clientelism in Argentina: Politics, poverty, and social policy*. New York: Cambridge University Press.

Williams, Colin C, Muhammad S Shahid and Alvaro Martínez. 2016. "Determinants of the level of informality of informal micro-enterprises: Some evidence from the city of Lahore, Pakistan." *World Development* 84:312–325.

Woods, Dwayne. 1988. "State action and class interests in the Ivory Coast." *African Studies Review* 31(1):93–116.

Wooldridge, J. 2002. *Introductory econometrics analysis of cross section and panel data*. Cambridge, MA: The MIT Press.

Young, Crawford. 1997. *The African colonial state in comparative perspective*. Yale University Press.

Yusuff, Olabisi Sherifat. 2011. "A theoretical analysis of the concept of informal economy and informality in developing countries." *European Journal of Social Sciences* 20(4):624–636.

Index

Printed in the United Kingdom by TJ Clays Ltd.